Managing *to Be* *Wealthy*

Putting Your Financial Plan—
and Planner—to Work for You

JOHN E. SESTINA
CFP, ChFC

DEARBORN™
A **Kaplan Professional** Company

Associate Publisher: Cynthia Zigmund
Managing Editor: Jack Kiburz
Project Editor: Trey Thoelcke
Interior Design: Lucy Jenkins
Cover Design: Elizandro Carrington
Typesetting: the dotted i

Published by Dearborn
A Kaplan Professional Company

The authors gratefully acknowledge permission to quote from the following:
- National Association of Personal Financial Advisors. "Financial Planner Interview." 1999. www.napfa.org. Buffalo Grove, Ill.: National Association of Personal Financial Advisors.
- Society of Actuaries. "Report of the Special Committee to Recommend New Mortality Tables for Valuation." Transactions of the Society of Actuaries. Volume XXXIII (1981): pp. 617–674. Chicago: Society of Actuaries.

Printed in the United States of America

01 02 10 9 8 7 6 5 4 3 2

Library of Congress Cataloging-in-Publication Data
Sestina, John E.
    Managing to be wealthy : putting your financial plan and planner to work for you / John
E. Sestina
      p.   cm.
   ISBN 0-7931-3716-0 (pbk.)
    1. Finance, Personal.   I. Title.
HG179.S424 2000
332.024′01—dc21
                        00-024631

Dedication

To Bobbi and Alison
and
to Fred, Beth, and Charlie

Why You Should Buy this Book

Do you wonder why your paycheck never seems to last until the end of the month? Have you lain awake nights wondering how to pay for your children's college? Or have you tried to make prudent investments, only to see the stock market go down along with your savings?

If so, you're not alone. Most of us struggle to make ends meet whether we're making $50,000 or $150,000. And when we seek advice, who can understand what the professionals are saying? It can be so intimidating!

This book will help you chart your way to financial freedom without putting you to sleep or confusing you. Before you can chart your specific financial plan, however, you need to know the basic concepts behind successful financial planning. What do you want to invest? What are the obstacles to your financial freedom? Why is it important to start saving now?

This book will teach you a proven, tested way to become financially independent using safe, low-risk investing. Isn't that what you need? Let your Uncle Harry brag about his latest "hot stock tip." You will be able to just sit back and smile, knowing that *you will manage to be wealthy*. After all, it's not how much you make along the way but whether you reach your goal of financial independence.

Contents

Acknowledgments

Thanks to the many people who used this book in its earlier drafts and editions while attending John Sestina's seminars. Their comments were most helpful, and their enthusiasm for the information was invigorating.

The encouragement and insight of Cynthia Zigmund, associate publisher at Dearborn, was especially helpful. Thanks also to Dearborn's Jack Kiburz, Sandy Holzbach, and Trey Thoelcke for their support in answering many questions. It is a pleasure to work with these professionals.

I would especially like to thank my marketing consultant, Sandra S. Nichols, APR. Since 1978 she has supported my efforts to educate consumers about their investment choices. I appreciate her creativity in developing ways to partner with the news media and others to spread the word about the new profession of fee-only financial planning.

Finally, a special thank you to the reference librarians of these central Ohio libraries: Upper Arlington Public Library, especially Ruth Browning, Ph.D., and Heather Phalen; Grandview Public Library; and Columbus Metropolitan Library. They were always able to find the information needed.

John E. Sestina
Dublin, Ohio

Financial Concepts You Need to Know

Would you like to lower your taxes, increase your investment return and your cash flow, and reduce your estate taxes? Would you like to be financially independent?

"Sure," you say, "who wouldn't! Where do I start?"

You start by learning how to plan your financial life now, instead of continuing to react to each financial circumstance that comes along.

What do I mean by "reacting?" Well, if you're like most people, you (or someone you know) has probably said:

"What am I going to do? I retire in five years, and I'm concerned that we won't have enough to live on, let alone do the traveling we've always talked about."

"My child starts college in three years. Where am I going to get the money for that?"

"My stockbroker says this is a great investment opportunity I shouldn't pass up. How do I decide whether or not it is?"

You get the idea. So many of us react to financial situations instead of planning for them. So many of us are intimidated by the financial language the experts use. But it doesn't have to be that way for you. You were smart enough to choose this book because you knew you needed some help. Keep reading, and I'll show you, as I've shown others for the last 30 years, how to manage to be wealthy. The first step is to prepare your own financial plan.

Creating Your Financial Plan

"Why do I need a financial plan? That sounds like too much trouble!"

You need a financial plan to guide you through the complex, constantly changing financial world. This book will guide you through preparing your financial plan and putting it into action. As a result, you control your money instead of your money controlling you. While preparing your plan will take time and effort, it will also keep your financial questions from keeping you awake nights.

Do you think your financial plan is set because you already have insurance, investments, an estate plan, tax planning, financial statements, a college fund, or a pension plan? That's part of the problem. Most people don't understand what a financial plan is. A good financial plan is all of the above plus an objective evaluation of your current financial picture, your goals, and what it will take you to reach those goals. When these factors are pulled together in an organized approach, you have a financial plan.

Before we can talk more about financial planning, you need to understand one basic principle. Whenever you are dealing with money or the government, there are certain words you must eliminate from your vocabulary: *fair, logical, reasonable,* and *rational.* Do the tax laws fit any of these descriptions? Of course not. Does the stock market always react logically? No. Do lending institutions seem reasonable if they continue charging high interest rates when the prime rate is down? No. The "rules" of the financial market don't seem to make much sense sometimes.

How Does This Relate to Investing?

Financial planning is *more* than investing. Investing, to some people, means buying stocks and bonds. To others it's oil wells or real estate. Everyone thinks of something different. I define investing as "putting your savings to work in order to reach your goals."

Why all this focus on investing? Because most people think you're going to hit your "financial home run" by investing. How many people do you know that have become millionaires by investing? I've had very few people who said they knew someone who had become wealthy by investing. Why? Because most people don't prepare a financial plan and then put it into action. They react to news reports or "hot tips" instead of following a plan. I'll talk about why this happens later in this chapter. Throughout the rest of this book, you'll learn how to avoid the mistakes that others make.

Why Are You Investing?

So why are you investing? People invest:

- To get ahead. We all want to improve our lifestyle.
- To save taxes. (But you don't save taxes through investing: *You save taxes with tools.* More about this in later chapters.) Remember that you're not looking for activity (the number of investments you buy or sell), you're looking for results (meeting your goals).
- To make money. Who couldn't use more?
- To save for the future. You may want to invest for your child's education or your retirement. We all want to enjoy the future, but we also want to enjoy today.

But what is the real reason? If you understand the real reason that you are investing, then you can be a success. The real reason that you invest is because someday you won't be working! That day will come because:

- Eventually your health may fail. If you are an 80-hour per week person, someday you may have to slow down. Your doctor may tell you, your spouse may tell you, or your body may tell you.
- If you're self-employed, your insurance company may either decide it won't insure you or will raise your premiums beyond your ability to pay. That's what's happening to many doctors and other professionals today.
- You may find yourself downsized.
- You reach the mandatory retirement age.
- You want to!

Financial Independence

If you follow the lessons in this book, you will learn to manage your money and your life so that eventually you can attain financial independence. If you want to work, you can. If you don't want to work, you don't have to. A financial plan will help you understand *what* you have now, *where* you want to be, and *how* you will get there.

An often-asked question is, "What should the average person have to retire on?" That's the wrong question. You're not average. You want to prepare *your* financial plan, not use your neighbor's or a computer program written by someone who's never met you.

Human nature makes us all easy targets. You receive calls from out of the blue offering great investment deals. Why are they calling you? Will a stranger look out for your best interests? The chapter on investing shows you how to make good investments, not "deals." Learning what financial planning is, what the terminology is, and what techniques are available to you will help you build your personal financial plan.

Are You Meeting Your Goal?

I'll be exploding some myths about money, taxes, insurance, and investments in this book. A common myth is this: People believe that if they can just do one thing right they will succeed. For example, if they can just earn a higher rate of return, or if they can just save more on taxes, they will have it made. These are short-term distractions from your long-term goal. The winner of the game is not who earns the highest rate of return or pays the least in taxes. The winner of the game is who makes his or her goal.

What if your goal is to set aside $1 million in ten years? The first year you put $100,000 in your savings account. The second year you put $100,000 under the mattress. The third year you hide $100,000 in the closet. Every year for ten years you put aside $100,000 and don't touch it. At the end of ten years, did you meet your goal? Yes! The focus should be on your long-term goal. That you met your goal is more important than what rate of return you earned or what taxes you paid.

Working through the financial planning process helps you find the money to meet your goals. When you do a financial plan, you will know that

- you don't have enough money and you will reach your goal later, or
- you have enough, and you can reach your goal sooner.

You may not like what you discover. You may have to revise your goals. At least you'll know where you stand and what you can achieve. You may be surprised at how much you can achieve.

Attaining Peace of Mind

Once you get started on a good financial plan, the pressure comes off. The best result is peace of mind. The ultimate products of financial planning are peace of mind and financial independence.

Having a financial plan means you won't wake up one morning and say, "What happens to my family if I die?" "Why are there more bills than money at the end of the month?"

A good financial plan is a road map, if you will, of how you are going to get to where you want to go. It will help you balance today's needs against tomorrow's available funds. Everyone has financial needs and wants that haven't been met. These financial problems don't have to overwhelm you. By working through this book, you will develop your personal financial plan.

Developing Your Plan

You will get as much out of this book as you put into it. You'll notice a lot of worksheets throughout. Don't be intimidated. I'll go through them one step at a time showing you how to build your financial plan. Complete the worksheets, make notes in the margins, and *use* this book. (There are more blank forms in the back of the book for you to use.)

If you make less than $50,000 a year, you can prepare your financial plan with the help of this book. If you earn more than $50,000, you should still work through this book. After completing the basics of your financial plan you will be prepared to meet with a financial advisor to figure out the complex parts of your plan. You will have the basic information ready, as well as your questions. This preparation will help you get the most from your advisor.

Once you have set up your financial plan, it will take only a few hours each week to manage to be wealthy. Anyone can learn to manage her or his money in spite of a busy schedule. Three obstacles to handling your own finances are:

1. "But I don't understand the language the experts use!" I will explain the concepts to you so that you can ask intelligent questions, understand what is happening, and become an active participant.
2. "But I've always let [my spouse, my stockbroker, my relative] manage my finances." Isn't it about time *you* understood your financial situation? It

doesn't have to be a mystifying process, even though many so-called financial advisors want you to think that.

3. Does it just sound too complicated? It is, but not because you're stupid. It's hard because it's complex! Financial markets are constantly changing. Just trying to figure out what each new tax law means will continue to generate tons of comments from tax experts and financial reporters. Even people who work in financial areas must constantly read and study to keep up.

Don't let this complexity discourage you. I will explain the confusing terms and sales pitches in everyday terms. You won't be able to sit down and prepare your first financial plan in a few hours, but you will be able to by the time you finish this book.

Obstacles to Reaching Financial Goals

What keeps people from meeting their financial goals? There are six common obstacles:

1. Taxation
2. Inflation
3. Death and disability
4. Ego
5. Lack of a plan
6. Leakage

How many of these apply to you?

Taxation

If you thought you were going to pay less tax under each new "tax relief" plan of Congress, you may have been surprised. In addition, state and local taxes are rising. Do you still need to reduce your taxes even under tax reform? Absolutely.

Do you know how to fund your retirement or your child's education with tax-deferred dollars? In Chapter 9 on taxes, you will learn about tools that can legally reduce or eliminate taxes.

Inflation

Inflation is also a major obstacle to meeting your goals. Many people don't realize how it eats away at their income. You must plan for inflation so that you don't end up with less than you need.

Inflation is one of the factors that gets individuals into financial trouble without even realizing it. Inflation is why you find that so many people who get a raise never quite get ahead. Even the slightest amount of inflation over a period of time can affect your lifestyle if you don't plan properly.

In Chapter 8, you'll learn that Americans save less and less. A 1999 report, "Overview of the Economy," from the U.S. Department of Commerce's Bureau of Economic Analysis says Americans' rate of savings in 1999 was 2.3 percent. You will learn how to keep ahead of inflation through consistent savings.

Death and Disability

Although no one likes to talk about them, death and disability can be devastating to a family that has not planned for these events. You may have estate plans. You should have a will. However, alone these are not enough. What would your financial situation be if a disability forced you to stop work for months, years, or perhaps the rest of your life?

How would you cope as you sit on the couch and watch your car being repossessed? How would you feel if your spouse had to go back to work or work two jobs? I know it's uncomfortable, maybe even painful, to talk or even think about these things, but you must. You will learn how to plan for death and disability. You will learn how having a financial plan will give you a greater sense of security than you have now.

Ego

Some people cannot reach their financial goals because of their egos. They buy cars to impress people. They live in a house they can't afford. They belong to a club simply to impress someone. They put their money into keeping up with the Rockefellers now and don't plan for their future.

I'll show you what happens if you increase your lifestyle one year too soon. You'll be shocked by the difference one year can make regarding whether or not you reach your goals. Ego is the hardest obstacle to overcome. For example, there are valid reasons for buying a house, but if you indulge your ego too soon or too much, that house will keep you from achieving financial independence. You will learn how having a bigger house is *not* necessarily the best investment you can make.

Lack of a Plan

Many people don't meet their financial needs simply because they lack a plan. They *react* to each financial event instead of planning ahead for their whole financial future. When they hear a hot stock tip, they buy stocks. When they hear gold is going up, they buy gold. However, they never consider which investments will help them achieve financial freedom and when and how to buy. You will learn a step-by-step process for setting up an investing plan and also how to avoid the common investment mistakes.

Leakage

Finally, "leakage" can be a hidden obstacle to meeting financial goals. Leakage occurs when you do not reinvest your profit or earnings from the investments made to meet your goal. What did you do with your last stock dividend? Did you spend it instead of investing it? Leakage of these dollars really adds up over time. For example, if you save $5,000 a year and earn 10 percent compounded annually, you would earn $500 the first year. It's so easy to spend that $500 on immediate needs and wants. If you spend this earned interest every year, after 20 years you will ony have the money you put in or $100,000. However, if you reinvest the interest every year, at the end of 20 years, you could have $286,375. Are those new clothes or golf clubs worth the difference of more than $186,000?

Leakage also occurs when you pick an arbitrary dollar amount as a goal, but you aren't really committed to the financial planning process. You keep sabotaging your goal by spending part of the money. For example, you think "If I only had $30,000, everything would be great." When you reach $30,000, you feel like you deserve a vacation and you spend $5,000. Now you only have $25,000. You figure if you build back to $30,000, you're still okay, but you've lost valuable time and the extra dollars from your money compounding (see Chapter 10 for The Amazing Compound Interest Story).

To avoid leakage, the savings and investments for your goal *must be untouchable* for any other reason except the long-term goal of retirement. When you spend part of this long-term money, you are eroding your nest egg.

Using the Income Cycle to Fuel Your Goals

You know that a financial plan is your road map to financial freedom, and you've seen some of the obstacles in the road ahead. What fuel will get you there? If you're going to reach your goal, then you have to use the financial gasoline that you have and that gasoline is your earnings. Figure 1.1 shows the income cycle, your cycle to financial success.

Let's look at the parts of this cycle: the earnings that come in and the expenses that go out.

Earnings

The next sentence is one of the most important you're going to read in any book on investing or financial planning: *Whatever your earnings are, they are.*

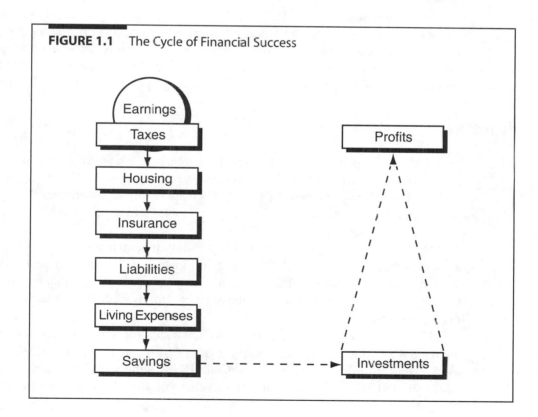

FIGURE 1.1   The Cycle of Financial Success

There aren't any more, there aren't any less. You can't live now on what you think the future will bring. How many of us have said, "I'm going to get a bonus next year." Or "I'm going to get a raise next year." Or "My business is doing really well so I'll have more money soon." Whether you like it or not, you can't live on more than you make. If it's not enough, make some more or change the way you live, but spend less than you earn.

It's surprising how many people don't know what they earn, especially if their pay is hourly, seasonal, includes sporadic bonuses, etc. They don't know what they spend because they don't keep track of credit card purchases or of how they spend the cash they carry around. Do you have any idea how much money your family needs for your current lifestyle? How can you plan if you don't know what you need to live on? If you're single, you need to get a handle on your own spending habits. If you're married, it's critical that both spouses know what's going on financially. If husband and wife communicate financially, then they make a team. But if one doesn't know, then they are handicapped. Your family needs to communicate.

I've seen it over and over. Let's say the husband is handling the family finances, and he dies. As a result, his wife doesn't know who the lawyer or the accountant is, she doesn't know about the trust, and she's struggling to understand all this while grieving at the same time. If you think it's uncomfortable to discuss financial matters with the family now, how painful is it going to be for them if you're gone?

Taxes   .

After your income comes in, you consume it in a variety of ways: taxes, housing, insurance, liabilities, living expenses, and savings. First, you pay taxes. "Oh, but I didn't pay any taxes. I got $1,000 back from the government!" Everyone pays taxes, and the majority of the time, Uncle Sam makes sure that he gets paid first from your paycheck.

However, when I say taxes, most people think federal taxes. Have the federal taxes been going up or down? They've gone down over the last ten years. How about state and local taxes? Most likely they've gone up. It's incredible how much they've gone up. Which do you have the most control over? State and local. Don't forget about them.

Here's an example to make the point. Let's suppose you have $10,000, and you have the option of buying a money market certificate of deposit (MMCD) or a U.S. Treasury bill (T-bill). What is a T-bill? It's simply a giant-sized savings bond worth $10,000. Forget about the fact that you buy the T-bill at a discount.

That's not the issue here. When it matures, it's worth $10,000. Which would you buy? What points should you consider in making that decision? Figure 1.2 outlines these points.

From the federal income tax point of view, is interest taxable on a certificate of deposit? On a T-bill? The answer is yes for both. Now the next question. If I buy a certificate of deposit, is the interest taxable at the state and local level? MMCD—yes; T-bill—no. So if you have $10,000 to invest, and if you assume they are both making comparable rates, and if you understand that state and local taxes are going up, then which one would you pick? The T-bill, of course. Don't forget T-notes and T-bonds, too. These are all "tools" you can use to save taxes. So when I talk about saving taxes in Chapter 9, I'll talk about "tools."

Housing

After paying taxes, the next thing people want to do with their money is buy a house. Why? We all need a place to live. Some of us buy a house to show the world how well we are doing. Many believe a house is an investment. I'll show you that a house is more often an expense rather than investment. If you own a house and have added up all the costs of owning and maintaining it, you may already know that.

How much does it cost to own a house? What it costs you each year to own a house (mortgage payment, taxes, insurance, repairs, and maintenance) is approximately 1.5 percent of its value. So when the market value of a house goes up, so does the cost of owning and maintaining it. In my case, whenever my wife and I sell a house, the water heater blows up the day we sell it. When you buy a house from us, you always know you get a good water heater. You'll learn more about housing costs in Chapter 6.

FIGURE 1.2   Comparison of Certificate of Deposit and Treasury Bill

	Money Market CD	T-bill
Invest	$10,000	$9,500
Pay federal tax?	Yes	Yes
Pay state and local taxes	Yes	No

Insurance

After you earn income, pay taxes, and buy a house, you usually spend money next on insurance. I'll discuss insurance in Chapter 7. How much do you spend on it over your lifetime? Do you know what it really costs? Are you buying protection or trying to use insurance as an investment?

Liabilities

Liabilities absorb your cash flow. Most people enslave themselves right from their financial infancy with a college loan. After getting their first job, most people buy a car, then a house. Already they are behind the financial eight ball. You'll learn how to get out from under that mountain of debt and use credit to help yourself in Chapter 8.

Whenever you go to buy something, *if you don't have the cash, you can't afford it.* You may not choose to pay cash for it. The key is: do you have money now to pay for it?

Living Expenses

After you've covered all these expenses, you can now "live." You need to buy the groceries and pay the utilities. You want to go to the places that are "in" this season. (Here comes that ego again.) You're trying to impress people, maybe before you can afford to do it. Chapter 2 will help you define your goals so you can reach them while still paying your bills today.

Savings

Last, but not least, you save, if there is anything left over. The problem is there's never anything left over. Look at how many years you've been working and look at your bank account.

What if, from the very first day you earned money, from that first babysitting or paper job, what if you had saved 10 percent of your earnings? What would you have now? You'd have a lot of money! Right now, you'd probably be financially free. So you have to learn that you don't save if there is any money left over, you save first. Make savings a priority expense every month.

Here's a simple example of how important savings can be to your financial independence. Let's say you know you'll need a new refrigerator in about ten years. There are three basic options to handle this situation:

1. Start saving for the refrigerator now.
2. Pay cash in ten years.
3. Borrow the money in ten years.

Assuming the cost today for a refrigerator is $1,000, and inflation will be 5 percent each year, the refrigerator will cost $1,629 in ten years if you pay cash for it then. If you start saving $112.50 per year now at an 8 percent return, you will have spent $1,125.00 of your money and earned $504.00 in interest in order to buy that refrigerator. What if you wait and borrow the money? At a 12 percent interest rate over four years, with annual payments of $536, the total cost of the refrigerator would be $2,144, which is $515 more than the actual cost of the refrigerator or $1,119 more than the cost for option 1 ($504 + $515). Doesn't it make sense to save ahead for purchases?

I know this planning sounds like it takes a lot of work. It does. This sounds like it takes discipline. It does. It takes discipline to become an Olympic athlete. It takes discipline to become a plumber. It takes discipline to become financially independent.

You must build your financial plan around your earnings. You only have so much money and only so many years to reach your goal so you must start today. The most important dollar you save is the first one. The first dollar you spend is the most expensive. If you spend that first dollar instead of saving it, look at all the compound interest you will lose over the years. In Chapter 10, I'll show you how important it is to understand how compound interest works.

This may not seem like fun so far, but I'm trying to teach you the basic concepts so you can prepare a successful financial plan. You've got to get the concepts fixed in your mind. If you get on the scale every day, you can see how much you weigh. As long as you get on the scale, you know your weight. If you don't get on the scale, you can pretend that you're a different weight, but your actual weight doesn't change. You can pretend that you're well off financially, but that doesn't change your earnings or savings. You must work to change your weight; you must do some work in order to become financially independent. Being able to make knowledgeable financial decisions is much better than being tempted to make those decisions based on hunches, today's headlines, and poor advice from well-meaning acquaintances.

Investments

After you have some savings, you get to make investments. I get irritated when people say, "But savings aren't investments." Yes they are. How can you have any money to invest if you don't save some money first? Chapter 10 covers savings and investments.

Now that you see how the income cycle works, let's look at the steps you must take to prepare your financial plan.

The Financial Planning Process

How do you set up your financial plan? You follow a six-step planning process:

1. What do you want? Identify your financial and personal needs.
2. What do you have now? Collect your information.
3. What's holding you back? Consider your problem areas.
4. How do you get what you want? Develop written recommendations and alternate solutions.
5. Put your plan into action.
6. Is it working? Review your plan at least once a year.

Here's a brief description of the process. You'll work through each step more thoroughly in Chapters 2 and 3.

First, write down your financial needs and dreams. Second, locate and evaluate your important documents. Third, as you evaluate your wish list and your financial information, identify any problem areas. What if your first child starts college in two years, and you don't have money saved for tuition?

Fourth, after completing your wish list and comparing it to what you have, write out ways to get what you want. You must write down your plan. Many of us talk about our dreams for the future. Putting them down on paper is the first step in making them a reality.

You may find that you start out with plan A and end up with so many revisions that it becomes plan E. That's fine. You need to consider all your options. Chapter 2 will help you to ask and answer questions such as: If I were disabled, what would change? If my spouse dies, what would change? If my kids go to college, what would change?

Fifth, following the strategies you've written down, put your plan into action. When you have financial questions, refer to the plan. Sixth, and finally, review the plan periodically to see if it is still what you want or if your financial situation has changed.

This all may sound a bit overwhelming when you look at the whole task ahead of you. By working on your plan one step at a time, however, you will be able to accomplish your goals.

The Book Is the Plan

The rest of this book will help you prepare *your* financial plan. Each time you find a worksheet, you will see an example of how to complete it. Then you can use the blank worksheets in the back of book to fill in your information.

Do you need further help in putting together your financial plan? It depends on your circumstances. If your financial situation is fairly simple and you earn less than $50,000 per year, then by the time you finish this book your plan should be complete.

If you earn more than $50,000 per year or your financial situation is complex, then you will benefit from the help of a professional financial planner. Refer to Chapter 12 to help you in choosing a competent planner.

Start Now

Putting together your financial plan the first time will be the hardest. But who cares more about your money than you? Make it a habit to give yourself a financial health exam every year, just as you would have a checkup with the doctor.

So what are you waiting for? It's time to show your money who's boss. Sharpen your pencils, gather your file folders, boot up your computer, and start now. Chapter 2 will tell you exactly what to do.

Summary

- Most people react to financial situations when they should be planning for them.

- Everyone needs a financial plan as a guide through the complex and constantly changing financial world. As a result of having a plan, you control your money instead of your money being in control of you.
- A financial plan is not just insurance or investments or tax planning. A good financial plan is a combination of these, plus an objective evaluation of where you are now, what you want and when, and what it will take to reach your goals.
- Many people think financial planning is investing; it's not. In future chapters you'll learn the important differences between these two terms and how to avoid the mistakes that others make.
- Your income cycle is important: you must save first or you will never reach your goals.
- Do not spend more than you earn.

2

What Do You Want?

What are your dreams? Do you want to tour Europe or go fishing when you retire? Do you want your children to go to Harvard or a state university? Do you want to leave millions through your estate or give your stamp collection to your favorite nephew?

Every person has a different dream, a different wish list of what they want for themselves and their family, for now and for later. What follows are questions to help you put your goals in writing, perhaps for the first time. Don't let these questions restrict you. If you don't see something listed that you want, put it in. This is *your* wish list.

Don't be afraid to dream big. We'll discuss the realities of how to get there later. For now, focus on your wishes.

Put It in Writing

Why do you need to do this? Good question. You're a busy person. Why take time to write things out that you already know? Here are several reasons:

- Writing down your dreams is the first step in making them happen. It makes them goals, not just dreams. Be specific in what you want. Don't say, "I want to retire with lots of money." Put a dollar amount on your goal.

"I need $50,000 per year in today's dollars when I retire." Or list what you want to do and the lifestyle you want and then put a dollar amount on that.

- Writing down your dreams will bring to light any gaps in information. How much insurance do you have? Where are all your policies? What are the total annual college costs today at the college your child might attend?

- Writing down your dreams and then sharing them with your family keeps everyone focused on the same goal. You may already have had these kinds of discussions with your family. If not, you may be surprised to find out that your family has different goals. What if your spouse wants to retire near the ocean while you love the mountains? Better to discuss this now rather than be surprised later.

- Writing down your dreams and informing your advisors will help them serve you better. The more they know about what you want, the more they can tailor their services to you. If you don't want to leave a large estate, your insurance agent shouldn't be trying to sell you more coverage "in order to have a large estate." If you want your spouse to be able to continue your business if you die, has your attorney included that in your will and gone over the paperwork with both of you?

- Writing down your dreams helps you keep up-to-date on what you want. When was your will last updated? Is your insurance coverage too much or too little? Have you had more children or have some moved away from home since you last considered all your financial affairs as a whole? None of us is the same person today as we were five years ago. Our dreams change. Our financial plan should keep up so those dreams can become reality.

Six Steps to Financial Freedom

"Okay, you've convinced me. I need to write down my goals. But then what?"

You'll use six steps in preparing your financial plan. Working through these steps and using the explanations in this book will put you on your way to financial independence.

Sound complicated? It's not really. You follow a similar planning process every day and don't realize it. Whether you're getting ready to paint the house or cook a meal, you must go through this process. Here are the six steps and two simple examples to show how they work.

Planning Process:

1. What do you want? Identify financial and personal goals.
2. What do you have now? Collect information.
3. What's holding you back? Consider problem areas.
4. How do you get what you want? Develop written recommendations and alternate solutions.
5. Put your plan into action.
6. Is it working? Review the plan at least once a year.

Paint the House:

1. Spruce up the house with a coat of new paint.
2. How many square feet need to be painted?
3. Are there any spots that need primer? How many square feet?
4. Possible solutions:
   a. Put on primer, then paint.
   b. Paint next year.
   c. Hire work done.
   d. Put on siding.
5. You chose option "a." Buy primer and paint sufficient for square feet you need to cover. Put on primer; then paint.
6. House looks great six months later. Pat yourself on the back.

Prepare a Meal:

1. Prepare lunch for four people.
2. What ingredients do I have?
3. I have only one pound of ground beef.
4. Possible solutions:
   a. Fix hamburgers. Use other ingredients for side dishes to make complete meal.
   b. Fix something else using ingredients on hand, or go to store first.
   c. Go out to eat.
5. Go out to eat.
6. Lunch was not that good. Option "c" can be chosen again, but not that restaurant.

Obviously, preparing your financial plan will take a little more thought. Here is a description of each of the financial planning steps and how they will help you build your financial plan.

One: What Do You Want? Identify Financial and Personal Goals

By now you know that you need to write down your goals. You may find some questions helpful in guiding your thinking. The rest of this chapter will cover those questions.

Two: What Do You Have Now? Collect Information

After writing down your goals, you will need to find and evaluate all your important financial data. Finding these documents may indeed be a "treasure hunt." Chapter 3 has a checklist to be sure you don't miss anything.

"But that sounds like a lot of work!" Yes, it will take time. But if you don't know where you're starting from, you can't make a plan to reach your goal. Remember, it's your money that you're going to manage. Who cares more about your money than you? If you want to make more money, it will take some work.

Chapter 3 shows you how to organize your financial data with a cash flow worksheet, a tax calculation worksheet, a spendable cash worksheet, and a balance sheet. Then you will learn how to evaluate the information each worksheet provides. If you don't know what a balance sheet is, don't despair. Chapter 3 explains the financial terms you need to know and has samples of how to fill out each worksheet.

Three: What's Holding You Back? Consider Problem Areas

Look at your financial problem areas. What is preventing you from achieving financial independence? You probably have struggled with one or more of these common problems:

- High taxes
- Too little insurance or paying for too much
- Inadequate cash flow
- Poor liquidity
- High debt
- Low rate of return

This book will help you tackle these problems and find workable solutions.

Four: How Do You Get What You Want? Develop Written Recommendations and Alternate Solutions

Once you've written down what you want and you know what you have now, what do you do next? You must analyze your situation and develop specific ways to meet your financial goals. In other words, how do you get what you want? As an example, if your investment rate of return is too low to meet your goals, one recommendation might be to raise your rate of return. With the help of this book, you will learn several ways to do that.

Five: Put Your Plan into Action

You may now feel like you're home free. However, a good financial plan only works if it's put into action. Continuing with the rate of return example, you must now choose a specific product that will meet your need for a higher rate *and* you must purchase that product.

Sound simple? This is where many people go astray in their financial planning. Some of you are great at planning on paper but put off taking action. Others of you want to take action right now without having a complete plan to guide the actions. Everyone needs both a good plan and the implementation of the plan. Having a professional financial planner to advise you and to help you put your plan into action may be your first good investment toward financial independence.

Six: Is It Working? Review the Plan

No financial plan should be carved in stone. Review it periodically with your spouse and financial planner. Adjust your plan to your changing circumstances, to the changing marketplace, and to the changing tax laws. A review once a year should be sufficient unless an unusual circumstance occurs, for example, a death in the family, a job and pay change, or an inheritance.

> You must be honest with your financial planner. A planner can't give you directions if where you're going is not clear. It would be like stopping on the street corner and asking the same planner for directions without explaining where you're going or what kind of transportation you're using.

Start Planning

Now that you understand the planning process, let's get started. Get out your pencil and at least five sheets of paper. Label the five sheets with the following headings.

1. Retirement plan
2. Education plan
3. Estate plan
4. Disability plan
5. Other needs

Here are some questions to get you started in each area. Remember to be as specific as you can. However, if you don't know how much something will cost, put down a guess and go on. Don't get too bogged down in details at this point. Later on, you'll be filling in more details about each wish.

Retirement Plan

1. What is your current age and at what age do you want to retire? How about your spouse? You may want to retire at 40 but realistically expect to retire at 55. Go ahead and put both numbers down. As you prepare your financial plan, you will find out which age is better for you. Do you think you're too young to be planning your retirement? If you're 21, prepare your plan according to the steps in this book, and put that plan into action, you probably can retire at age 40.

It's never too late to start your financial plan. Any planning for retirement, even if you have just retired, is better than no financial planning.

2. Do you want to retire all at once or gradually cut back your work hours? If you retire from one job, do you plan to start a business or work at a different job, but for fewer hours? Will you be making more, less, or the same income? In other words, do you plan to continue to earn income or do you want to live off investments, pensions, and Social Security?

Remember that retirement doesn't have to mean rocking chairs. I know many retired people who put in full days managing their own money or continuing to work at what they enjoy. You don't have to put yourself in mothballs just because you retire.

3. How much do you need to live on? This is a difficult question because none of us has a crystal ball regarding the future. While inflation is relatively low as of this writing, there are no guarantees.

So how do you decide how much money you need? For now, use the following simple equation to estimate your costs. (In Chapter 3, you'll learn how to do a more detailed estimate of your retirement needs.)

How much money do you need now to maintain your standard of living?	$_____
Those costs that will increase	+_____
The most money you might need	$_____
Those costs which may be eliminated or reduced	−_____
The least money you might need	$_____

For example, if you plan to retire to a warm state and spend most of your time there, costs for heating and winter clothes will be reduced, if not eliminated. Air conditioning costs may be more than you currently pay. Because you are getting older, it is likely that your health costs will eventually increase. Depending on your health insurance arrangements, you may need to add a large amount to your needs estimate to cover increased health costs.

As for inflation, you can beat it! In the investment chapter you will learn specific ways to make your investments grow faster than inflation. That way if you estimate how much it would cost you per year if you retired today, your money should have the same purchasing power later.

4. How many years of retirement do you need to fund? Most of us would like to live to a healthy old age, but how do you predict your life span? I've always told my classes that the ideal retirement plan for my wife and I goes like this: *We both die on the day that we spend our last nickel.*

For yourself, there's no need to get out a crystal ball. The insurance companies have already done life expectancy tables on people who have insurance. Use one as a guide to determine how many years you will live (see Appendix A). Obviously, if your grandparents and parents all lived to a hundred, then you may want to add a few more years to your life estimate, and congratulate yourself that you picked the right ancestors.

5. What do you want to do when you retire? You may want to continue your life just as it is today. Or you may plan to drastically change everything. Or you're in between. Whatever you have dreamed of doing in retirement, write it down. Writing your dreams down is the first step in making them reality. Plus it will help you plan your preparations for retirement, both financial and psychological. If you want to paint, but have never picked up a paintbrush, maybe now is the time to take a beginning art course. You may find you love it, you hate to sit still, or you're allergic to paint.

Education Plan

    1. How many children will go to college? This is a more difficult question than it may seem. You may hope your children become doctors or lawyers, but they may become plumbers (and probably make more!). Still, if your children are young, all these decisions are far in the future. For now, it's probably better to assume they will go and plan accordingly. Do you want to return to college? Add yourself to your education plan.

    2. What are their current ages? Will you have more than one attending at a time?

    3. How many years until they start college? List years to enrollment for each child.

    4. How many years will they attend college? There are two-year and four-year schools, graduate schools, and professional schools. Do they want to go to a vocational school? How many years do you need to fund?

    5. What are the possibilities for scholarships, grants, and other financial aid? Obviously, the older the children are, the better idea you will have as to their potential for financial assistance. Have you looked into these ways of paying for college or do you want to consider them?

    6. What is the current cost of college? Choose the college that they might attend and find out the current cost for one year. Remember to include tuition, room and board, books, lab fees, and personal expenses in your estimate.

    7. What is the rate of increase for tuition? At present, most college tuition increases are more than the current rate of inflation. You'll need to keep an eye on these increases as you reevaluate your financial plan each year.

Estate Plan

1. Do you have a current will? Does your spouse?

2. What if you die first? How much you want to leave for your family may depend on factors such as whether your spouse works outside the home and would continue doing so, and the ages of your children, if any.

3. What if you are a full-time homemaker and die first? What services such as housekeeping and child care would need to be covered? If you also work outside the home, what income, insurance, or other benefits would need to be replaced?

4. What if both of you die at the same time? What do you want to do with your estate?

5. Do you need to pay off bills? Are there mortgage(s), business obligations, and so on that must be paid?

6. How much ready money would be needed right away to handle day-to-day expenses? How long does it take an estate to be probated in your area? Will any other bills become due during this time?

7. Do you need a dedicated college fund? Look again at the previous questions for your education plan in light of your estate plan.

8. If one of you dies, would the other one want to sell the house in that first year or stay there for at least a year?

9. Do you want to leave anything to family, friends, other people, charities, colleges, and so on?

10. What do you want to leave behind: money, real estate, and/or personal property?

11. Who will get what? Do you want to divide things equally between people? Do you want to give percentages? Do you want to specify priorities for the distribution of your estate or specify that someone would get a minimum of so many dollars in case your estate is worth less than you anticipated?

12. Are there any strings on any bequest? Do you want to give a lump sum, a certain amount each year, or a bequest made only if certain requirements are met?

13. Do you want to exclude someone specifically?

Disability Plan

1. What happens if your income is gone? What would you do if your income stopped for a short time (less than two years), for more than two years, or for the rest of your life (permanent disability)? Where would you get the money to live on?

2. What happens if your spouse's income is gone? Consider the same three scenarios.

3. What costs could you eliminate or defer for any of the above scenarios? Do you have insurance to cover lost wages?

4. What percent of your current income could you live on for any of the above scenarios? For example, if you had no income for two years, would you need 80 percent or 100 percent of your current income to live on? Some people would be able to tighten their belts and get by. Others might need more than their current income if their medical insurance did not cover any increased costs of the disability. What would be right for you?

Other Goals

In addition to the previous basic needs, we all have other goals we would like to reach. Maybe it's adding onto the house or buying a bigger one. Maybe it's buying a new car every three years or taking a vacation every six months. These are legitimate goals, too. Be sure to write them down.

We all need to provide enough for our retirement, education, estate, and disability plans, but it's important to keep a balance between the future and today. After all, you are living in the here and now. One of the many benefits of a good financial plan is that when you follow it, you can enjoy today more, knowing you've planned for the future.

Review Your Plans with Your Family Members and Advisors

Sometimes this is the hardest part. You may find out you and your spouse have very different goals. It's better to know it now than later, even at the expense of unpleasantness now. If you want to leave your estate to charity and your spouse doesn't agree, you need to talk out that decision now and/or revise your goals.

On the other hand, you may be pleasantly surprised to find out that both of you have always wanted to try your hand at painting, but somehow it's never come up in your day-to-day conversations.

> **A** couple should be in agreement on the general direction of their goals. If they have different goals, that's okay. If their goals are conflicting, a financial planner cannot help until they resolve their conflicts.

Discussing your plan with family members may uncover items that have been overlooked. Perhaps a special relative should be included in your estate planning. This is why businesses frequently have planning retreats. It helps to clarify who you are, where you are going, and how you are going to get there. That is what your financial plan will do for you.

Including your advisors in this goal-setting is good common sense. How can they help you achieve what you want if they are not clear on what that is? You may have always told your stockbroker to invest conservatively. Does that fit with all the dreams you've listed or do you need to take a more aggressive stance? If you want an estate of $5 million, then you may need to make your insurance dollars work harder for you by buying more term insurance instead of whole life. These choices will be discussed more fully in Chapter 7.

You Know What You Want

As you can see by now, a financial plan must start with a list of what you want. Before you go on to the next chapter, review what you've written down on your five sheets under the headings listed above. You may want to revise the retirement sheet based on what you wrote later on the disability sheet and so on. These are your goals; revise them until they are right for you and your family.

Now it's time to add more substance to those dreams by filling in the details in Chapter 3.

Summary

What do you want out of life? You need to write down your goals in order to achieve them, to find gaps in information, to let your family know what you want, and to help your advisors serve you better.

There are six steps to financial freedom. To prepare your financial plan, you and your spouse should work through each step:

1. What do you want? Identify financial and personal needs.
2. What do you have now? Collect information.
3. What's holding you back? Consider problem areas.
4. How do you get what you want? Develop written recommendations and alternate solutions.
5. Put your plan into action.
6. Is it working? Review the plan at least once a year.

Review your plan with your financial advisors. Consider their suggestions, but the final decisions are for you and your spouse alone to make.

What Do You Have Now?

Do you know what your net worth is? Do you know what your total debt is? Do you have a rough idea of how much you'll owe in taxes this year?

If you answered yes to all these questions, then you probably have your financial information well organized and you will breeze through this chapter. However, most of us have only a vague idea of the answers to these and other questions about our financial data. This chapter may take effort. However, it will be rewarding to finally know the answers.

In this chapter you will work through a checklist of the financial information you must find. You may discover you're missing some data, and you'll need to fill in those gaps. Next, you'll do cash flow planning, including formulating an estimate of how much in taxes you'll owe this year. The spendable cash worksheet will give you the benchmark data you need to analyze new financial proposals. Finally, there is the balance sheet. You'll calculate what your "bottom line" is: how much you're worth right now. Then when you review your financial plan next year, you'll be able to see how much you've gained or lost over the year.

So let's get started! Where is that financial information of yours?

Materials You'll Need

First, you'll need a few materials to help you get organized: a financial calculator, at least 16 file folders to start, an accordion file, and a 13-column ruled accountant's pad for your cash flow worksheet. While a financial calculator is not a must (you can do the calculations needed with an ordinary calculator using the reference tables in Appendix A), you will be able to calculate percentages and other results more easily with a financial calculator. If you have a computer, a spreadsheet program will allow you to keep track of all these details.

Information You'll Need

Figure 3.1 shows the financial information you must collect and put into your folders. If an item doesn't apply to you, go on to the next item. You may not need a folder for every item on this list. In fact, you may wish to start with the 16 main headings listed so you don't get overwhelmed. For some items, such as general insurance, you may need a folder for each type of policy.

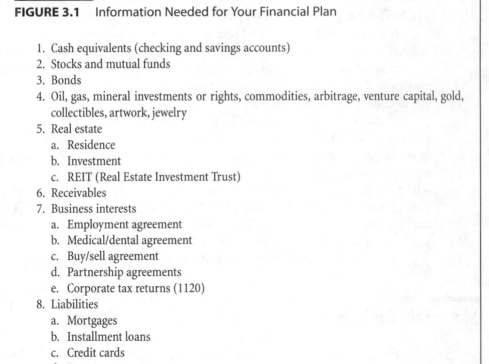

FIGURE 3.1   Information Needed for Your Financial Plan

1. Cash equivalents (checking and savings accounts)
2. Stocks and mutual funds
3. Bonds
4. Oil, gas, mineral investments or rights, commodities, arbitrage, venture capital, gold, collectibles, artwork, jewelry
5. Real estate
   a. Residence
   b. Investment
   c. REIT (Real Estate Investment Trust)
6. Receivables
7. Business interests
   a. Employment agreement
   b. Medical/dental agreement
   c. Buy/sell agreement
   d. Partnership agreements
   e. Corporate tax returns (1120)
8. Liabilities
   a. Mortgages
   b. Installment loans
   c. Credit cards
   d. Leases

9. Life insurance
10. Health and accident insurance
    a. Hospitalization/major medical
    b. Expense reimbursement
    c. Disability
11. General insurance
    a. Homeowners/PCP (Property Comprehensive Policy)
    b. Automobile
    c. Office
    d. Professional liability
    e. Umbrella
    f. Fidelity
    g. Marine
12. Estate planning
    a. Wills
    b. Trusts
    c. Powers of attorney
    d. Legal documents
13. Retirement planning
    a. Defined-contribution pension (also called "money purchase")
    b. Defined-benefit pension
    c. Profit sharing
    d. Keogh
    e. IRA
    f. 401(k)
    g. Public employee retirement system
    h. State teacher retirement system
14. Education planning
15. Income planning
    a. Personal tax returns (1040)
16. Miscellaneous

Finding the Information

If you have your actual stock certificates, put a copy of them in the proper folder (the originals should be in your safe deposit box). If a broker holds them, put the latest brokerage statement in the folder. If your bonds are in your safe deposit box, put copies of them in the proper folder. If you have bearer bonds, put a copy in the folder. Wherever the information is, you need to get it.

You will need to pull out your insurance papers. Get out those policies and blow the dust off of them. In Chapter 7, I'll show you what all those fancy terms mean in your policy and why some companies hope you remain ignorant about them.

Do the same for all your financial information. Why do all this work? You need to know what you have now. The only way to do that is to have the information all in one place and complete the worksheets in this chapter. It will be worth the effort just to have all your financial data together for review.

> **B**e sure that your planner asks you for the actual documents to confirm that your understanding of each item is correct. For example, you may think that an account is jointly owned when, in fact, it is not. There are significant consequences to your estate plan if the ownership is not correct for the plan you are creating.

Obviously, all this information is valuable to you so keep it in a safe place in your home. Keep the information all together until you've completed your financial plan. You'll need to refer back to various items as you work through the rest of the book. If you have to keep going back to your safe deposit box or someplace else to look up some detail, you will lose your momentum.

How long will it take to work through this chapter? A lot depends on the complexity of your financial affairs. If you're single with few investments, then a few hours may be enough. If you're married with children, have many investments, own your own business, and have a complex estate, then you will need to set aside time each day to work on it until you complete this chapter. Also allow enough time to review the results of this chapter's work with your spouse and financial advisor. They may catch items you missed. Don't get discouraged! Planning for your future is a lot easier than not having a plan for your future.

Identify the Information Gaps

Were you able to find every piece of information? Most of us usually come up short on one or more items. The checklist in Figure 3.2 may help in finding things. You may smile at some of the locations, but people do put things in the strangest places.

Do you have a favorite secret storage place of your own? Check it. We sometimes put things in temporary safe places

> **I**f your planner doesn't care about the details, he or she may miss some important piece of your total financial picture, or your planner may not know the significance of the detail. Sometimes the person asking the questions demonstrates intelligence or knowledge by the questions asked.

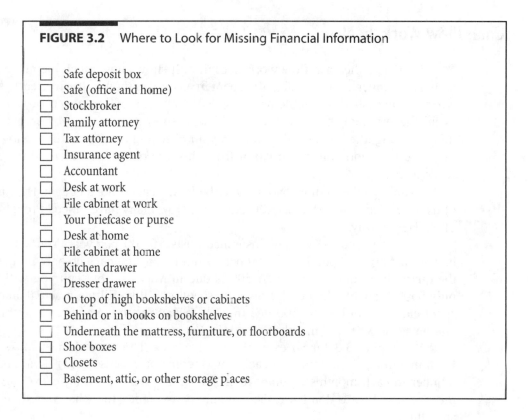

FIGURE 3.2   Where to Look for Missing Financial Information

- ☐ Safe deposit box
- ☐ Safe (office and home)
- ☐ Stockbroker
- ☐ Family attorney
- ☐ Tax attorney
- ☐ Insurance agent
- ☐ Accountant
- ☐ Desk at work
- ☐ File cabinet at work
- ☐ Your briefcase or purse
- ☐ Desk at home
- ☐ File cabinet at home
- ☐ Kitchen drawer
- ☐ Dresser drawer
- ☐ On top of high bookshelves or cabinets
- ☐ Behind or in books on bookshelves
- ☐ Underneath the mattress, furniture, or floorboards
- ☐ Shoe boxes
- ☐ Closets
- ☐ Basement, attic, or other storage places

until we can get to the safe deposit box or other permanent storage place. Then we forget and that temporary place becomes permanent.

After you've checked all these places and still can't find something, then it's time to figure out how to get the document replaced. Almost any document from birth certificates to bonds can be replaced if you have some other proof of ownership or can provide specific information about the item. Use the phone, write a letter, or make a visit. Take the time now to get this information.

Cash Flow Planning: When, Where, and How Much?

Now that you've got all your information together, it's time to start completing the worksheets. Use the blank worksheets in Appendixes B and C. Read through the following descriptions of how to fill in each worksheet, then get to work.

Cash Flow Worksheet

Complete the cash flow worksheet first. It shows how much income comes in and how much money is actually spent in any given month. It will clearly show where your cash flow problems are so you can take action ahead of time and avoid the problem in the future. It will also show you where you might have money sitting idle for several months in your checking account earning a low rate of interest. In addition, information from this worksheet will be used for other worksheets.

I know you're saying, "Not another budget!" This is not a budget. How many of us have tried to follow a budget? All of us. How many have failed? Probably all of us. Here's why.

Let's say you know your insurance costs $6,000 per year. You start your budget in April and put down $500 per month for insurance. The only problem is the quarterly insurance bill of $1,500 is due in May, and by then you will have only $500 available. In a cash flow worksheet, you'll be filling in actual amounts spent each month (the $1,500 due in May to pay for the quarter), not estimated amounts (the $500 per month if you did a budget).

See Figure 3.3 for an example of what a cash flow worksheet looks like. Each month has a column, and each row (income or expense item) should have a number in each month's column. *Remember these numbers are just to illustrate the concept.* Please don't use these numbers as guides for what you should be spending!

At the bottom, the total expenses and net income are calculated, and the cumulative surplus is shown. Note that negative numbers are shown in parentheses (see April's net income figure at the bottom of the worksheet). This is a common accounting practice.

Let's go through the categories shown on the left and see what is needed. "Cash available" is liquid cash, what you could get tomorrow morning from your savings or other cash accounts. This is used for the first month that you fill out the worksheet. For the second month and forward, your "cash available" is whatever the "cumulative surplus" amount is at the bottom of the worksheet. "Salary" is what is reflected on your pay stubs.

Income

People whose income is erratic think a cash flow worksheet is only for those who earn a salary. Not true. It's even more important for someone who has variable income to go through this exercise. Once most self–employed people put

FIGURE 3.3   Sample Cash Flow Worksheet

SAMPLE	MAR	APR	MAY	JUN	JUL	AUG	SEP	OCT	NOV	DEC	JAN	FEB	TOTALS
1 Cash available	5,000												5,000
INCOME													
2 Salary	6,000	6,000	6,000	6,000	6,000	6,000	6,000	6,000	6,000	6,000	6,000	6,000	72,000
3 Self-employment net income													
4 Investment income													
5 TOTAL INCOME	6,000	6,000	6,000	6,000	6,000	6,000	6,000	6,000	6,000	6,000	6,000	6,000	72,000
6 TOTAL CASH	11,000	6,000	6,000	6,000	6,000	6,000	6,000	6,000	6,000	6,000	6,000	6,000	77,000
EXPENSES													
7 Taxes — personal property	0	0	0	0	0	0	0	0	0	3,000	0	0	3,000
8 Taxes — real estate	0	0	0	0	0	0	0	0	0	4,000	0	0	4,000
9 Home maintenance	200	200	200	200	200	200	200	200	200	200	200	200	2,400
10 Food	100	100	100	100	100	100	100	100	100	100	100	100	1,200
11 Household expenses	500	500	500	500	500	500	500	500	500	500	500	500	6,200
12 Medical/dental	150	50	250	150	50	50	150	50	50	150	50	50	1,200
13 Clothes	700	500	500	500	500	1,500	500	500	1,500	500	500	500	8,200
14 Charitable contributions	200	200	200	200	200	200	200	200	200	200	200	200	2,400
15 Auto — gas/repairs	200	200	200	200	200	200	200	200	200	200	200	200	2,400
16 Home mortgage	1,400	1,400	1,400	1,400	1,400	1,400	1,400	1,400	1,400	1,400	1,400	1,400	16,800
17 Telephone — home	100	100	100	100	100	100	100	100	100	100	100	100	1,200
18 Electric — home	400	200	200	150	150	200	250	300	400	400	500	400	3,650
19 Water — home	65	65	150	150	48	48	100	48	65	65	65	65	1,140
20 Cable — home	48	48	48	48	48	48	48	48	48	48	48	48	576
21 Business expense	400	400	100	400	100	100	400	100	100	400	100	100	2,700

(continued)

FIGURE 3.3 Sample Cash Flow Worksheet (continued)

SAMPLE	MAR	APR	MAY	JUN	JUL	AUG	SEP	OCT	NOV	DEC	JAN	FEB	TOTALS
22 Education	0	0	0	0	0	0	0	0	0	0	0	0	0
23 Insurance — life	0	1,500	0	0	1,500	0	0	1,500	0	0	1,500	0	6,000
24 Insurance — home	0	0	0	0	0	0	0	0	0	0	0	0	0
25 Insurance — car	200	200	200	200	200	200	200	200	200	200	200	200	2,400
26 Insurance — personal umbrella	0	0	0	0	0	0	0	0	0	0	0	0	0
27 Gifts	50	50	50	50	50	50	50	50	50	50	50	50	600
28 Vacations	0	0	0	0	2,000	0	0	0	0	0	0	1,500	3,500
29 Miscellaneous	200	200	200	200	200	200	200	200	200	200	200	200	2,400
30 Lessons	245	245	245	0	0	0	245	245	245	245	245	245	2,205
31 Camp	0	1,000	0	0	0	0	0	0	0	0	0	0	1,000
32 Bank loan #1	239	239	239	239	239	239	239	239	239	239	239	239	2,868
33 Bank loan #2	300	300	300	300	300	300	300	300	300	300	300	300	3,600
34 Bank loan #3	150	150	150	150	150	150	150	150	150	150	150	150	1,800
35 Bank loan #4	200	200	200	200	200	200	200	200	200	200	200	200	2,400
36 TOTAL EXPENSES	6,047	8,047	5,532	5,487	8,587	6,037	5,732	6,882	6,447	12,847	7,047	6,947	85,839
37 NET INCOME	4,953	(2,047)	468	513	(2,587)	(37)	268	(882)	(447)	(6,847)	(1,047)	(947)	(8,639)
38 CUMULATIVE SURPLUS	4,953	2,906	3,374	3,887	1,300	1,263	1,531	649	202	(6,645)	(7,692)	(8,639)	

down an amount that they expect to earn in a particular month, I've found that they will work to make it come true.

If you have dividends, you should know when they are paid. If you have interest, you should know when it is paid. That's the "income" part of the worksheet.

Expenses

You'll need many rows to list expense items. You may have more or fewer than the example. Use it to help you think of all possible expenses.

Some expenses you pay every month and others are only paid occasionally. Periodic expenses may include car insurance, property and personal property taxes, safe deposit box fees, sanitation fees, some business expenses, and so on.

Examples of expenses that you pay every month usually include: income and payroll taxes; household expenses such as heating, electricity, and phone; fixed real estate costs such as condominium fees, rent, and mortgage; food; gasoline; credit cards; business expenses such as wages, benefits, and office expenses; and so on.

The cash flow worksheet helps you plan around the irregular income. Using life insurance costs as an example, let's say the quarterly payment is due in April. In April's column, you put down $1,500. For March and May, you put 0, because you don't pay anything then.

Utilities. "My utilities? I'm not on the budget plan." Well, get out your past bills, and you'll see a pattern. You spend more in the winter and less in the summer on utilities, unless you have air conditioning.

Clothing. Most people spend in cycles. When do you buy the children's clothes? You probably buy most of them in August before school starts and before Christmas.

Gifts. You know when the birthdays and holidays are. You know the discussion you always have: "How much should we spend on Cousin Susie? Do we spend more or less on Aunt Matilda?" Now you can figure this out ahead of time and plan what you're going to spend.

Vacation. Everyone needs a vacation. Everyone needs time away to recharge their batteries.

Plan Your Future Cash Flow

You should start your worksheet by filling in the current month, or if you prefer, you can do a January–December worksheet. This should be future cash flow, not a history of past spending.

For your first month, "Total Cash" is what you already have in the checkbook plus any other income that month. You do that for each month. What happens the next month? You overspend. That happens to lots of people.

When you know your cash flow, then you can see if you have money sitting there not earning enough interest. If you see that you've got extra money sitting in your checking account every month, then you should put it where it will earn more money. In Figure 3.3, notice that there is a surplus of $2,900 or more for March through June. One of the principles of financial planning is that the longer you have your money someplace, the more it earns. So if you look at your cash flow and see that you don't need that money for three months, you can put it into a certificate of deposit, a 13-week Treasury bill, or a money market mutual fund for that length of time and earn a higher rate of return.

Plan Your Cash Reserve

I'm always asked, "How much should I have in reserve?" That depends on your cash flow. Money in reserve is money you can get out quickly for emergencies. You may have heard that you need six month's income in reserve. Why six months? Because some expert said that once, and now it's been quoted ever since. It doesn't make sense. This is *personal* financial planning. What do *you* need? Your cash flow worksheet will help you answer that and other questions about where your money is going.

This sample worksheet shows one of the benefits of doing a cash flow worksheet. You can see that there are eight months with a negative cash flow. The result? By the end of the year, this person is in the hole by $8,639. The government may be able to operate on a deficit budget, but you can't afford it.

The cash flow worksheet will highlight these potential problems for the coming year. Then you can take action before a problem occurs. You can either increase income or decrease expenses so that you make sure that you can live on what you earn and have money to invest for your future.

Now take out your 13-column accountant's paper or open up your spreadsheet. In the second column, start with the current month and write in a month in each column heading. Then in the first column, enter your own income and expenses categories and start filling in the numbers. Don't forget to include all the taxes you pay, such as federal and state income tax and other payroll taxes.

If you have a computer, there are excellent software programs such as Quicken and Money that are more sophisticated than spreadsheets. Not only will they handle the cash flow worksheets and other worksheets, but they will allow you to do "what if" scenarios. Because they recalculate automatically, you can see the consequences of the change.

Income and Expenses Worksheets

The Income and Expenses Worksheets in Figures 3.4 and 3.5 will help jog your memory on all the different sources of income and all the different ways you can spend that money. For your own worksheets, be sure to enter the yearly amount for each item that you will receive or spend in the coming year. You'll notice that the data from the totals column of the cash flow worksheet can be used to assist in filling out the income and expenses worksheets. If you still don't know the amount for a particular item, make an estimate or check last year's tax forms or other data from last year.

Now you know what your cash flow is and what your annual income and expenses are. Next, you need to calculate your tax bite.

FIGURE 3.4   Annual Income Worksheet

EARNED INCOME

    Salary   _____

    Self-employment   _____

    Retirement   _____

    Other earned income   _____

INVESTMENT INCOME

    Interest — taxable   _____

    Interest — federal and state exempt   _____

    Interest — federal tax exempt   _____

    Interest — state tax exempt   _____

    Interest — money market fund   _____

    Dividends   _____

    Capital gains   _____

    Annuity   _____

    Other   _____

(continued)

FIGURE 3.4 Annual Income Worksheet (continued)

OTHER INCOME

    Social Security   _____

    Alimony received   _____

    Unemployment compensation   _____

    Other — not taxable   _____

    State and local income tax refund   _____

    Other — taxable   _____

BUSINESS INCOME

    Sales   _____

    Gross receipts   _____

    Fees   _____

    Other   _____

UNCLASSIFIED INCOME

_____   _____

_____   _____

_____   _____

_____   _____

_____   _____

_____   _____

_____   _____

_____   _____

FIGURE 3.5   Annual Expenses Worksheet

INCOME & PAYROLL TAXES

    Federal Income Tax (FIT) — withheld   _____

    FIT — estimated payments   _____

    FIT — payment with return   _____

    State Income Tax (SIT) — withheld   _____

    SIT — estimated payment   _____

    SIT — payment with return   _____

    Local income tax   _____

    Social Security tax   _____

    State disability insurance   _____

    Income tax penalties   _____

HOUSEHOLD EXPENSES

    Fixed real estate   _____

    Maintenance and repairs   _____

    Real estate taxes   _____

    Home improvement   _____

    Furniture and decorating   _____

    Utilities   _____

    Personal property taxes   _____

    Vacation home expenses   _____

    Other   _____

PERSONAL EXPENSES

    Food   _____

    Personal allowances   _____

(continued)

FIGURE 3.5   Annual Expenses Worksheet (continued)

PERSONAL EXPENSES (continued)

    Medical   _____

    Dental   _____

    Clothing and personal   _____

    Sales tax   _____

    Charitable contributions _____

    Political contributions   _____

    Other   _____

TRANSPORTATION EXPENSES

    Automobile   _____

    Other vehicles and equipment _____

    Other transportation   _____

INVESTMENT/PROFESSIONAL EXPENSES

    Investment management fees _____

    Accounting fees   _____

    Legal fees — deductible   _____

    Legal fees — not deductible _____

    Notary fees   _____

    Rental investment expense   _____

    Other   _____

INTEREST

    Interest — home mortgage   _____

    Interest — consumer loans   _____

FIGURE 3.5   Annual Expenses Worksheet (continued)

INTEREST (continued)

       Interest — credit cards   _____

       Penalty — early withdrawal   _____

       Bank service charge   _____

JOB RELATED EXPENSES

       Unreimbursed business   _____

       Business education   _____

       Membership   _____

       Professional subscriptions   _____

       Moving   _____

       Child care   _____

       Other   _____

OTHER EXPENSES

       Education   _____

       Alimony paid   _____

       Child support   _____

       Casualty losses   _____

       Other   _____

BUSINESS EXPENSES

       Cost of goods   _____

       Advertising   _____

       Bad debts   _____

       Bank service charges   _____

(continued)

FIGURE 3.5   Annual Expenses Worksheet (continued)

BUSINESS EXPENSES (continued)

Transportation   _____

Commission   _____

Dues and publications   _____

Employee wages   _____

Employee benefits   _____

Freight   _____

Insurance   _____

Interest   _____

Laundry and cleaning   _____

Legal and professional   _____

Office   _____

Pension and profit sharing   _____

Rent   _____

Repairs   _____

Supplies and materials   _____

Taxes   _____

Travel and entertainment   _____

Utilities and telephone   _____

Other   _____

Tax Calculation Worksheet

Figure 3.6 shows an example of how to calculate your taxable income. Check with your financial planner, accountant, or an IRS publication for the current year's standard deductions, personal exemptions, and tax schedule.

Be aware that there are income phaseouts for the standard deduction, personal exemption, and itemized deductions. Check with a competent advisor for the

FIGURE 3.6   Tax Calculation Estimate

	Joint	Single
Income	$41,360	$41,360
Standard deduction*	7,200	4,300
Personal exemptions (Joint — 4; Single — 1)*	11,000	2,750
Total deductions from adjusted gross income	18,200	7,050
Taxable income (line 1 − line 4)	23,160	34,310
Schedule or table tax*	$ 3,474	$9,606.80
Tax bracket	15%	28%

*1999 numbers used for illustration only. Use the current IRS numbers.

current limits. Chapter 9 discusses the major effects of recent tax laws. Always check with your tax advisor about your specific situation.

Spendable Cash Worksheet

Next you need to calculate your spendable cash. An example is shown in Figure 3.7. You'll use the data from your other worksheets to fill in this form.

What's the purpose of this worksheet? Notice that there are two columns to the right of each item description. The first one is for where you are now. The second one is for you to use when you are evaluating a financial choice you must make. This sample shows the effect of putting money into an IRA. Income taxes are reduced, and spendable cash is increased by $860.

You will be able to see how your cash flow increases or decreases depending on a particular financial strategy. If you want to buy more life insurance, what does it do to your spendable cash? If you want to increase your retirement plan contributions, what does it do to your spendable cash? This worksheet will answer those kinds of questions for you.

In filling out this worksheet, note that depreciation, exemptions, and nontaxable income (lines 21, 22, and 23) are first taken out and then added back in. These items are deductible, but you didn't actually spend the cash for them. Your accountant and/or financial planner will estimate your depreciation for you using IRS Form 4562. Exemptions are shown on IRS Schedule 1040. Nontaxable income includes items such as scholarships.

Now it's your turn to fill out your spendable cash worksheet (Appendix E).

FIGURE 3.7 Sample Spendable Cash Worksheet

	Current	Proposed
ADD INCOME:		
1. Business		
2. Salary or salaries	$41,360	$41,360
3. Investment		
4. Other		
5. TOTAL INCOME	41,360	41,360
LESS:		
6. IRA		4,000
7. Keogh		
8. Corporation retirement plans		
9. 401(k)		
10. Public employee retirement system		
11. State teacher retirement system		
12. 403(b) tax-deferred annuity		
13. Medical/dental plans		
14. Disability plans		
15. Business expenses		
16. Depreciation (Form 4562)		
17. Normal deductions	3,760	3,760
18. Exemptions (Schedule 1040)	7,600	7,600
19. TAXABLE INCOME	30,000	26,000
LESS:		
20. Income taxes (for illustration only)	4,640	3,780

FIGURE 3.7   Sample Spendable Cash Worksheet (continued)

ADD BACK FROM ABOVE:

   21. Depreciation (Form 4562)

   22. Exemptions (Schedule 1040)   7,600   7,600

   23. Nontaxable income

LESS:

   24. Retirement savings   4,000   IRA

   25. Medical/dental expenses

   26. Disability insurance

   27. Life insurance

   28. Education

   29. Certain living expenses

   30. SPENDABLE CASH $28,960 $29,820

   31. CASH FLOW INCREASE   S860

Balance Sheet: What Is Your Financial Worth?

Finally, you need to fill out a balance sheet. Figure 3.8 shows an example. I realize by now you may expect to be seeing numbers in your sleep, but stick with it. You're almost done with these baseline worksheets. Then the fun starts.

What is a balance sheet and why do you need one? It's a snapshot of your financial status taken once a year (or more often if you have major changes during a year). The balance sheet is the yearly measure of how you're doing. As you work toward your goals, your net worth will increase. You will be able to see what you are achieving by comparing this year's net worth with next year's.

So sharpen your pencil or boot up your computer one more time and start filling in those blanks.

FIGURE 3.8 Balance Sheet

ASSETS Date: _____

CURRENT ASSETS

    Cash on hand   _____

    Checking accounts   _____

    Money market accounts   _____

    Savings accounts   _____

    Treasury bills   _____

    Life insurance cash value   _____

    Escrow account   _____

    Other current assets   _____

TOTAL CURRENT ASSETS   _____

MARKETABLE INVESTMENTS

    Common stocks   _____

    Preferred stocks   _____

    Treasury bonds   _____

    Corporate bonds   _____

    Municipal bonds   _____

    Unit investment trust   _____

    REIT (Real Estate Investment Trust) shares   _____

    Mutual funds   _____

    Traded stock options   _____

    Warrants   _____

    Futures contracts   _____

    Other marketable investments   _____

TOTAL MARKETABLE INVESTMENTS   _____

FIGURE 3.8   Balance Sheet (continued)

LONG-TERM INVESTMENTS

Real estate   _____

Farming interests   _____

Oil and gas investments   _____

Tax shelters   _____

Leasing investments   _____

Research & development ventures   _____

Venture capital investment   _____

Annuities   _____

Deposits   _____

Long-term receivables   _____

Mortgage receivables   _____

Interest-free loan receivables   _____

Stock purchase plan   _____

Executive stock options   _____

Investment collections   _____

Precious metals   _____

Mineral royalties   _____

Closely-held businesses   _____

Other long-term assets   _____

TOTAL LONG-TERM ASSETS   _____

RETIREMENT/DEFERRED ASSETS

IRA   _____

Keogh account   _____

(continued)

FIGURE 3.8   Balance Sheet (continued)

RETIREMENT/DEFERRED ASSETS (continued)

    Retirement plan   _____

    Deferred compensation plan   _____

    Other retirement plans   _____

TOTAL RETIREMENT/DEFERRED ASSETS   _____

TRUST AND ESTATE ASSETS

    Trust assets   _____

    Estate assets   _____

TOTAL TRUST AND ESTATE ASSETS   _____

PERSONAL/NONEARNING ASSETS

    Residence   _____

    Vacation property   _____

    Automobiles   _____

    Home furnishings   _____

    Other personal property   _____

    Noninvestment collection   _____

    Other vehicles and equipment _____

    Other nonearning assets   _____

TOTAL PERSONAL/NONEARNING ASSETS   _____

BUSINESS ASSETS

    Cash account   _____

    Checking account   _____

    Accounts receivable   _____

    Short-term investments   _____

    Deposits   _____

    Inventory   _____

    Land   _____

FIGURE 3.8   Balance Sheet (continued)

BUSINESS ASSETS (continued)

    Buildings   _____

    Furniture and fixtures   _____

    Manufacturing equipment   _____

    Transportation equipment   _____

    Office equipment   _____

    Other fixed assets   _____

    Other assets   _____

TOTAL BUSINESS ASSETS   _____

UNCLASSIFIED ASSETS

    Unclassified assets   _____

TOTAL UNCLASSIFIED ASSETS   _____

TOTAL ASSETS   _____

LIABILITIES

CURRENT LIABILITIES

    Credit cards   _____

    Demand notes   _____

    Margin accounts   _____

    Other   _____

TOTAL CURRENT LIABILITIES   _____

LONG-TERM LIABILITIES

    Home mortgage   _____

    Home improvement loan   _____

    Other real estate mortgages   _____

    Automobile loans   _____

    Student loan   _____

(continued)

FIGURE 3.8   Balance Sheet (continued)

LONG-TERM LIABILITIES (continued)

    Loan on life insurance   _____

    Investment liabilities   _____

    Interest-free loan payable   _____

    Other long-term liabilities   _____

TOTAL LONG-TERM LIABILITIES   _____

BUSINESS LIABILITIES

    Accounts payable   _____

    Accrued expenses   _____

    Prepaid orders   _____

    Employment taxes   _____

    Accredited FICA tax   _____

    Other payroll taxes   _____

    Long-term loans   _____

    Other liabilities   _____

TOTAL BUSINESS LIABILITIES   _____

UNCLASSIFIED LIABILITIES

    Unclassified liabilities   _____

TOTAL UNCLASSIFIED LIABILITIES   _____

TOTAL LIABILITIES   _____

NET WORTH (TOTAL ASSETS − TOTAL LIABILITIES)   _____

Evaluate Your Data

By now, you should have quite an impressive stack of wish lists and worksheets. You may also feel like you're ready to sit for the CPA exam. Rest easy. The worst of the intense calculations are over. Now comes the moment of truth when you compare those dreams with the financial facts.

You have to get to this point so you know where you stand. Whether you may find out you're better off than you thought or not, at least now you'll know the facts.

Develop Recommendations and Alternate Solutions

So how do you get to where you want to go? That's what the rest of this book is about—helping you lower those taxes, increase your investments, improve your cash flow, and reduce estate taxes.

Now you know how much you've got. The next step is to compare goals with reality. Look at each specific item on your wish list. How close or how far are you from achieving it? How much more do you need? Get some more blank paper and start writing down your recommendations and alternatives as you read through the rest of the book.

In Chapter 4, I'll go into detail on calculating how much you need for education and then describe specific strategies to get you to that goal. In Chapter 5, I'll show you how to calculate just how much you will need for retirement. Then I'll describe all the ways that you can put aside money for an enjoyable retirement.

In Chapters 6 through 8, we'll look at how to reduce housing, insurance, and liabilities costs, and still live the good life. You'll learn how to reduce taxes legally through the use of a variety of tax tools in Chapter 9.

You'll learn how to plan your investment strategy to increase your returns and your peace of mind in Chapter 10. And finally, in Chapter 11, you'll learn how you can almost take it with you by leaving more estate for your beneficiaries and less for Uncle Sam.

Yes, this book has a few more calculations in it, but that's what financial planning is about. To make more money, you'll have to keep pushing those calculator buttons.

Set Priorities

I'll mention this again later, but it's important now to consider your priorities. If you can't have it all, which is more important to you: sending your children to college or leaving a large estate to your heirs?

Which is more important, having that expensive car now or having a comfortable retirement later? We all have to make these choices, but now you'll understand the impact of each decision on your financial situation.

Conclusion

For the majority of you, this will be your worst year. From now on your financial situation will improve. You may have to eat more ground beef and less steak, but you will see continuous improvement in your spendable cash situation and on your balance sheet.

Make savings a regular habit and pay yourself first. Your money for investments comes from these savings. You may have to tighten your belt a bit now, but then you'll be able to loosen it a few notches as you go along. You'll be working towards your dreams, and your lifestyle will improve, too.

It's your money. Set your priorities and stick to them no matter what. Then when your stockbroker says, "I've got a great investment deal!" you can run through the calculations and respond according to your financial plan, not a spur-of-the-moment reaction. When your insurance agent says, "I've got this great new insurance package," you can look at your financial recommendations and make an informed decision. What a feeling of confidence and success you'll feel. You are in control of your financial affairs. You've set your goals, and you're moving confidently towards them!

Summary

1. Locate all your financial data, set up a storage system, and have the information available to you at any time. Determine your net worth and how much insurance you have. Use the checklists and forms to help you determine where you're at and where you want to be. Be sure to complete all the following forms:
   • Cash flow worksheet
   • Income and expenses worksheet
   • Tax calculation worksheet
   • Spendable cash worksheet
   • Balance sheet
2. Include your spouse and financial advisors in these processes. They are important participants and can bring different perspectives to bear on your plan.

4

Planning to Send Your Children to College

In this chapter, I'll show you how to calculate what it will cost to educate your children when they reach college age. You'll also learn the various ways you can provide for that education at the lowest possible cost.

How Much Will a College Degree Cost?

Figure 4.1 shows how college cost increases from 1986 to 1997 compare to the rate of inflation as measured by the changes in the Consumer Price Index.

As you can see, both public and private college costs usually have been increasing at a higher rate than inflation since 1986. Pretty sobering, isn't it? The following step-by-step plan will help you analyze your needs to fulfill your goal of sending your children to college.

Remember the work you did in Chapter 2? Go back to those goals you wrote down under Education. In this chapter, you'll fill in the details on exactly how much it will cost to meet your goals.

First, you must answer these questions:

1. How many children will go to college?
2. What are their current ages?
3. How many years until each one enters college?
4. How many years will they attend school?

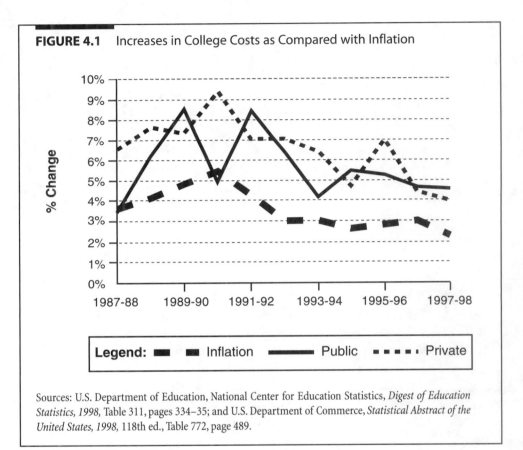

FIGURE 4.1   Increases in College Costs as Compared with Inflation

Legend: ■ ■ Inflation   ——— Public   ■ ■ ■ ■ Private

Sources: U.S. Department of Education, National Center for Education Statistics, *Digest of Education Statistics, 1998,* Table 311, pages 334–35; and U.S. Department of Commerce, *Statistical Abstract of the United States, 1998,* 118th ed., Table 772, page 489.

5. What is the current cost (tuition, fees, room and board) of the college they will attend? (You can get this from a college catalog—many libraries have them, or you can call the college and ask.)

6. Look again at Figure 4.1 showing increasing college costs and choose a rate of increase that you are comfortable with. I don't want to tell you what specific number to use. Some of you may feel 12 percent is right. Some may want to choose a higher or lower number based on your beliefs about inflation and other factors. (This is *personal* financial planning. I can show you what historical rates have been. I can tell you what I or others feel the future rate of increase may be. But these are your goals you're setting, not mine.)

As an example, consider a family with two children, and see how they might do the calculations. First, use Figure 4.2 to gather the basic facts.

Next, go to the reference tables in the back of the book and look up the inflation adjustment factor (Appendix A, Table A.1). Find the column heading with the rate of increase that you chose (in this case, 8 percent). Read down that column until you find the row with the number of years until entry (in this case, 8 and 10 years). The number you find is the factor you will use to help you calculate the future cost.

Do your children have special needs? Whether they have asthma or a learning disability, you already know what additional resources you have needed up to this point. If your child is younger or has just recently had special needs arise, you should contact your support group or special needs professional consultant and your financial planner to estimate what additional funds to factor into your plan.

For example, the factor for the older child's costs for the first year is 1.8509 and the second year is 1.9990. The factor for the younger child's first year and the older child's third year is 2.1589, and so on. You will need to look up this factor for each year your children are in school. Then you multiply the current cost times the factor for each year to get the cost for that year. Figure 4.3 shows how to do the calculation. Notice that in years 10 and 11 the current cost doubles because both children are in college for those two years.

Now get out paper, pencil, and your calculator and figure out your own costs using the blank worksheets in Appendix E. You need to know these numbers in order to develop a savings plan.

FIGURE 4.2   Baseline Data for Estimating College Costs

	Older Child	Younger Child
Current age	10	8
Number of years until entry	8	10
Number of years in school	4	4
Current cost of college/year*	$5,000	$5,000
Rate of increase of costs*	8%	8%

*Numbers are for illustration only. Investigate what the current costs and increases are at the schools you're considering.

FIGURE 4.3   Calculating the Future Cost of School

Year	Older Child's Current Cost	Younger Child's Current Cost	Total Cost	Inflation Adjustment Factor (8%) (Table A.1)	Future Cost
0–7	$0	$ 0	$0		$0
8	5,000	0	5,000	1.8509	9,255
9	5,000	0	5,000	1.9990	9,995
10	5,000	5,000	10,000	2.1589	21,589
11	5,000	5,000	10,000	2.3316	23,316
12	0	5,000	5,000	2.5182	12,591
13	0	5,000	5,000	2.7196	13,598
TOTALS	$20,000	$20,000	$40,000		$90,344

NOTE: The actual amounts are rounded to the nearest dollar.

Where Will the Money Come From?

There are several alternatives for funding your children's education. The worst way is to wait until the child enters college and then try to come up with the money. I've seen people bankrupt themselves trying to put their kids through college.

A second way is to put money aside each year, starting now, until they are finished with school. This is the method that most of you should probably use. More about how to do that later.

The third way is to set aside a lump sum now that will grow to be the right amount by the time they enter school. This method is the least expensive and so the best if you can afford it. Let's look at what the three methods will cost.

Pay as You Go

From Figure 4.3 we estimate it will cost a total of $90,344 to put these two children through college. You can plug in your own figures to estimate your education dollar needs.

Save Each Year

If the family decided instead to start saving today, how much do they need to save each year? We figured the future cost. Let's assume that they invest the money to earn 8 percent every year, and all the principal and interest are left to compound.

To calculate the savings needed now, you'll need to multiply the amount needed by an annual investment factor from Table A.3 in Appendix A. To simplify the math, let's choose one rate of increase and keep it the same each year. It is possible with a computer program to calculate different increases every year. Figure 4.4 shows how the calculation is done.

In Figure 4.4, the future cost (from Figure 4.3) is multiplied by the annual investment factor to find the amount needed for that specific year. By totaling those amounts, we get the specific amount that we must start saving now. Remember in this example, each year the family will need to save money for the six total years that their children will be in college.

Notice that in year 8, the need decreases by $870 because the first year of college is completed for the daughter. In year 10, the decrease is $1,671 ($870 + $801) because the first and second years of college for the daughter are completed.

So, as the children enter college, you need to save less each year for this goal. You can then route this money into another goal or spend it!

FIGURE 4.4   How Much to Save for Education Each Year

Year	Future Cost	Annual Investment Factor (8%) (Table A.3)	Need for a Specific Year	Save Each Year
0–7	$0		$0	$5,858
8	9,255	0.0940	870	4,988
9	9,995	0.0801	801	4,187
10	21,589	0.0690	1,490	2,597
11	23,316	0.0601	1,401	1,296
12	12,591	0.0527	664	632
13	13,598	0.0465	632	0
TOTALS	$90,344		$5,858	$60,664

NOTE: The actual amounts are rounded to the nearest dollar.

Invest a Lump Sum Early

The third method is to put a lump sum aside now and let the interest accumulate until the children start college. Then, as they start, only the amount needed for that year is withdrawn. As shown in Figure 4.5, this method requires the least investment by the parents.

Using the lump sum method, you would need to invest only $40,000 today at 8 percent interest. In eight years you will have the estimated $90,000 needed to fund two college educations. Figure 4.6 shows a comparison of the three ways to fund a college education.

Notice the difference in total costs. Remember, whichever method you choose, this is the net amount (after taxes have been taken out). How much do you actually have to earn? To calculate the gross amount you would need, divide the net amount by

Expect your children to earn part of their education funds. It can encourage a work ethic, make them responsible for whether they can have the benefits of a college education, and increase their commitment to make the most of their college years. Discuss this goal with your planner so they understand that you don't expect to fully fund your children's education. Your planner can evaluate whether some of the strategies mentioned in this chapter, such as splitting, are appropriate for you.

FIGURE 4.5 Lump Sum Calculation

Year	Future Cost (8%)	Lump Sum Investment Factor (Table A.4)	Need Today to Fund
0-7	$0		$0
8	9,255	0.5403	5,000
9	9,995	0.5002	5,000
10	21,589	0.4632	10,000
11	23,316	0.4289	10,000
12	12,591	0.3971	5,000
13	13,598	0.3677	5,000
TOTALS	$90,344		$40,000

NOTE: The actual amounts are rounded to the nearest dollar.

FIGURE 4.6 Comparison of Alternatives for Funding Education

Year	Pay As You Go	Save Each Year	Invest Lump Sum
0	$ 0	$ 5,858	$40,000
1–7	0	5,858	0
8	9,255	4,988	0
9	9,995	4,187	0
10	21,589	2,696	0
11	23,316	1,296	0
12	12,591	632	0
13	13,598	0	0
TOTALS (NET)	$ 90,344	$60,664	$40,000
BEFORE TAXES (GROSS) (30%)	$129,063	$86,663	$57,143

NOTE: The assumption is that the investments grow at 8 percent each year.

(1 − tax rate). If the tax rate is 30 percent, 1 − 30% = 0.7. So you would divide the net amount by 0.7. The gross amount (before taxes are taken out) for each payment method is shown at the bottom of the table. Looking at this gross amount needed should convince you that the pay as you go method is a terrible choice. Even worse, if you borrow money each year that you need it at 10 percent for five years, you would pay $164,521 (gross), almost three times the lump sum method!

Review Your Goals

Now you know the facts. Go back and look at your original goals for education. You may need to revise them based on these facts.

Do you want or need to fund all of your children's education? If they are in high school now, what are the possibilities for scholarships, work-study, etc.? If it isn't possible to meet your education goals, what can you do?

There are always five alternatives when it looks as if a goal is not reachable:

1. Increase your income.
2. Reduce your taxes.
3. Reduce your spending.
4. Change your goal.
5. Take more risk with your investments.

There it is in black and white. No more or no less. You must choose one or more alternatives from this short list. As you will see in later chapters, there are dozens of ways to put these alternatives into action.

For the rest of this chapter, let's focus on specific ways to meet your education goal. The first rule in meeting any financial goal is: *The sooner you save the better.* Let compound interest do the work for you. You've seen from previous calculations what a difference it makes. It's not too soon to start saving for college when your child is born (or before).

Who Controls the Money?

Will the education fund be under your control or your children's? Everyone has different feelings about this issue, but it's vital that you give some thought to it. There are several reasons for concern about who controls the education fund.

Will They Really Go to School?

First, will the fund be used for education? We all hope that our children will grow up to be a credit to us and make a contribution to society. But let's face it; sometimes despite all your good parenting efforts they may turn out the very opposite of what you had hoped. If the education funds are in their names, kiss the money good-bye. I realize this may seem pretty cold-blooded to some of you. As I go on to discuss your other goals in subsequent chapters, you'll see how you need to have your money working hard for you. If you don't control the money, you may have to reduce or eliminate some other goals.

So here's the issue. If your children decide not to go to college, would you give them that amount of money anyway? If they control the money, then the money is theirs. If you control the money and they say, "I'm dropping out of school, but I still want the money," then you can decide whether to give them all, some, or none of it. You have retained control for a longer period of time and that gives you more flexibility.

Who Pays the Taxes?

If the money is in the children's names, they pay the taxes on the investment earnings, usually at a lower rate. However, this is not such a clear advantage due to tax law changes as discussed in the next section.

This issue of control may be clear-cut for you or hard to decide. Be sure to think through what it will mean to you and your family.

Effects of Recent Tax Laws on Your Education Goal

Understanding and working with the complicated changes of the recent tax laws will be discussed in detail in the tax chapter. What follows is a brief summary. These changes will significantly affect how you do your education planning.

Income Tax Deductions and Exemptions

A child who has earned income can take the maximum standard deduction for individuals. This standard deduction reduces the amount of wages that are taxed. Earnings above these amounts are taxed at the child's rate, no matter what the age. If a child has no earned income, then the standard deduction is limited to $700 (for 1999). For example, if a child earned $900 and had unearned income of $800, his standard deduction would be $900, the greater of $700 or his earned income.

If a child has income and can be claimed as a dependent on her parents' return, she cannot claim a personal exemption (different from a deduction) on her own tax return. If a child cannot be claimed as a dependent, then she can use the standard personal exemption.

Taxing a Child's Unearned Income

You may have heard the phrase "kiddie tax." All children under 14 can make up to $1,400 of unearned income and be taxed at their own tax rate. The first $700 has no tax. The second $700 is taxed at the child's tax rate. All unearned income above $1,400 for children under 14 is taxed at the parents' tax rate. It doesn't matter where the money for the investments comes from: a paper route, grandparents, and so on. Whatever the source, all unearned income is taxed as described above.

These rules mean that you must pay close attention to your children's current unearned income and redo any past arrangements. You also need to plan for their future unearned income in order to decrease the tax bite.

Taxing Scholarships

Any scholarship monies received that cover more than tuition, fees, and books are taxed at the child's rate. This includes special scholarships for athletic, musical, or other skills.

Student Loans

The interest paid on student loans is tax deductible.

Other

As I go on to discuss specific strategies for meeting your goal, I'll point out other effects of tax changes. Always check with your attorney and financial planner to be sure you use the following techniques correctly.

Resources for College Aid

There are many resources for funding higher education. Whole books have been written and consultants specialize in finding college funds. Here's a brief summary of some options you should consider.

1. Parents who work at a college or university may be able to take courses or have family members take courses at reduced or no cost.
2. Different states provide differing amounts of state aid. For example, California state schools are free to residents.
3. Work/study programs provide an opportunity to earn money while working on campus.

Unless you have a very low income or are independently wealthy, you will need to help your child find student aid. However, do consider what expectations you have for your child. Do you want to fund their entire college costs or do you want them to earn part of the expenses? Remember that if they earn part of the money, they may better understand the sacrifice necessary to earn a degree. Start teaching them early about the value of money.

Education IRA, HOPE Credit, and Lifetime Learning Credit

The most recent tax changes added three new options for education planning. However, it will take some research and/or the advice of some financial advisors to decide which of these options to use and in which order.

Education IRA

The term "IRA" is misleading here because this account has nothing to do with retirement. It's a savings account for post-secondary education expenses for you, your spouse, or your children. Contributions are limited to $500 each year and are paid with post-tax dollars. There is an income phaseout for allowable contributions.

Anyone may contribute to an education IRA. However, no money can be contributed in a tax year in which money is put into a qualified state tuition program for that person.

Withdrawals are tax-free if they are used for higher education expenses. By the time the student is 30, the account must be empty. If not, the money is taxed at the student's regular tax rate with an additional 10 percent penalty. However, the account may be transferred to other family members. There also are rules to cover transfers due to death or divorce.

Check with your advisor to see if this is worthwhile for your situation. Having an education IRA may affect the student's eligibility for financial aid.

HOPE Credit

The HOPE Credit provides a $1,500 credit on the family tax return for each student enrolled in post-secondary education. It can only be used for the first two years. This credit is available to married couples with adjusted gross incomes (AGI) up to $100,000, or singles with an AGI up to $50,000.

This credit cannot be used in the same year that you use an education IRA or a Lifetime Learning Credit.

Lifetime Learning Credit

This credit can reduce a family's tax liability by up to $1,000 through 2002 and up to $2,000 each year after that. The income limits are the same as those for the HOPE Credit. The Lifetime Learning Credit can be used for four years. Each person in the family can use it, including the parents.

Each of these options has many rules and exceptions attached to them. Please check with a qualified financial advisor before you choose to use an education IRA or the credits.

Income Shifting to Save Taxes

In the past, it usually made sense to shift income from family members in a higher tax bracket to those in a lower tax bracket. The "kiddie tax" changes this old rule. However, there are still ways to use income shifting techniques to help you build an education fund.

Be sure that you have first decided where you stand on the issue of control. Any gift of money must be permanent. If you don't want the child to control the money yet, then income shifting is probably not for you at this time. Come back to this section when you are ready to transfer control of the money.

Will Shifting Save You Taxes?

You will first need to see if income shifting will provide you any tax advantages. For 1999, if you are in the 28 percent tax bracket and your unmarried child has income of more than $25,750 (include the income you plan to shift), then you are both in the same tax bracket. Income shifting will not save you any taxes.

However, a more typical case has the child in the bottom bracket. You may be in a higher bracket. If that's the case, you have a good reason to pursue income shifting aggressively.

Income Shifting Techniques: What You Still Can Do

Here are several ways to shift income to your children for their educational or other needs. The first three strategies are only for those who own their own business (either a full-time or sideline business).

Use Property to Control Income

If you are self-employed or own a business, you can control the amount of income produced by a particular piece of property, for example, the equipment you use in your home office. Give it to the children or a trust and rent it back from them. Then you can pay smaller lease payments during the early years before the child turns 14. However, this strategy isn't free from challenge by the IRS so discuss it with your financial advisors.

Sideline Business

A second business is an ideal way to shift income to your children. Make them part owners and pay them from the profits (see Appendix D for the reasons why you might consider a sideline business).

Depending on how your second business operates, you will usually have one of these three formats:

1. Use a partnership if the business manages a piece of rental property, for example, real estate. Make your children limited partners with no say in management but a predetermined share of profits.
2. Use an S corporation if the business is service-oriented but you are not actively involved in it. In order to give your children profits without power, you can issue nonvoting stock to them.
3. Use a regular incorporation if the company is a service business in which you do much of the work. This is the only business structure that will work for you because the law requires that you get paid the value of your services in an S corporation. That rule might effectively wipe out the income-shifting potential of the business.

Most professionals do some writing for professional journals or other trade publications. Suppose you write an article and plan to sell it to a magazine. Give all rights in that article to your children before you complete the sale; then any sale profits are theirs, not yours. Because they own the property, they pay the taxes on the profit. Be sure to check with an attorney specializing in copyright law to be sure you handle this transaction correctly.

Employment of the Child

Beyond the personal satisfaction of seeing your children learn to function in the world of work, there are tax advantages to employing them. First, the under-14 "kiddie tax" only applies to *unearned* income. They can *earn* more without having to worry about that rule. Second, they can open a deductible IRA and begin deferring taxes on their income.

What can your children do as work? They can take phone calls, file correspondence, deliver documents, check your bookkeeping, or even clean the office. Be sure it is useful work and is documented by a written record of hours worked and the work done. Keep in mind that the pay must be reasonable. Don't try to pay a child $20,000 a year for sweeping the floors. Learn what the child labor laws are that will apply to your situation.

If your second business is not incorporated, you will not have to pay Social Security taxes or federal unemployment taxes for children under 18 who work for you.

However, if your business is incorporated or if the children are self-employed (for example, they baby-sit or mow lawns), then they must pay Social Security tax. This tax must be paid even if they don't owe any income tax.

You should also be aware that if you pay someone, or if someone pays your child, more than $600 per calendar quarter, the child can be considered an employee. Thus you or whoever "employs" your child as a baby-sitter or lawn mower should deduct the proper amount from the wages, add an equal amount from his or her own pocket, then send the total to Social Security. Check with your tax advisor for the proper procedure for determining if your child is an "employee" and, if so, how to pay the amount due.

Remember that any child receiving a regular paycheck from an employer will have Social Security tax withheld automatically, just as adults do, and that that money is not refundable.

Loan the Money to Your Child

You can loan your child $10,000 to cover college costs. As long as he or she does not use the income to acquire income-producing property and as long as college tuition is the primary reason for the loan, there may be no income tax consequences. The money is used for college and five years or so later the loan is paid back. You need not charge any interest.

Second Mortgage or Home Equity Loan

You can take a second mortgage or home equity loan to cover college costs. In the liability chapter, we'll discuss these options in more detail including cautions against them. Be forewarned: use the money for college, not to buy a depreciating asset like a car.

Split Annuity

An annuity is a series of payments of a fixed amount for a specific number of years. You can use a "tool" called a split annuity to save for education and to defer taxes. Here's the concept. You buy two annuities in one package. An "immediate annuity" begins sending you monthly checks right away. About 40 percent of your money is put into this annuity. The remainder of your money is put into a "deferred annuity." You can fund a child's education through a split annuity.

As an example, let's say you buy two annuities for $50,000, paying 7.5 percent. You put 40 percent of that $50,000—or $20,000—into the immediate annuity. The other $30,000 goes into the deferred annuity. Each month you receive a check for $300 from the immediate annuity and pay your child's education costs. About 66 percent of this interest is not taxable because it is a return of your principal. At the end of the annuity period, you are paid back your original $50,000.

For comparison, what if you put $50,000 into a CD, also paying 7.5 percent interest? The child uses the interest from that CD, also about $300 a month, to pay for education. However, 100 percent of that $300 interest is taxable.

With a CD, you still have the $50,000 at the end of the term, but 100 percent of the earnings are taxed. With the annuity, you have the same rate of return, but the majority of the interest is not taxable because it is return of principal. Figure 4.7 shows the comparison

FIGURE 4.7   Comparison of a CD and a Split Annuity

	Initial Amount	Amount at End	Interest is Taxable
CD	$50,000	$50,000	Yes
Split Annuity	$50,000	$50,000	No

The beauty of this investment is that you put in $50,000 and you get $50,000 back after 59½, and you've funded your child's college with the interest, most of which is not taxed.

After the cash value accumulates for a few years, you can borrow against the policy at a very low interest rate. This is an advantage over single premium variable life insurance.

There is an early withdrawal penalty. If you take a lump sum distribution before reaching age 59½, you pay a 10 percent penalty to Uncle Sam. To avoid the penalty, talk to your insurance agent about more payouts or buy another annuity with the money.

Another limitation is a penalty on withdrawal from the "immediate" annuity for the first seven years. If you withdraw, you must pay a penalty of 7 percent the first year, 6 percent the second, and so on.

You can also buy an annuity that defers the entire payout until just before the child starts college. This has two advantages. First, the yield increases. Second, if your child does not go to college, you can leave the money in.

Tax Deferral to Save Taxes

If your child is 14 or older, you don't need to worry about how much unearned income there is. However, you still will want to defer taxes just as you would for yourself. If your child is under 14, there are several ways to defer income until they turn 14.

There are many tools that can be used to defer taxes. Remember, tools save taxes, investments don't save taxes. You choose the tool based on considerations of deductibility and tax deferral. For example, one tool is an IRA. The money in an IRA is put into an investment such as a mutual fund, bond fund, and so on. Tax deferral techniques are covered in more detail in Chapter 9. Following is a brief discussion of deferral as it relates to your education fund.

Avoid Current Taxable Income

Some investments do not produce current taxable income, for example: growth common stocks, tax-exempt municipal bonds, Series EE Bonds, land, and certain insurance items.

If you have growth-oriented investments, you could initially own the investments. If the investments appreciate, then you make gifts of the investments to a child. In this way you will retain control over the money for a longer time.

Avoid zero coupon bonds. The interest must be reported and the taxes paid yearly at the parent's marginal rate.

Because of the "kiddie tax," you will want to pay particular attention to the unearned income of your children who are close to age 14. If your child is almost 13, consider a certificate of deposit for 18 months. The interest will be deferred until the child turns 14.

Trusts

Another technique is to set up a trust that accumulates income year after year. The trust can be designed so that it does not pay out income to your child until after the year he or she reaches 14.

Trusts must make quarterly estimated tax payments and file tax returns on a calendar-year basis. The first portion of trust income will be taxed at the trust's lowest tax bracket.

Trust expenses are subject to the same limitation as individuals. Fees for items such as tax preparation, administration, and investment advice are lumped in with "miscellaneous" charges. Only the amount over 2 percent of the trust's adjusted gross income is deductible.

Be sure to give the trustee flexibility in distributing income to take advantage of the best tax bracket. It will depend on your specific situation as to whether the individual tax rate or the trust tax rate may be used to minimize your tax bill. Always check with your tax advisor to be sure the trust does what you want it to do.

Gifting: How to Get the Money Back to the Child

You may gift up to $10,000 each year to each child. Your spouse may also gift $10,000, giving you a yearly gift total of $20,000 for each child. When you gift the money, you lose control over it, so be sure that is what you want to do. Let's say each child needs $10,000 each year for college costs. Then you could gift $10,000 each year to each of them and have them pay the costs. If the money is paid directly to the college, then there is an unlimited gift amount for qualified education expenses.

Before you use gifting, discuss it with your financial planner and attorney to be sure you understand how to do it correctly and what the consequences are.

Conclusion

You can fund your child's education, but it will take disciplined savings and use of appropriate income shifting and tax deferral techniques. Be sure you have considered the issue of who controls the money. A successful education plan must coordinate between income tax, control, and gift tax considerations.

Summary

1. The costs of a college education have been increasing at a faster rate than the rate of inflation. In order to have enough money to pay for these rapidly rising costs, you need to plan carefully now.
2. Determine your needs by finding out the current costs at the university your child will probably attend.
3. Calculate future costs and how much you need to save using three different methods of funding: pay-as-you-go, save each year, and invest a lump sum early. If at all possible, avoid borrowing money for your child's education.

5

Planning for Financial Independence: "Retirement"

The most important goal of this book is to assist you in achieving financial independence. When you can manage to be wealthy, then "retirement" doesn't have to mean gray hair and rocking chairs. It can mean financial independence.

In Chapter 1, you learned the real reason why people invest: "because someday I'll no longer be able to work." You want to achieve financial freedom so that if the boss says, "You're fired!" it doesn't matter. If you want to work at your current job or a more appealing one, you can. If you don't want to work you don't have to. Remember, as you work through the calculations in this chapter, your goal is financial independence. The choice to retire will be up to you. So while the words "retire" and "retirement" will be used for the rest of this chapter, remember what they really mean to you.

Now it's time to learn the truth about the cost of financial freedom. Hide the keys to the liquor cabinet, abandon the ice cream and candy stores, and let's begin. Estimating how much money you will need for retirement and then how much you'll need to save each year to meet that goal may be a shock. It's better to find out what it takes now rather than later. The sooner you start saving, the less you have to save each year because of compounding interest. We'll discuss more about how to get the most from your savings in Chapter 10.

In this chapter, I'll review the information you need to gather, and you'll learn how to calculate the following estimates:

1. How much you need for retirement living expenses.
2. How much your current retirement savings will be worth when you retire.

3. How much you still need to save each year in order to accumulate a lump sum by the time you retire that will earn interest equal to the amount in item 1.

What if you think you can't save as much each year as you need? You'll see how strategies such as deferring taxes on your savings interest can greatly reduce the amount you must save each year and still meet your goal.

Review Your Retirement Goals

Before you can plan for your retirement, you need to know what you want. If you only read through the first three chapters and didn't put your thoughts down on paper, please go back and do it now. Chapter 2 has specific questions that need to be answered before you can move ahead through this chapter.

Did you retire from one job to start a business you've always been interested in, expand a second business you've had on the side, or become a volunteer for a cause? Or did you just want to retire? Whatever you choose, you're in control with financial independence.

Now that you've finished your cash flow worksheet, look again at your retirement goals. You may want to revise them up or down now or wait until you've completed the following calculations. Be sure you have reviewed these goals with your family.

> **W**hen you are planning for retirement, be honest with yourself about the different possible outcomes over the decade or more ahead of you. Consider at least one scenario where your health changes. How would this change your plan? Work with your planner to prepare a spendable cash worksheet showing how your finances would change.

Your Cash Flow Worksheet Is Crucial

If you have not already done your cash flow worksheet, please stop reading and go back to Chapter 3. You need those numbers. How can you estimate what it takes for retirement if you don't know what it takes to live on today? I know you will be tempted to skip all that hard work and just say, "Oh, I make $50,000 a year so that's what I need to live on." *Don't make that mistake!* While completing the cash flow worksheet takes time, it's your life and your money you're planning for.

Who cares more about them than you? This information is the foundation for your present and your future.

Many people think they know what they spend each year. In fact, they have absolutely no idea. You may spend less than your income, but the sad fact is that many people spend more than they earn. *Until you do a cash flow worksheet, you will not know the truth.* That's what this book is all about—finally finding out the truth about your finances, setting goals, planning how to reach them, and then putting your plan into action. So bite the bullet and go back to Chapter 3. I'll wait for you.

Assumptions for This Retirement Planning

Before you learn how to calculate how much to save for retirement, you need to understand the following assumptions upon which your plan will be built:

1. Social Security is not figured into any of these calculations. I believe you need to rely on yourself, not on the government, to take care of you. I'm not debating the need for this program or its future. I'm just saying you should be prepared to provide all your retirement funds because it will give you peace of mind and control over your future.
2. You should use conservative numbers that will give you peace of mind. It's better to overestimate your needs than underestimate them. Use inflation numbers, rates of return, or other variable numbers that you're comfortable with—not necessarily those in the examples. It's your future and your money.
3. Remember the cardinal rule: You will *not* touch your retirement fund principal. You will live off the interest. This way you should never run out of money no matter how long you live. There are calculations that include living off the principal and interest, eventually reducing your fund to zero. Those calculations are beyond the scope of this book and require the input of specialized professionals.
4. To show you how to estimate your retirement fund, one inflation rate, one investment rate of return, and one tax rate are used. These rates are assumed to stay the same for all the years from now until retirement (in the following examples, 30 years) and for all the retirement years. Obviously that would never happen in real life.

    The following example is meant as a guide to show how much you may need to save for retirement. Work through this calculation to understand what is involved in deciding how much you need for retirement. For your own situation, choose rates that you are comfortable with so that your estimate will give you an amount that should be more than you need. For exact calculations, there are computer programs available or you can discuss your specific circumstances with a qualified financial planner.

5. Government policies, the economy, and other financial factors will not change drastically from those of the past.

Questions to Answer before Doing the Calculations

First, you must know what it takes to live today. That was the reason for doing your cash flow worksheet. Now using that worksheet and your wish list, consider what will be different when you retire. Take another sheet of 13-column accounting paper (or start a new computer spreadsheet program) and do an estimate of what your cash flow might be when you retire.

Estimating Retirement Cash Flow

Use the following questions to help you decide how to adjust the numbers. Don't worry about the effects of inflation now. I'll show you how to allow for that later. For now, look at each item and estimate the changes in your cash flow worksheet when you retire.

1. Will the house be paid off or will you move to a smaller house with lower monthly payments? Will you have a fixed or variable rate mortgage or will you be paying rent?
2. How many people must you support? You may have a houseful of children now, but you will have only you and your spouse when you retire.
3. Will you do less traveling or more?
4. Will you spend less or more on clothing, cars, meals, and miscellaneous items?
5. What other costs will increase or decrease, such as health insurance?

Of course, the one variable that you cannot predict is your health. Most people over 60 years old remain in good health for many years. If you know that your health costs will increase because of family history or other factors, then you may want to increase those costs for this estimate. Make the changes that seem right for you.

For the following example, living expenses are assumed to be $18,000 per year in today's dollars, not including paying taxes.

Other Basic Factors That Will Affect Your Retirement Needs

Now you have answered the first question, "In today's dollars, how much do you need to live on?" These questions also must be answered in order to calculate your retirement needs:

- What is your present age?
- At what age would you like to retire?
- How many years do you have until retirement?
- How long will you live? Use the life expectancy table in Appendix A that describes 50 percent mortality, modifying it as you see fit depending on your personal and family history. This question is included to make you think about how many years of retirement you will have. As stated before in assumption 3, all the following calculations are based on the assumption that you will withdraw only the interest to live on. Because the principal will not be touched, you will know that you should always have money to live on whether you are 73 or 93.
- What do you think the inflation rate will be in the future? In the past 30 years, the average annual increase in inflation has been about 6 percent (see Figure 5.1). You may want to use a higher or lower figure. Pick a reasonable number that makes you comfortable. Even though for the past 70 years inflation has averaged 3 percent, I use the shorter time frame. If I am wrong, the client has more money. Next look up the inflation adjustment factor in Appendix A, Table A.1.

Example: 6 percent inflation and 30 years gives a factor of 5.74.

It is possible to do these retirement calculations using a varying rate of inflation and a computer program to handle the various rates you choose. Those calculations are beyond the scope of this book. A qualified fee-only financial planner can help you in doing this more complex calculation if you feel it is needed. Table A.5 is a payout table showing how long the money might last depending on the lump sum you start with and the same interest rate earned each year.

- What rate of return will you earn on your investments? Again, you must pick one rate in order to do the calculations that follow. Ask a qualified financial planner to help you if you want to vary the rates of return over time. In choos-

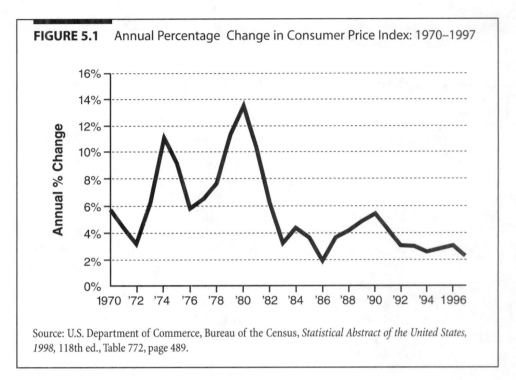

FIGURE 5.1   Annual Percentage Change in Consumer Price Index: 1970–1997

Source: U.S. Department of Commerce, Bureau of the Census, *Statistical Abstract of the United States, 1998,* 118th ed., Table 772, page 489.

ing a rate, pick one that is conservative for you. If your money earns more, it will be a pleasant surprise. In the following example, the gross rate of return is 7 percent. Gross return includes capital gains, dividends, and interest.

Don't Forget about Taxes

- What is your tax rate? Refer to Chapter 3 for a simple way to calculate your taxes. If you didn't originally include federal, state, and local taxes in your cash flow worksheet, go back now and include taxes. You must know all your living expenses—including all your taxes—before you can do the rest of the calculations. You may want to increase or decrease the tax rate, depending on your circumstances.

   Lacking a crystal ball, the only thing to do is to pick the highest tax rate you think you will pay. According to the U.S. Department of Commerce, the maximum effective rate limitation on taxes levied to date was 94 percent during World War II. The current top rate is 39.6 percent. Who knows what it might be when you retire? For this calculation it's better to pick a rate that is too high and end up with more money rather than underestimate and be scrambling to pay your bills.

How Much Do You Need to Retire On?

Now that you have looked up or decided on the answers to all of the above questions, you can calculate how much money you will need for the first year of retirement.

Gross Annual Retirement Cost in Today's Dollars

To find out your gross annual retirement cost, take the total of all living expenses and divide that by (1 − highest tax rate you expect). In this example, the living expenses are $18,000, and the highest tax rate is 30 percent, so the calculation looks like this:

Example: total living expenses/(1 − highest tax rate) = gross annual retirement cost
or
$18,000/(1 − 0.30) = $25,714.29

Let's round it to $25,714. This is only an estimate. If you expect to live on $18,000 after taxes are taken out (net), then you would need $25,714 before taxes (gross).

At the end of the calculations on the next few pages, you will see how much you must save each year in order to have $25,714 per year in inflated dollars at retirement.

Gross Annual Retirement Cost in Inflated Dollars

Next multiply the gross annual retirement cost from above by your inflation adjustment factor.

Example: $25,714 × 5.74 = $147,598 (inflated gross annual retirement cost)

In this example, $147,598 will be needed in inflated dollars in 30 years to cover living expenses and taxes.

What Lump Sum Will Yield the Required Annual Retirement Cost?

Next, find out how much you must have in a lump sum in order to live off the interest only. Take the gross annual retirement cost in inflated dollars from above and divide it by the gross rate of return.

Example: $147,598/0.07 = $2,108,543 (lump sum needed)

So, in order to earn $147,598 in interest each year (at a 7 percent gross rate), you must have more than $2.1 million as a lump sum in your retirement fund!

That sounds like a lot of money, doesn't it? Well, it would be now. We all tend to forget the effects of inflation. Remember the 20¢ postage stamp? That was in 1981. In 1971, a stamp cost 8¢. If you're over 40, do you remember when ground beef was 39¢ a pound? That was in 1962. Figure 5.2 shows how the actual value of the dollar has declined in the past 40 years.

Inflated prices, for the most part, creep up on us. So believe the calculations. If you want to live on $18,000 in today's dollars and all the other numbers are as shown above, then you need to have more than $2.1 million the first year of retirement. The net (after-tax) yield will give you the equivalent of $18,000 each year.

Figure 5.3 shows a summary of the example calculations so far.

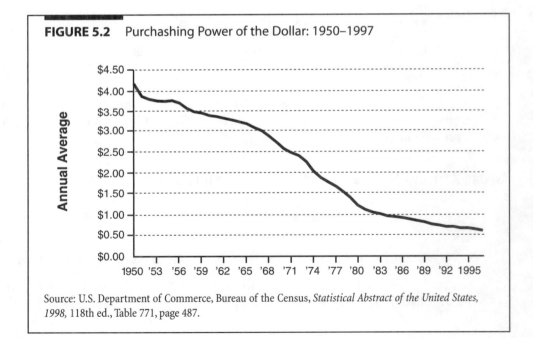

FIGURE 5.2   Purchashing Power of the Dollar: 1950–1997

Source: U.S. Department of Commerce, Bureau of the Census, *Statistical Abstract of the United States, 1998,* 118th ed., Table 771, page 487.

FIGURE 5.3   Retirement Fund Calculations: Basic Data

BASIC DATA

Retirement age	65 years
Present age	35 years
Years until retirement	30 years
Life expectancy }	72 years – male
(Table A.7) }	74 years – female
Annual living expenses needed for retirement	
(today's dollars)	$18,000
Inflation rate	6% or 0.06
Inflation adjustment factor for 30 years at 6%	
(Table A.1)	5.74
Gross rate of return	7% or 0.07
Tax bracket	30% or 0.30

CALCULATIONS

Living Expenses /(1 – tax rate) = Total living expenses plus taxes

Example: $18,000/(1.00 – 0.30) = $25,714

Total living expenses plus taxes $25,714

Inflation adjustment factor for 30 years @ 6% (Table A.1)   5.74

Inflated gross annual retirement cost $25,714 × 5.74 = $147,598

(Inflated gross annual retirement cost)/(Gross rate of return) = Inflated total retirement fund needed

Example: $147,598/0.07 = $2,108,543 (inflated total retirement fund needed)

How Much Do You Have in Savings?

Now that you know how much you need, how are you going to get there? Well, first you need to look at how much you already have saved. Go back to your balance sheet in Chapter 3. Whatever you have saved for retirement so far should be listed there under "Assets: Retirement/Deferred Investments." You also may want to include other investments—marketable, long-term, and so on. Whatever you currently have in a lump sum that is set aside for retirement, find those numbers in your balance sheet and total them. Don't include future contributions, just what you have now. If you didn't complete the balance sheet before, do it now. If you don't start with solid data, your final estimate will be unreliable.

If your pension or profit-sharing plan will calculate an annual benefit for you, then you would subtract that yearly amount from the annual inflated dollar amount that you calculated you would need (in this example, $147,598). Or if they tell you what the lump sum is worth when you retire, then you would subtract that from the total retirement fund needed.

A cautionary note: if you get information from your company saying how much your benefit will be in the future, ask what it includes. Some companies will include Social Security as part of the benefit shown. You want to *know just what the company will pay you.* If you happen to also qualify for Social Security, then that's just that much extra.

I prefer to fund my own retirement and not expect the government to take care of me. The United States has a savings rate lower than most developed countries. I suspect that is because too many of us expect the government to take care of us instead of taking care of ourselves. Don't misunderstand. The Social Security system has helped many people who could not help themselves. But those of us who can take care of ourselves should.

If you don't know your projected benefit, you can calculate it. Next you'll learn how to do the calculation of future worth based on how much you have contributed to date.

For this part of the example calculations, let's assume that your current retirement savings are in a taxable investment. The advantages of tax deferral for your retirement savings will be covered later in this chapter.

Gross versus Net Investment Rate

Whenever you are determining the value of your savings, you must consider the effect of taxes. If the interest is taxable, then you need to calculate your actual net rate (after taxes are taken out). Take the gross investment rate of return and multiply it by your total tax rate (include federal, state, and local taxes). The result is the percent lost to taxes. Subtract that from your gross rate to get the net rate. Figure 5.4 will show you a sample calculation.

To simplify the calculations, let's round up to 5 percent for the net rate of return. That will make it easier to look up the various factors in the reference tables in the Appendix. If you want to calculate a specific factor more precisely, say for a net rate of 5.6 percent, then use the formula shown in Appendix A for the specific reference table you are using.

FIGURE 5.4   Net (After-tax) Rate of Return Calculation

Gross (before taxes) rate of return × tax rate = Percent lost to taxes

EXAMPLE:	0.07	Gross rate of return (7%)
	× 0.30	Tax rate (30%)
	0.021	Lost to taxes (2.1%)

Gross rate of return − percent lost to taxes = Net rate

EXAMPLE:	0.070	Gross rate of return (7%)
	− 0.021	Lost to taxes (2.1%)
	0.049	Net rate of return (4.9%)

Future Value of Current Retirement Savings

Next you calculate what the current retirement savings will be worth when you need it. Let's say you have $10,000, the gross rate of return is 7 percent, the net rate is 5 percent, and you earn interest for 30 years. This next point is crucial. *You must leave it alone!* You don't touch the principal *or the interest.* You let it accumulate. You don't buy a new car with it. You don't take a trip with it. You don't buy new clothes with it. The money is not available. If you leave it alone, then today's $10,000 will grow to $43,200 in 30 years (using the after-tax rate of 5 percent).

However, if each year you take the interest you earn and spend it, how much will your money be worth in 30 years? Only what you have now, $10,000. See how important it is that you leave the principal and interest alone? See the calculation in Figure 5.5.

FIGURE 5.5   How Much Will Your Current Savings Be Worth?

Net (after-tax) rate of return	5% or 0.05
Years until retirement	30 years
Current retirement savings	$10,000
Compound interest factor, 5% (Table A.2)	× 4.32
Future value	$43,200

Your $10,000 today increases to about $43,000 in 30 years. Now take the total retirement fund needed, $2,108,543, and subtract the $43,200. You still need $2,065,343 to retire.

How Much Do You Still Need to Save Each Year?

Where will that $2 million come from? It comes from your savings which you then put into investments. Next you'll learn how to calculate how much you need to save each year to accumulate that $2 million. You must know how much you need before you can decide how to invest. You'll get to the "fun" part, reducing taxes and investing, in a little while.

You know you need $2 million. You know you have 30 years in which to save at a net (after-tax) rate of 5 percent. Once more, go to reference Table A.3 in Appendix A and look up the correct factor. If you end up with an after-tax rate with more than two decimal places, you may want to round down in order to simplify your calculations. Or you can use the correct formula in Appendix A to calculate the factor.

To find out how much you need to save each year, multiply the amount you still need by the factor for savings needed now. Then, to see how much you would need including taxes, divide the net savings needed by (1 − tax rate). Figure 5.6 shows the calculations.

There it is in stark black and white. Each year for the next 30 years, this person will need to save more than $31,000 and must earn about $45,000 before taxes to put that amount in savings.

Now you need to do your own calculation to see what your needs are.

FIGURE 5.6   How Much to Save Each Year to Reach Retirement Goal

Still needed for retirement fund	$2,065,343
Annual investment factor for a net rate of 5% (Table A.3)	× 0.0151
Net savings needed each year (taxes not included)	31,187
Tax rate	.30
Total gross savings per year (Net savings / (1 − tax rate))	$ 44,553

What If You Can't Make That Savings Goal?

Don't let these numbers fluster you; this is not a cut-and-dried process. Go back and look at all the assumptions you had to make in reaching this final number. Maybe you were pessimistic and put inflation at 10 percent. Reducing that number (only if you are comfortable doing so) will reduce the final amount you need. There's nothing I can do to change the historical inflation numbers. However, there are things you can do to lower your bottom-line savings goal and still retire. Here are your four alternatives:

1. Earn more money
2. Reduce your taxes
3. Increase your rate of return
4. Change your goals

Can You Earn More Money?

The most obvious solution is to make more money. Assess your skills. Should you be earning more at your present job or seeking a better-paying one? If you already are working a number of jobs, you're at your limit. If you only have one job, can you take a second job or better yet, start your own (sideline) business? I'll discuss starting a business in more detail later, and you'll see why they have so many advantages for increasing income as well as reducing taxes.

Can You Reduce Your Taxes?

If you've been earning money, paying taxes, and then trying to save, you'll learn how to use tools to save taxes. Some examples of tools are an IRA, a 401(k), or a pension plan. By using a tool, you save first. The tax is deferred; you have more left over to spend. There are ways to reduce your taxes legally. I'll deal with them in Chapter 9.

If you pay less in taxes, then you increase your net rate of return. You will need less for your total fund so you don't have to save as much. Figure 5.7 shows an example, in summary form, of the difference that tax deferral can make. All variables are the same as in the previous calculations except for the tax deferral.

In this example, each year for 30 years the retirement savings are kept in a tax-deferred tool. The $10,000 would grow to $76,100 instead of only $43,200.

FIGURE 5.7   Effect of Deferring Taxes on Your Savings Goal

Gross rate of return	7%	7%
Net rate of return	5%	7%, defer taxes
Annual retirement living expenses including tax	$ 147,598	$ 147,598
Total lump sum for retirement fund (annual amount / gross rate)	2,108,543	2,108,543
In 30 years, $10,000 becomes	− 43,200	− 76,100
Still needed	2,065,343	2,032,443
Annual net savings needed	$ 31,187	$ 21,544
Annual gross savings needed	$ 44,553	Same as net savings

You would have to save only about $22,000 per year instead of almost $45,000. That's quite an incentive to learn about tax deferral!

Can You Increase Your Rate of Return?

In addition to decreasing the tax bite, can you increase the rate of return on your investments? If you've been earning 5 percent in a savings account, can you earn 7 percent by putting your savings in a long-term certificate of deposit? If you've been earning 7 percent, can you earn 9 percent in a different investment? Increasing your rate of return will mean you have less to put in savings, as shown in Figure 5.8.

By increasing the gross rate of return from 7 percent to 9 percent per year and deferring taxes through a tool, the total lump sum needed is less. The $10,000 would grow to $132,700. Then you would have to save only about $11,000 per year or about one-fourth of the amount needed in the original calculation where the interest was taxable. See how good financial planning can help you manage to be wealthy?

Of course, you will have to determine what level of investment risk is comfortable for you. Usually, the higher the long-term rate of return, the greater the short-term risk of the investment. If increasing your long-term rate of return from 7 percent to 9 percent means you lose sleep because the investment has more short-term risk, then don't do it.

FIGURE 5.8	Effect of Higher Rate and Tax Deferral on Savings Goal		
	Pay Taxes	**Taxes Deferred**	
Gross rate of return	7%	7%	9%
Net rate of return	5%	7%	9%
Annual retirement living expenses including tax	$ 147,598	$ 147,598	$ 147,598
Total lump sum for retirement fund (annual amount / gross rate)	2,108,543	2,108,543	1,639,982
In 30 years, $10,000 becomes	− 43,200	− 76,100	− 132,700
Still needed	2,065,343	2,032,443	1,507,281
Annual net savings needed	$ 31,187	$ 21,544	$ 11,003
Annual gross savings needed	$ 44,553	Same as net savings	

However, most people can increase their present rate of return without greatly increasing their risk just by having a financial plan. You'll learn the details in Chapter 10 on investing.

Can You Change Your Goal?

Finally, can your goal be changed? As you read Chapter 2, you wrote down your dreams. I believe that most of us can achieve our goals if we make a commitment to reach them. And remember that you still have more strategies to learn about. The rest of this book will cover all the information you need to know about reducing taxes, improving your investment savvy, and meeting your goals.

For now, go back to your retirement goal and reevaluate it. Take a hard look again at your education goal and other goals. What are your priorities? If you can only fund one goal, which one should it be? Maybe you can fund part of two goals. The decisions are up to you.

This is why personal financial planning is so important. Don't be fooled into thinking some $50 computer printout will be right for you. You need to do your own calculations.

Here are three possible ways to change your goal.

1. Retire later. Maybe you wrote that your goal was to retire at 55. If you wait until 60, you will need to save less per year now.

2. Live on less per year. Perhaps you included in your estimated retirement costs that you would travel six months a year. If you reduce that to three months, it will lower the amount of money you need to live on. Maybe there are other costs that are luxuries and not necessities. Can they be reduced?

3. Retire from one job and start or expand a second business for income. Perhaps you could retire from one job and, rather than earning no income, start working part-time at another job. That plan would reduce the amount you need to save.

Now you understand the importance of having done all that homework in Chapters 2 and 3. Decide what, if any, changes to make in your goals. What assumptions about your retirement or your current lifestyle do you want to change?

But What About . . . ?

However, before ending this chapter, I know there are some of you who are saying,

- "But what about inflation?"
- "Why can't I just live off the principal and interest when I retire? Then I won't have to save as much now."
- "What if my health fails?"

Inflation and Retirement

"What about inflation after I retire?" That's a good question. Most of us remember the double-digit inflation of 1974 and 1979–1981. Unfortunately, no one has a crystal ball when it comes to inflation. All you can do is look at past trends. Historically, inflation has averaged about 6 percent a year in the last 30 years.

The previous calculations assume that inflation will be a level number. So, even based on history, that's wrong. It's done that way for two reasons. First, it makes the calculations simpler to do and understand. By now you'll agree you have been keeping those calculator keys humming as it is.

Second, inflation should be less of a problem for you after you retire. When you retire, you tend to slip out of the mainstream of inflation. What are the things that cause inflation? Housing, clothing, travel, and so on. What tends to happen when people retire? Depending on their health of course, the first four or five years they travel and do all the things they've been saving up all their lives to do. After they've been around the world several times, they cut back on their travel. They may not need a new car as often, and they keep the house in good shape by puttering around, taking care of it.

For all these reasons, it is likely that you will not be spending money on the major components of inflation. You will still be in it a little, but you're not in the mainstream buying the big ticket items.

Inflation is usually only an issue when you are accumulating money, not after you have accumulated it. That has to do with the way you structure your portfolio. In Chapter 10, you'll learn an investment strategy that can be modified—depending upon your risk tolerance—so that you always beat inflation by about 2 percent per year after taxes. If you can do that, you're a winner.

Remember that every year you're dealt a new deck of cards for inflation, taxes, and so on. The issue is not this year's rate of return but whether or not you reached your goal.

Using Up Your Retirement Fund

Here's one of the basic questions this book helps you answer. "On the first day I retire, how much money do I need in one lump sum so I can live for the rest of my life?" Remember that an important assumption is that you do not touch the principal but live off only the interest.

What if you want to live off the interest and the principal because you can't meet your goal any other way or you don't want to leave that lump sum to someone else? Then, in the example above, let's say you might only need $1.5 million instead of $1.8 million. The amount doesn't drop as much as you might think.

> **D**oes your company offer a pre-retirement seminar or workshop? Take advantage of the opportunity to learn more about the specific details of your company's retirement plan. Be sure to pass on the details to your financial planner so they can factor in any updates or changes to your company's plan.

There is one major problem with the approach of living on principal and interest: You have to figure out how long you're going to live! If you live longer than that, you're out of money! That's why there is a life expectancy table in the Appendix. You were surprised, weren't you, to see how short a life span the insurance companies have given you.

So to do such a calculation, you must decide when you will die. Look at your family to see the age of the longest living person of your sex. When I do a mortality projection, and I don't know that information, I will use age 85. Now, at age 86, you'd better be dead, because there will be no money left.

In simple terms, that's what your insurance company does. You could buy an annuity from them and let them worry about it and do the calculations. However, you'll probably do better on your own. First, you're not paying them a commission and thus reducing your savings. Second, you may make a better rate of return than they will give you.

A payout table is included in Appendix A if you want to do the calculations. However for peace of mind, I expect that most of you would rather plan to live off the interest only.

Health Concerns

Because the news tends to focus on the bad things that happen, we read or hear more about retired people with health problems. Actually, according to experts, most people over 60 are in good health. However, it is a concern which is, unfortunately, beyond the scope of this book.

There are entire courses devoted to health planning for the retired. Look into such courses available from your local senior center, social service agency, or the American Association of Retired Persons. They will address health and other related issues that you should consider. Be an educated consumer.

If health factors are a viable concern, various solutions are available and can be included in your planning.

Conclusion

By now you should know how much money you need to save each year to fund your retirement goal. As you continue to read the following chapters, make notes as to which tools and strategies will help you better meet that goal. As you learn how to manage to be wealthy, you will be able to meet your goal sooner, increase your goal, or reduce your per-year savings requirements for that goal.

Summary

1. Review your retirement goals from Chapter 2. Write down what you expect your retirement cash flow worksheet to look like.

2. In doing retirement calculations, make choices about the inflation rate, investment rate of return, and so on. Check your balance sheet to see how much you already have saved. Then calculate what the future worth of those dollars will be.
3. Calculate how much you will need to save each year.
4. If it looks like you cannot reach your goal, consider these four alternatives:
    *   Earn more money.
    *   Reduce your taxes.
    *   Increase your rate of return.
    *   Change your goal.

    By using one or more of these strategies, you *can* meet your goal of financial independence.

6

A House Is Not Always a Good Investment

I always ask the people in my seminars, "How many of you think that a house is a good investment?" Usually, about half or more of the class will raise their hands. My next question is, "Who told you that? Your banker or your real estate agent, right?" Everyone agrees. "And they can't both be wrong, can they?" Then everyone chuckles.

Your banker and real estate agent are in the business of selling mortgages and houses. Of course, they're going to tell you to buy your first house or trade up to a larger one. That's how they make their living.

When did this start? Go back before 1950 and look at newspapers and magazines. Try to find a financial expert then who said that a house is a good investment. It's only since World War II that the idea of buying a house as an investment has been "sold" to us.

Here's a comparison. I own a Mercedes, but is that a good investment? Every time I've sold my Mercedes since 1970, the car has sold for what I paid for it or more. But is it an investment? The answer is no, because of the cost of owning that Mercedes. Every time I drove into a dealership, they smiled because it cost at least $500. The cost of owning the car far exceeds the fact that I sold it for what I paid for it. The point is: I drive a Mercedes because I can afford it, not because it's a good investment. *I own a house because I can afford it, not because it's a good investment.*

There are certain things that are real investments, and there are certain things that are just ordinary things or assets. The car is a perfect illustration because no one would argue that the car you drive every day is an investment. The house fits in that same category. Your home is an ordinary asset, not a real investment. I want you to understand the difference between real investments like a rental property and personal property like a house, a car, or your television.

Now if you happen to buy the right house at the right time in the right place and then sell it at the right time, then you can probably increase the amount of money you originally put into the house. That's a lot of "ifs." It's about the same as saying "Buy low and sell high" in the stock market and look what happened to people in October 1929 or in 1987.

The point is this: Most people who buy a house spend more on the house than they realize and overextend themselves because they mistakenly think they are making an investment.

When you're making a financial decision, there are two aspects to the decision. There is the economic aspect, which is $1 + 1 = 2$. That's usually the point that I'm coming from in providing advice to you. However, another aspect is just as valid, and that is the emotional aspect: "I feel better." Owning a house is a "feel better" decision, not an investment decision.

I'm not saying, "You should only rent; never buy a house." I don't rent; I bought a house. However, I don't want you to place your future in an "investment" house. I want you to invest for your future with real investments, as I discuss in Chapter 10.

The True Cost of Home Ownership

How much does a house really cost you? Experts say that when you own a house, you spend approximately 1.5 percent to 2 percent of the cost of the house per month on the mortgage principal and interest, taxes, insurance (PITI), and maintenance. "That sounds high," you say. The problem is that unless you do a cash flow worksheet and a balance sheet, you may not realize all that you spend on the house.

Basic Maintenance and Repair Costs

Remember the cost of the hot water heater you replaced, the roof that had to be fixed, or the paint for the outside of the house? Those are just some of the basic maintenance and repair costs. What about the extra bathroom you put in, or the addition you had built? Then add that extra furniture, carpet, and drapes. It all adds up to more money than you realize. As we move from an apartment to a house, we all buy these things.

Outdoor Living and Transportation

In addition you need a lawn mower, a hose, a sprinkler, equipment to fertilize the lawn, a ladder, and garbage cans. You might add a gas grill or a deck or patio. Remember outdoor furniture. You probably will need a second car because you bought that nice house in the suburbs instead of living in an apartment close to work.

Now, of course, these costs aren't money spent on the house. However, would you have bought all these things if you had stayed in that apartment? Of course not. It all adds up to increased expenses when you own a house. Let's look at a simple example.

Learn more about the housing market in your particular area. Anything I might include in this book about specific areas would probably become out-of-date quickly. Your local newspaper, real estate agents, and lending institutions are the best sources of current mortgage rates, what parts of town are selling well, the average selling price of a home, and the average number of days a house is on the market before it sells. Use the Internet to search for specific houses and other real estate information. If you don't have a computer at home, your public library can provide access to the Internet. Ask your planner to recommend professionals such as loan officers and real estate agents.

Comparing the Cost of a House with That of an Apartment

Suppose a house is worth $100,000. The extra monthly cost is $1,500–$2,000. How would this house compare with an apartment? Table 6.1 shows the comparison between this house and a $900 per month apartment.

Could you find a nice apartment for $900 that would be equivalent to a $100,000 house? In most parts of the country, probably yes. If you did, you would have $600 left over to save and invest. If you had an extra $600 each month and could get an 8 percent rate of return, then in 20 years that extra money would grow

---

FIGURE 6.1   Calculation to Compare a House and Apartment

Value of the house	$100,000
Principal, interest, taxes, insurance, and maintenance/month	$\times$ .015
Extra cost of the house	1,500
Equivalent apartment	– 900
Extra cash	$600

to about $353,000. In 30 years, it would be around $894,000. Think what you could do with that money! Is your house really worth that loss of savings?

I'm convinced that the number one reason most people today are behind the financial eight ball is because they are living beyond their means, usually by owning more house than they should. When people tell me they can't save any extra money, one of the places to look is your house. Do you really need to have a $150,000 house when a $100,000 one may do fine? The difference in the mortgage and upkeep costs could be money to save for your retirement. Can you afford to own and maintain an expensive house? Will you reach financial freedom if you must spend a large part of your money on that house? You need to think seriously about these questions. The true cost of a house may be that you never reach financial independence.

Valid Reasons for Owning a House

Now, don't go out and immediately sell your house. Of course, there are perfectly valid reasons for owning a house. Buy a house because you like it, because it is a comfortable place in which to live, because you want a yard for the kids to play in, because you want pets and the landlord won't let you have them, or because your hobby is ham radio and you can't put an antenna up in an apartment. But don't buy a house solely as a real investment and don't buy more house than you can afford.

Living Beyond Your Means

How many couples do you know where both partners are working so they can afford a nice house? It all gets back to that obstacle, ego, that I talked about in the first chapter. People try to satisfy their egos and end up depleting their savings. They are never going to reach their true goals if they must scrimp and save to pay for a house that's beyond their means.

Let's look at it another way. An expensive car is a joy to have, *if* you can afford it. Many luxury cars have appreciated over time. However, would you send your wife to work to support a Mercedes-Benz? Would you ask your husband to work a second job for a Porsche? If you wouldn't do it for a car, why do it for a house?

A House as an Investment

Even after you read all these reasons, someone will still say, "But what about . . . ?" Their main arguments always involve interest deductions and an inflation hedge.

The "Interest Deduction" Argument

"But what about the tax deduction for interest?" someone always asks in my seminars. Interest is an expense, not a deduction. If you are rationalizing your home ownership on the interest deduction argument, let's look at a comparison in Figure 6.2. The factors to consider are: is it a tax shelter, does it appreciate, and can you deduct maintenance?

When you own your home, you are able to deduct the interest you pay on the mortgage. However, on a rental property, you can also deduct depreciation. When you own your home, its market value may appreciate. Even if you are willing and able to sell it for the appreciated price, what do you do? You buy another house to live in, and your money is tied up again. When you sell a rental property, there is no urgency to buy soon in order to have a place to live so you are able to make an informed economic decision and not an emotional decision.

Finally, when you own your home, you pay the plumber when the hot water tank goes out. When the plumber does work on your rental property, the repair cost is deductible.

Based on these three factors, the smart investor would buy a house or apartment to rent to someone else. If you buy a duplex, you can live in one side and deduct the other. Better yet, buy a multiple unit building. Of course, you must consider whether you want to be a landlord and who would do the maintenance and repairs, you or someone you hire. I discuss real estate as an investment in Chapter 10.

FIGURE 6.2   Owning versus Renting

Factors	Owning	Renting
Tax shelter?	Interest	Interest and depreciation
Appreciation?	Yes	Yes
Deduct maintenance?	No	Yes

Owning a House Is Not a Hedge against Inflation

Over the long-term, a house's increase in value barely keeps up with inflation. Suppose you had bought an existing home in 1986 for the national average price of $80,300. Figure 6.1 shows what happened from 1986 to 1997 to existing home prices. It also shows you how that $80,300 would have increased if it had been invested in six-month T-bills or long-term government securities. By 1997, you would have had about $24,000 to $59,000 more than the house might have been worth by investing in either of those two products. Imagine what you might have earned if you had invested in the stock market during the same period.

If you had sold this hypothetical house by 1988, you might have made the same return on it as on the other investments. However, what do most people do when they sell their house? They buy another house. The money is tied up again. In 1990, the rate of increase for existing home prices was 2.9 percent while six-month T-bills were earning 7.5 percent and long-term government securities were at 8.6 percent. Figure 6.3 compares home value inflation compared to investment interest.

When you buy a T-bill or T-bond, you know ahead of time what rate of return you will get and when you will get it. That's peace of mind. When you buy a house, no one can predict what your rate of return will be or how quickly you will be able to sell your house (when you will get your money). In the late 1970s, most people would have said that buying a house in Houston or Dallas was a good investment. Then oil prices went down, and the housing market followed.

Can a house be a real investment? Sure, if you treat the buy/sell decision on the house as an economic decision. For example, I know one client who sold his personal residence when market values were rising (after a slump of four or five years). He planned to rent until the real estate market settled back down. Then when the prices declined, he planned on buying another house. Notice that he made economic decisions, not emotional decisions about that particular house. Most of us are unable to do that because owning our personal residence is an emotional decision. That's perfectly acceptable; just be honest with yourself about your reasons for owning a house and about how much house you can afford.

Buy Now or Buy Later

The next argument that usually comes up relates not so much to the so-called investment as to the timing of the house purchase. We've all been told to buy a

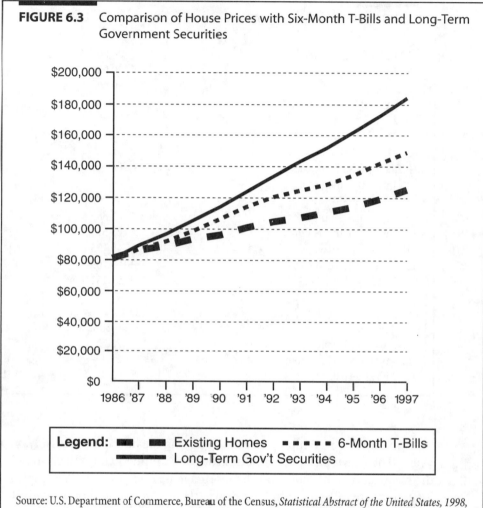

FIGURE 6.3   Comparison of House Prices with Six-Month T-Bills and Long-Term Government Securities

Legend: ▬ ▬ Existing Homes   ▪ ▪ ▪ ▪ ▪ 6-Month T-Bills
▬▬▬ Long-Term Gov't Securities

Source: U.S. Department of Commerce, Bureau of the Census, *Statistical Abstract of the United States, 1998*, 118th ed. (1998); and U.S. Department of the Treasury, "Federal Reserve Bulletin," vols. 71–84 (1986–98).

house as soon as you can. "Buy now when interest rates are low." Not true. Even if you wait to buy a house, you will still come out ahead because of compound interest as shown in Figure 6.4. Here's a very simple example:

FIGURE 6.4   It's Cheaper to Buy Later

1. Cost of house today	$100,000
2. Down payment	20,000
3. Mortgage	80,000
4. Interest	10%
5. Length of loan	30 years
6. Monthly payment	$702

	Assumption A	Assumption B
— But if you wait 10 years		
7. Invest that money at	7%	8%
8. Inflation	5%	7%
9. Future cost of house	$162,889	$196,715
10. Invest monthly payment	121,515	128,439
11. Invest down payment	40,193	44,393
12. Total available to buy	$161,709	$172,831
13. Would still owe (#9 – #12)	$1,181	$ 23,884
— If you had bought the house		
14. Tax bracket	30%	30%
15. Mortgage balance after 10 years	$72,750	$72,750
16. Invest tax savings from interest deduction	29,877	31,456
17. Mortgage balance left	$42,873	$41,294

In these two examples, instead of buying the house immediately, you wait ten years. The down payment is put into savings immediately. Each month you save the same amount of money as the mortgage payment. Under Assumption A with a 7 percent rate of return and 5 percent inflation, you would only need $1,181 more to buy the house while the mortgage on a house bought today would still have $42,873 remaining. Total savings would be $41,692 (balance left – cash needed). With Assumption B and higher rates, you would save $17,410.

Now of course during these ten years you would have to pay rent to live somewhere else. That cost of living comes from all the money you didn't have to pay for taxes, insurance, and all those maintenance and repair costs on a house. However, if you stayed in the same house the entire time, chances are you would be living well below your means. Every situation is different and must be individually addressed.

Be sure to evaluate what compound interest can do for you. You don't have to rush out now and buy a house that you may not be able to afford anyway. By waiting, you may be able to save more money and still buy the house, if that's one of your goals.

Making the Most Use of Your Cash Flow

If you decide to buy a house, and most of you will, then you can make the most of your cash flow by putting less down on the house. This use of credit to increase your buying power is a form of leverage—the same principle people use in investment real estate. This can be dangerous when the market goes down. You owe more money. However, in a home purchase, using a lower down payment allows you to make better use of your cash flow. The most efficient use of your cash is to invest it rather than to tie up the money in your house. For example, if your mortgage payment would be $700 but you can lower that to $500, then you can use the $200 difference for investing to reach your goal. If you will spend that $200, however, then you should not do this.

An additional benefit of leveraging your home is inflation. If you live in your present home for an extended period, the mortgage payment will become less and less a portion of your cash flow. Inflation will reduce the real cost of these payments.

If you decide to use leverage when buying your house, you will probably want to make the down payment enough, usually 20 percent, to avoid being required to escrow your taxes and insurance. You must balance this concept against other financial factors, such as existing debt or whether you've met your goal. If you've met your goal, you don't have to worry about using your cash flow efficiently. Here's where a financial advisor can help you look at different scenarios and choose your best strategy.

Shopping for a Mortgage

It's funny that people will spend more time choosing clothes or discussing the latest game than selecting a mortgage company. There are many useful books on how to buy (or sell) your house. Spend some time at your public library and then shop around for a mortgage. There are many mortgage resources online, including mortgage calculators where you enter the purchase price, number of years, and interest rate, and get back the payment amount (for example, www.kiplinger. com/calc or www.finance.com, click on the real estate tab at the top, then go to the real estate tools).

Buying a home is probably the largest purchase you will ever make. I'll give you a brief outline of the process. Your assignment is to compare mortgage lenders and their terms so you get the best mortgage.

First, remember you're not buying a house for the tax benefits. Use the calculation examples that follow or see the payment calculation examples in any homebuying book to determine what you can really handle. *You don't have to spend what the lender or agent says you can afford.* Remember: Live within your paycheck!

Types of Mortgages

Conventional or Fixed Rate

If you're buying a house for the long term, then a fixed-rate mortgage has advantages. The payments are the same for the entire term of the mortgage, usually 15 or 30 years.

Which length of time is better? Well, you will pay less interest over 15 years. However, you're locked into that payment schedule. If an unexpected illness, job loss, or other financial hardship occurs, the mortgage is still due.

Even if you have a 30-year mortgage, you can reap the benefits of a shorter term mortgage by paying more in principal according to your cash flow. First, you need to be sure you have a mortgage that will allow additional payments of principal (most will). Second, make sure that the additional amount you pay is credited to the paydown of the principal (indicate this on the payment coupon that you send in).

Variable Rate Mortgage

Although the rate changes with the current interest rate, there is usually a limit on how much it can change within one year and over the life of the loan. If interest rates are high or you don't expect to own the house very long, a variable rate might be right for you.

Balloon Mortgage

This mortgage has a fixed rate, but the loan term is shorter than a conventional mortgage. For example, the loan might have payments using a 15-year to 30-year payment schedule, but at the end of 5 years, the remaining amount is due.

Land Contract or Purchase Money Agreement

The seller finances the mortgage and keeps the title until the full amount is paid. In a purchase money agreement, the seller finances the mortgage, but the buyer is given the title. When the real estate market is not good and interest rates are high, these mortgages are popular.

Biweekly Mortgage

By making payments every two weeks instead of once a month, the buyer effectively makes thirteen monthly payments. If the two payments equaled a normal monthly payment, a 30-year mortgage would be paid off in 21 years.

Graduated Payment Mortgage

Set up for first-time homeowners, these mortgage payments begin at a lower rate. Then they increase until they reach a payment that stays the same for the rest of the loan.

Closing Costs

The number of different closing costs you will have to pay can be overwhelming. Here's a brief definition of each term.

Application Fee

This fee is collected when you apply. It covers loan processing costs and is nonrefundable unless the lender turns down your application. This fee can be negotiated or even waived.

Appraisal Fee

A professional appraiser determines the market value of the house for the lender. The lender wants to know that the property is worth at least the loan amount. The appraiser may use sales of "comparable" houses to establish the value of the house you're buying in addition to an inspection of the property you're buying.

Credit Report Fee

The lender orders a detailed credit report from one or more of the credit reporting companies. This report shows all credit transactions you have made for the last seven years, if you paid on time or were late, and other credit risk factors that may concern the lender.

Loan Origination Fee

The bank or mortgage company that originates the loan keeps this fee as part of its profit.

Discount Fee (Points)

A point is 1 percent of the mortgage amount. This fee increases the lender's total yield. The seller pays points for VA and FHA loans. The buyer pays the points for a conventional mortgage. On a new mortgage, points can be deducted from your income tax for the year the loan began. When refinancing, you must deduct the points over the life of the loan. Points can be negotiated. Generally, the lower the interest rate, the more points you pay. However, in a highly competitive market, it is not unusual for points to be waived.

Processing Fee

This fee covers the lender's processing costs and overhead. Again, its rate can be negotiated.

Survey Fee

The professional survey provides a legal basis for the property boundaries. There are different levels of detail given in the survey report, depending on the type of survey done. The fee depends on property location and size.

Mortgage Title Insurance

This special type of insurance for the buyer and lender guarantees that the property is transferred without liens or rights-of-way.

Prepaid Interest

At closing, the buyer prepays the interest from the closing date to the date of the first mortgage payment.

Mortgage Insurance

Often a lending institution will try to sell you mortgage insurance. It is a declining benefit term life insurance policy to cover your mortgage in case you die. Try to avoid this cost. If you need insurance to cover the mortgage, then make that choice based on your whole financial plan, not piecemeal as it would be here.

Private Mortgage Insurance (PMI)

If the down payment is less than 20 percent of the sales price, the lender usually requires the borrower to pay this cost. A private insurer provides the insurance to the lender. As soon as you have 20 percent equity in the house, write the lender and have it remove this insurance.

Recording Fees
The county or town charges a fee to record the deed and mortgage.

Prepaid Property Taxes
Because property taxes are usually paid ahead, this prorating of taxes reimburses the seller for taxes already paid on the property.

Escrow Reserve for Property Taxes
Next year's taxes are put into an escrow account to be sure that they will be paid. Depending on your downpayment amount, you may be able to avoid this. Be sure to ask, especially if you can earn more interest on the money than the account is paying.

Escrow Reserve for Hazard and Flood Insurance
As with the property tax escrow, the money is put into an escrow account so that the insurance can be paid. Find out what down payment is required to avoid escrow. However, you should set aside the money to pay the insurance when the bill arrives. Your cash flow worksheet can help with planning for this expense.

Real Estate Transfer Tax/Revenue Stamps
When property is transferred from one party to another, the transaction is taxed.

Saving Money on Your Mortgage

Whether you have a mortgage now or are just looking for your first home, you can save money on a mortgage by reducing your payment or reducing your total liability. Use some or all of the methods below.

Reduce Your Payment
Can you reduce or eliminate tax or insurance escrow costs? Can you refinance at a lower rate or shop around for a better rate for your new mortgage? If you put a larger down payment on the house (usually 20 percent or more), then you can avoid extra costs such as private mortgage insurance or mortgage term life insurance. However, you will have to weigh this against the advantages of putting down a small down payment so you will have more money to invest.

Reduce Your Total Liability

Can you increase the monthly payment you make? A 15-year mortgage costs you less in total interest paid. Can you make a lump sum payment? Do you know that you will be able to make a large payment in the future, perhaps when a CD matures?

Whatever your strategy, remember to keep the big picture in mind. Don't make a decision that might save money on your mortgage but would cost you financially in another way.

How Much Can You Afford?

Frequently, home buyers are told that they can afford a house that costs two and one-half to three times their gross incomes. That should be your maximum. You need to focus on what amount you can really handle. Go back to your cash flow worksheet and look at these three amounts:

1. How much do you have for a down payment?
2. How much do you have for a monthly payment?
3. What other debts do you have?

Ratios to Calculate

Next, figure out these two ratios:

1. Mortgage Payment/Monthly Gross Income. This ratio should be 28 percent or less.
2. Overall Debt/Monthly Gross Income. This ratio should be 36 percent or less.

Lenders usually say you can afford the smaller of these two numbers. As an example, let's suppose your monthly gross income is $4,000. The ratios listed above are calculated as:

1. 28 percent × $4,000 = $1,200 maximum monthly
2. 36 percent × $4,000 = $1,440 maximum overall debt

Then you subtract other debts from this maximum overall debt. So if you have a $500 car payment and a $100 credit card payment, you would subtract $600 to get an $840 maximum monthly payment. In this example, a lender would allow the smaller number or an $840 monthly payment. I want to warn you that, in general, if you cannot come up with the mortgage and down payment, you should not buy that particular house.

Just as we warn you not to buy a house if you don't have the down payment or sufficient assets to get the loan from a creditable institution, you should not sell your house under any arrangement to someone who can't qualify.

Once you have these numbers, then you can ask a mortgage lender or a REALTOR® what price house you can buy. Don't let them talk you into more than you want. You know your circumstances and your level of financial discipline. Don't let that obstacle, ego, get in the way of sound financial decision making.

Refinancing an Existing Mortgage

Should you refinance an existing mortgage? You can usually save money if: 1) the new rate will be at least 2 percent below your current rate, and 2) you keep the house for the number of months it takes to recover the closing costs. Figure 6.5 shows an easy example of how to calculate this break even point. Don't worry about the actual rates used in this example. Just focus on how to calculate *your* possible savings.

Remember that the monthly payment savings will be offset by the lump sum closing costs until you reach the break even point. In the example in Figure 6.5, you would have to keep the house almost two years to benefit from refinancing.

FIGURE 6.5   How Much Can Refinancing Save You?

Example: Suppose you refinance a house worth $100,000 at a new rate of 8 percent

Current monthly payment at 9.5%	$840.85
Proposed monthly payment at 8%	− 733.76
Monthly pretax savings	107.09
1.00 − 0.30 (tax bracket)	× 0.70
Monthly after-tax savings	74.96
Lost investment return	− 10.00*
Net monthly savings	64.96
Total refinancing cost	$1,500.00

Months to break even ($1,500 / $64.96) = **23 months**

* $1,500 × .08 return = $120 per year / 12 months = $10 per month.

Paying Off the Mortgage Early

Along with the myth of a house as an investment, you may have been told or have read that you should prepay your mortgage. "Build up your equity and save thousands of dollars in interest," the experts cry. Let's look at these five points you ought to consider before you start paying more towards the mortgage.

1. Are you meeting your goals? If not, why tie up more money in your house when that money should be put towards meeting your goals?

2. If you are meeting your goals, can you earn a better rate elsewhere? How does the interest rate on your mortgage compare with what you could earn in a certificate of deposit, T-bill, or other investment? Remember to factor in the effect of taxes on your mortgage interest rate. If your tax bracket is 30 percent and your mortgage rate is 10 percent, then your after-tax mortgage rate is 7 percent ([1 − bracket] × rate = after-tax rate). If you can find an tax-free investment earning 10 percent, why prepay your mortgage?

3. Are you sure that your house will continue to appreciate at or above the rate of inflation? This assumption is one of the cornerstones of the prepayment advice. If you own a home in a good location and homes like yours have been selling at appreciated prices, it's hard to think that it won't always be that way. However, the housing market has cycles just like any other investment. Then there are external factors. Recall the plunging housing market in Texas when oil prices fell. There are no guarantees when you have money tied up in your house. When you put your money in a certificate of deposit, your rate is guaranteed.

4. Consider liquidity. A house is not a liquid asset; a T-bill is. Don't tie up money that might be needed for emergencies.

5. What about the tax deduction for your mortgage interest? Even with tax reform and lower tax rates, the tax deduction reduces the actual cost of the interest to you.

Are there some advantages to prepaying? First, if you can't save any other way, perhaps prepaying will force you to save something. Second, if you only intend to stay in the house for a few years, you might want to build up your equity faster (but look at the interest rates). Finally, if you have excess cash flow and have considered all of the five points above, you may want to prepay.

Home Equity Loans

A home equity loan is a second mortgage. While there may be valid reasons for having one (education, business, or financial hardship), remember that failure to repay means you could lose your home!

The interest on a home equity loan is deductible up to certain limits. No other consumer loans are deductible on your income taxes. This makes home equity loans very enticing as an extra source of cash. Don't ever use a home equity loan to pay for a depreciating asset such as a car, furniture, or a vacation. It's not worth the risk.

Buying and Selling

Whether you are buying or selling, remember that this is a financial transaction. It's okay to buy a home for emotional reasons, but try to keep your emotions in control during the process. Falling in love with the house before you've thoroughly checked it out is the worst thing to do. When you are selling, it's hard to be objective about the strong and weak points of a home that has so many memories. There are many good books and magazine articles on this subject, so I'll just mention the main points of buying and selling. Also, it's wise to have a lawyer review the contract.

Buying a House

Real estate agents say the three most important points in selling a house are "location, location, and location." Unless you plan to retire in this house, keep in mind that the location will help you sell it later.

Start following the mortgage rates and prices before you need to buy so you will have a feel for the market. Then you will know when the rates are a good buy and how one house compares with another. Have a lender preapprove you so you'll know how much house you can afford.

Be sure to have a home inspection, preferably by a licensed engineer. It is worth the extra cost to know whether that ceiling crack is cosmetic or indicates structural damage.

Selling a House

Whether you decide to use a real estate agent or sell the house yourself, do the less expensive things first before putting your home on the market.

Clean out the closets, have a yard sale, or donate to a charity; get the clutter out of the house. Repair all those small things you've ignored: the leaky faucet, the squeaky hinges, the torn window screen. Clean up inside and outside. If washing the walls doesn't improve their looks, then start painting with a neutral color.

If the house has problems, don't cover them up. Be honest about what you've done to fix the problem. Get a repair estimate so you have a basis for negotiation on the sale price.

> Even though the rules have changed regarding the deduction for a house sale, don't throw away those records! Ask your financial planner to show you what you must keep to establish the basis (the original cost) of the house.

Home Improvements

Before you add a jacuzzi or any other improvement to a house before selling it, do your homework. Some improvements will return 90–100 percent of their cost in the sales price while others may actually detract from selling the house. Several magazines do yearly surveys of the value of home improvements when selling a home. Check out your local library for the latest research.

When you are buying a home, don't guess at the cost of doing home improvements. Check the magazine articles at your library for average costs of typical improvements. Then talk to local contractors to see what the price range is in your area.

What Taxes Will Be Due from Your Home Sale?

Be sure to check with your tax advisor for the latest laws regarding the exclusion of profits from the sale of your home. The current exclusion for married joint filers is up to $500,000 and $250,000 for single filers. This exclusion can be used once every two years. If you have been deferring profits from previous sales, check to see if those profits plus your current gain will exceed the exclusion. You will owe tax on the amount above that.

Conclusion

Don't buy your principal residence for an investment, but treat it like one. Your home is an ordinary asset and not a real investment. Pull out your cash flow worksheet and re-evaluate the true cost of your house. Is it worth it to mortgage your future, your retirement, and your other goals, just to have this house today?

If you don't currently own a house, carefully evaluate whether to buy one now or wait until you can afford it. If you already own a house, what can you do to cut costs? Is a move to a less expensive house necessary in order to have more money for savings and thus meet your goal of financial independence?

Summary

You should own a house because you can afford it, not because it's a good investment. Your home is an ordinary asset, not a real investment. When you're making a financial decision, there are two aspects to the decision: the economic aspect, and the emotional aspect. Owning a house is a "feel better" decision, not an investment decision.

People say, "A house is the biggest investment you will ever make." What they should really say is, "A house is the biggest expenditure you will ever have." Most of us don't know the true cost of a house. Every month you spend about 1.5 percent to 2 percent of the house's value on the mortgage principal and interest, taxes, insurance, and maintenance. However, unless you do a cash flow worksheet and a balance sheet, you may not realize all that you spend on the house.

In addition to those costs, add in the new roof, the extra bath, the lawn mower, the second car you had to have, and so on. It all adds up to a significant expense over the long haul. You don't see it unless you sit down and analyze the expenses. For the same cost of our house, many of us could live in a very nice apartment and still have money left to save.

This doesn't mean you should immediately sell your house. There are very good emotional reasons why you want to own a house. Buy a house because you want a yard for the kids or a big garden, but don't buy a house for an investment.

Too many two income households today are trying to support a house they can't afford. Remember that one of the obstacles to achieving financial independence is ego. Don't satisfy your ego with a house and risk your long-term goals.

Treat your house like you would a car. Would you send your spouse to work just so you could have a Porsche?

The most frequent comments about house ownership include the "tax deduction" argument and the "inflation hedge" argument. Looking at the facts shows you the fallacy of these arguments. If you want a true tax deduction, buy a duplex apartment. If you want a hedge against inflation, put your savings into a tax deferred tool which invests in T-bills.

If you do buy a house, and most people will for valid reasons, buy only what you can afford—not what your ego wants. Put down the lowest amount possible on the purchase. Save the rest in a tax-deferred tool, and you have used leverage to your benefit. Compare mortgage rates, types, and closing costs to save money.

Does it pay to refinance? Probably, if the new rate will be 2 percent below your current rate. Do the calculations to see how many months it will take to break even.

Consider my five points before you prepay your mortgage. You may get a better return on investment by putting that money in savings.

A home equity loan is a second mortgage. Don't use the money to buy something that depreciates, such as a car.

Remember that buying and selling is a financial transaction. Keep your emotions and ego under control. Don't commit to a home improvement until you do your research. Consumer articles at the library will help you determine the value of a home improvement.

7

Life and Disability Insurance

Review Figure 3.3, the Cash Flow Worksheet, and Figure 3.7, the Spendable Cash Worksheet, in Chapter 3. When you're just starting out, you usually have few investments but still need insurance. Insurance fills the gap between what you have and what you need to protect your loved ones. See Figure 7.1 to evaluate your needs. Using the worksheets in Chapter 3 will help you see how much you can spend for insurance (cash flow) and how any particular insurance policy expense will affect your spendable cash.

Take the time to do some "what if" scenarios. For example, if you have children, what if one of you dies? What changes regarding your income or expenses? Filling out a worksheet for possible scenarios helps you to see how your insurance needs might change.

As your investments increase, then you need less insurance. However, most of us are still somewhere in the insurance-gap years.

In this chapter, you'll learn what the two types of life insurance are and their variations, the two types of insurance companies, how agents earn their money, tax considerations, why you need disability insurance, and how to find and evaluate the best buys in insurance.

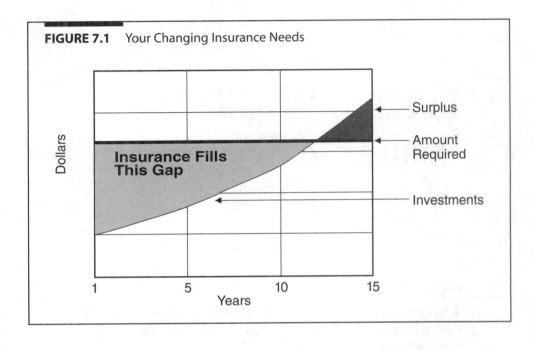

FIGURE 7.1   Your Changing Insurance Needs

Types of Life Insurance

Life insurance seems to come in as many varieties as ice cream these days, but the names are not much help in describing what they will do for you. There are only two types of insurance—term and cash value.

Term Life Insurance

With term insurance, you are only buying protection in case you die. The insurance company is betting that you will stay alive; you are betting that you will die in one year. If you don't die, you lose. If you do die, you lose. I realize that may sound a bit crass, but that's what insurance boils down to.

Remember that the most valuable dollar you have is the first dollar right now. You want to spend the least amount necessary for insurance. As you'll learn in Chapter 10, if invested properly, that first dollar can be worth thousands by the time you retire.

You want control of how much you need in insurance. As your investments grow, you should need less insurance. If you have a cash value policy, you bought protection and savings so you're stuck with the policy unless you want to take a loss on all you paid so far. So you keep paying for a product that isn't giving you the most bang for the buck.

Credit Life Insurance

One type of term insurance you will see frequently is credit life (decreasing term). Avoid it. It's the most expensive, and you have no control over the value of the insurance. The protection decreases each year whether you want it to or not. This is the type of insurance you are offered when you take out a car loan, for example. It's better to plan for your entire insurance coverage. Buy one policy rather than buying insurance piecemeal for each loan you take out.

Cash Value or Whole Life Insurance

Cash value life insurance is sold by many names: whole life, single-premium whole life, universal life, variable life, and many hybrid forms. You need to understand that they all boil down to a product that offers protection plus something else, usually a savings program. The result is you get less protection for your dollar.

Let's look at the specific details of the four main types of cash value insurance: whole life, universal life, variable life, and single premium.

> **A**sk your financial planner what to do with your whole life policy. You may be able to cash in life insurance that you don't need. Your financial planner can calculate any taxes due if you cashed in that unneeded policy.

Whole Life

The death benefit is fixed when you buy the policy. You pay a fixed premium on regular payment dates. You have no investment choices and the rate of return on the cash value is not given. You may take out a loan against the policy at a fixed or variable rate of interest.

Universal Life

With universal life, you choose an initial death benefit which you can raise or lower each year. The premium can be fixed, or it can be a variable amount that you can increase or reduce periodically or even skip occasionally. You have no investment choices. The rate of return is generally guaranteed at a base amount. Any higher rate will vary. The rate the agent quotes to you will probably be before the costs are deducted. You can make partial withdrawals for a fee and from 6 percent to 8 percent interest.

Keep in mind that if you do not pay enough in premiums to cover mortality charges (the basic charges to cover the cost of insuring you), the company will subtract what they need from your cash value or the policy will lapse.

Variable Life

You choose the initial death benefit when you buy the policy. If the investments you choose do well, the death benefit could increase. You pay a fixed or variable premium periodically. This type of insurance has two fees: a "mortality and expense charge" and an "investment management expense" that other types of life insurance do not have.

You can choose between stock, bond, and money market portfolios and can change your choice by writing to the company. The investment choices look like mutual funds. There is no guaranteed rate of return because it depends on how the investments do. You can get a loan from equity at an interest rate of 6 percent to 8 percent.

Joseph Belth, former insurance commissioner of Pennsylvania and professor emeritus at Indiana University, points out that with this policy, your beneficiary's best hope is that you will die when the market is going up.

Single Premium Adjustable Whole Life

Like whole life, the death benefit is fixed when you buy the policy. The premium is a lump sum payment of anywhere from $5,000 to $1 million. You have no investment choices. The rate of return on the cash value is 4 percent, generally guaranteed. This rate usually will change every one to three years. You can take out a loan from equity usually at 2 percent to 4 percent net interest on your original investment and at no interest on your own earnings.

A single premium whole life policy should not be used for short-term needs (under ten years). If you cash it in early, it costs you part of the premium. The first year you would lose 9 percent; 8 percent the second year; and so on. If surrender charges continue more than seven years, don't buy the policy.

If you want this policy because of the loan privileges, be sure to find a policy that guarantees a no-net interest rate on your earnings and no more than 2 percent on your original premium.

Single Premium Variable Life

You choose the death benefit when you purchase the policy. It can increase if the investments do well, but it will not drop below a base amount. You pay a lump sum premium of from $5,000 to $1 million. You can choose among stock, bond, and money market portfolios and change your choice by writing to the company. There is no guaranteed rate of return. Usually there is no interest on loans against earnings. Other loans will run 2 percent to 4 percent.

Only buy this policy for the long term. Most of the premium covers expenses during the first ten years. If you have chosen the stock investment, don't borrow much. You could lose a lot in a volatile market. The most the company will give you is a return that equals your loan interest on the amount of the policy loan.

Hybrid Policies

There are many different names and variations of cash value life insurance. Each year a "NEW" variation seems to appear. Here are four hybrid policies being sold currently.

1. Modified life. This policy is whole life with a lower premium in the early years.
2. Limited payment life. You pay premiums for a limited number of years on a whole life policy.
3. Family income policy. This policy combines decreasing term and whole life insurance.
4. Adjustable life. You are allowed to switch between term and cash value insurance.

Recommendation

What do I recommend? In general, term insurance is a better buy. Because the marketplace is so fluid, I can't recommend a specific type of term. The best buy today will probably not be the best buy tomorrow. Do your homework and compare policies using the strategies I describe later in this chapter.

To compare term with cash value policies, find the best buy in term insurance. Then ask for a comparison of that term policy with a cash value policy. Be aware that a particular company's term policy will not compare favorably with its own cash value policy.

Remember: You want to buy basic protection, not make an investment. Do your tax sheltering with tools, not insurance.

The premium is based on the standard mortality tables. An example of such a life expectancy table is given in Appendix A. Other risk factors, such as smoking and illness, are also considered in determining your premium.

Your best bet may be through a professional or social association (e.g., Elks, Soroptimists, etc.) to which you belong that also offers term insurance. It will probably have good rates because of a large member pool. Also, it may offer additional coverages you might not get individually.

> **A**sk your planner to evaluate whether you have the best buy for your money in life insurance. The National Association of Insurance Commissioners has adopted the "interest-adjusted net payment cost index" and the "surrender cost index" to use in comparing costs. Your planner can calculate these indexes in order to make an apples-to-apples comparison of different policies.

If you don't belong to a professional association, check to see what is available in your business and related businesses. Some professional associations have less strict membership requirements (support of their aims, interest in the field, and so on) than others (licensure) so it will pay to investigate.

Types of Insurance Companies

There are two types of insurance companies. One pays dividends and is known as participating or par. You can do five things with the dividends.

1. Take cash.
2. Use them to reduce the premiums (this is the best option).
3. Leave them in to accumulate with the company.
4. Purchase additional cash value insurance. If you are under 45, a dividend-paying policy may be cheaper.
5. Purchase one-year term insurance.

The other type of company is called non-par and does not pay dividends.

Tax Considerations

Life insurance does not go through probate. For federal estate tax purposes, it is taxable. Each state has different estate tax rules. For example, in Ohio, where I live, an estate is not taxed on the insurance if it is properly set up and the beneficiary is not the insured's estate.

Tax Shelter

Life insurance is sometimes sold as a tax shelter. The advantages to this include:

- Earnings on cash value grow tax deferred.
- You can borrow the earnings from the policy tax free. The interest is tax deductible.
- The beneficiary can get policy proceeds free of federal income tax.
- The premium is generally fixed when you take out the policy and does not increase.

The disadvantages include:

- You get a decent return only after holding the policy for several years.
- The insurance company makes all investment decisions (except with variable life policies).
- This product suffers from a lack of liquidity. You can only get the money out as a loan. Generally you can't take out as much as you put in for a considerable time; the exception is single-premium life.
- The death benefit is usually fixed when you buy a policy. Because of inflation, what sounds like a lot of money when you take out a policy may be chicken feed by the time it is paid.

How Insurance Agents Earn Money

Insurance agents are paid a percentage of the premiums on the policies they sell, not by volume. They get paid to *sell* insurance not necessarily to find the best policy for you. They make more money if you buy a whole life policy, as shown in Figure 7.2.

It doesn't take much thought, does it? You want to buy insurance to protect you, not to pay someone else's commission.

Sales Pitches You Will Hear

Here are the seven most common sales pitches that agents use to sell you life insurance.

1. *Peace of mind and no risk.* Life insurance policies are not insured by the U.S. government. Most states have guaranty funds which pay claims and

---

FIGURE 7.2   Which Policy Would You Sell?

Term Insurance

Premium $100   Commission 35% the first year
                                     5% thereafter

Cash Value Insurance

Premium $1,000   Commission 50% the first year
                                     10–15% for the next 10 years
                                     3–5% for the policy life

---

will continue your coverage if an insurance company is declared insolvent. Some states—including California, New Jersey, and Ohio—have no such funds. Check with your state insurance commissioner to see if your state has a guaranty fund. If your insurer goes out of business, you or your beneficiaries might not receive everything you paid for.

2. *If you buy term insurance, all you have to show for it are receipts, just like renting instead of buying a house.* However, if home prices are too high and rents are reasonable, why not rent? Likewise, why pay too much for whole life when term insurance will meet your goal.

3. *Sell your municipal bonds and buy single-premium whole life so your earnings will be automatically reinvested.* You can invest in municipal bond mutual funds which also reinvest automatically, don't have all the extra charges, and have more liquidity. Take your savings and buy term insurance.

4. *Loans against a single-premium policy's cash value have zero net interest, and there are no federal taxes on the loan.* You must be careful not to borrow most of the cash value or you will no longer have a policy. In addition, you will owe tax on the difference between what you paid for premiums and what you borrowed. Not all insurance companies warn you that you are about to borrow too much.

5. *Life insurance is a tax shelter, plus you earn double-digit interest rates.* No company can guarantee double-digit rates. The high initial rates you are quoted are teaser rates intended to sell you a policy. The high rate quoted is usually before expenses are deducted. Not all companies will tell you about all these expenses unless you specifically ask. Furthermore, the high interest rate may only be good for a year or perhaps only a

month. When you look at policies, forget those that quote a rate much higher than current rates or Treasury bonds or quality corporate bonds. Higher rates mean higher risk.

6. *The insurance is free because this is such a fantastic investment.* You don't get something for nothing. Insurance companies are in business to make money; somewhere there is a charge to cover the cost of payout and the company's profit. This charge will come out of your "fantastic" investment if the charge is not shown elsewhere. How good an investment is it, really?

7. *Due to the changes in the tax code, you need to buy life insurance.* Nothing in the recent tax laws has changed the way you should buy life insurance. Buy it for protection. Do your investing elsewhere unless this is the only way you can discipline yourself to save.

Disability Insurance

Everyone needs disability insurance. The odds are greater in middle age that you will be disabled than die. Most of us think of getting life insurance first.

Even if your company provides you with some disability insurance, don't be lulled into a false sense of security. Based upon my experience, you will still need to get your own policy. Most company disability policies either don't have enough coverage or are too limited by their restrictions.

> **A**sk your planner to look at your company's disability plan to see if you need additional coverage. Be sure to get recommendations on disability insurance for your partner if he or she does not have it or if the insurance is inadequate.

What do you need? Look for noncancelable, guaranteed renewable insurance with an inflation rider, provision for partial/residual benefits, and "own occupation" definition of disability. That's a mouthful, isn't it! Let's define the terms so they make sense.

Noncancelable

The policy can never be canceled regardless of your circumstances. A change in your health or job might cause some policies to be canceled if they do not have this provision. In addition this guarantees the premium and benefit amount.

Guaranteed Renewable

At the policy renewal date, the company must allow you to buy the policy again until you reach a certain age, such as age 65.

Inflation Rider

This will give you some protection against the effects of inflation by increasing the benefit on an annual basis while you are disabled. The increase can be calculated with either compound or simple interest and can be guaranteed or tied to the Consumer Price Index (CPI).

Partial/Residual Benefits

These can be either an integral part of the policy or added as a rider. This provision will pay a reduced benefit based on the insured's percentage loss of income. For example, a physician earning $10,000 per month who suffers a 50 percent loss of income would receive 50 percent of the monthly benefit *stated in his policy*. Note that some policies require a period of total disability to qualify for this benefit. This requirement usually can be eliminated by adding a rider.

Own Occupation

This definition of disability means the insureds will receive their benefits if unable to perform the duties of their own occupations *even* if they are earning income from a different occupation. Some policies have an *own occupation* definition of disability for only the first year or two of disability. Thereafter, there is an *any occupation* definition. For example, a physician who is disabled and unable to perform surgery but can teach would collect full disability benefits for two years. Thereafter, other earned income would reduce or eliminate the benefits.

Understanding Terminology

As you can see, when shopping for disability insurance, you can really lose if you don't understand the terms. Check your company policy to see if it covers all five areas and beware when making future purchases.

Finally, one point to help you in finding a policy. With disability insurance, expensive is often better. Shop by benefits offered, not premium price.

How to Evaluate Insurance Companies and Policies

Here are four ways to evaluate both the companies and the policies before you buy.

1. Go to your library and check the reports of the insurance rating agencies such as Weiss Research (www.weissratings.com), Duff & Phelps (www.dcrco.com), Moody's (www.moodys.com), Standard and Poor's (www.standardandpoor.com), and A.M. Best (www.ambest.com/index.html). Be sure to look at more than one report because some agencies are easier in their ratings than others.

2. Write to the Insurance Forum, Inc., P.O. Box 245, Ellettsville, IN 47429 or call 812-876-6502 for information on its newsletter edited by Joseph Belth, former insurance commissioner of Pennsylvania. A few issues each year are devoted to the consumer. Back issues are available. Be advised that the calculations do take time but they are useful. See if your library has this newsletter.

3. Check with your state's insurance commissioner to see if there is state backing for insurance companies.

4. There are several companies that will provide you with a list of insurance policies to meet your specifications (age, sex, amount, and so forth). Check recent issues of consumer magazines for the details or ask your reference librarian.

The ABC Technique

Use this ABC technique to help you evaluate any business proposal. It will help you decide which insurance policy to buy, which investments to purchase, and answer some of the other questions you will have in implementing your financial plan.

What do you do? You can do much of the "detective work" yourself with the ABC approach shown in Figure 7.3. Let's say that you need disability insurance. Call Agent A. You say, "Agent A, I need disability insurance. Don't come over. Send me a proposal." You call up agent B and C and say the same thing. Now you

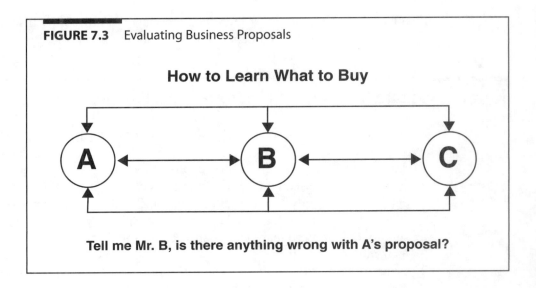

FIGURE 7.3 Evaluating Business Proposals

How to Learn What to Buy

Tell me Mr. B, is there anything wrong with A's proposal?

have three proposals. (This works for oil wells, real estate, insurance, or anything you need to compare.)

Then you go to B and say, "While I was waiting for your proposal, I received A's proposal. Would you mind telling me what's wrong with this proposal?" What do you think B will do? He'll tell you what is wrong with A's proposal. You go to C and show her B's proposal. And you go to A and show him C's proposal. You'll learn which is the best proposal.

You're not doing this to embarrass people. You're not doing this to take advantage of them. You're trying to learn. You're doing this so you can understand. You'll know the terms and you'll know the right kind of insurance or investment to buy.

It's your money. No one cares as much about your money as you do. I manage my clients' money. Many times I lose sleep over it. But I still don't care as much about their money as they do.

Conclusion

Buy life insurance for protection, not for investment. Term insurance should give you the best value for your dollar. Take the time to evaluate policies and shop for the best buy.

For your other insurance needs—health, disability, homeowner's or renter's, automobile, personal liability, and professional and malpractice—you will need to take the same care in evaluating and choosing the policies.

Summary

Although life insurance seems to have many varieties, there are only two basic types: term and cash value. With term, you buy protection and only protection in case you die. In general, term insurance is a better buy. Cash value insurance is protection plus something else, usually a savings program. You get less protection for your dollar, plus a lower rate of return. There are four main types of cash value life insurance: whole life, universal life, variable life, and single premium. Spend as little on life insurance as possible.

Credit life is a type of term insurance that is expensive and gives you no control over its value. This is the type of insurance you are offered when you take out a car loan; avoid it!

Consider the tax consequences of your life insurance policies; they do not go through probate but are taxable for federal estate tax purposes. State estate laws differ.

Everyone needs disability insurance because the odds are greater in middle age that you will be disabled than die. Don't be lulled into thinking your company disability insurance will take care of you. Most company policies don't have enough coverage or have too many restrictions.

To evaluate companies and policies, check the existing reports mentioned and use the ABC approach.

8

Liabilities

What is a liability? It's anything that you owe to someone else, whether it's money, property, or services. A debt is money that you owe to someone else in re-payment. Rent is not considered a debt, assuming it is paid on time.

How much do you owe? By now, you should have completed the worksheets in Chapter 3, so you can refer back to them for a list of your liabilities. If you haven't yet pulled out your financial records or filled out the worksheets, please stop now and do so. Without the basic facts, you cannot reach your financial goals.

The Effects of Consumer Debt on Interest Rates

According to the U.S. Department of Commerce, the savings rate in the United States dropped from 6.2 percent of gross domestic product in 1992, to 1.8 percent in the first half of 1999. We are also running up higher levels of debt. In short, we have been spending more than we earn. You must live within your means.

Many of you are probably aware of how greater consumer debt can affect in-terest rates. For those of you who were not aware of the connection, here's a brief review of how supply and demand drives interest rates.

Let's say you want to borrow some money to buy a house. However, the same day you apply for a loan, ten other people also apply for loans. The bank only has a limited amount of money to loan. In effect, you and the other people are demanding more than the available supply. What happens to rates? They go up because of the demand. When you add higher consumer demand to the demands of the government for loans, you can see why rates will rise. When there is less demand for loans, interest rates go down.

Good Reasons to Borrow Money

There are three good reasons to borrow money:

1. You have a genuine emergency. For example, the furnace stops working in the middle of winter, the roof gets damaged in a storm and needs immediate repairs, or a medical emergency occurs. These are all justifiable reasons for borrowing money. Make sure it is a *real* emergency and not just an excuse to increase your spending.
2. You need to establish a credit history. Everyone needs to have a credit history so that if an emergency occurs, as just discussed, you will be able to get a loan. Everyone needs a personal credit history. If you're married and all the credit is in one spouse's name, what happens if the credit holder dies, is disabled, or you get divorced? It will be much more difficult then to establish a personal credit rating.
3. You borrow from yourself and pay yourself interest. Let's say you have money in an investment paying 9 percent and a car loan will cost 11 percent. It makes sense to use the investment money to buy the car. Then you pay yourself back with the monthly payments that you would have had to pay to someone else.

Bad Reasons to Borrow

Unfortunately, most of us borrow for bad reasons. Here are seven:

1. You spend it on a wonderful vacation. Unfortunately, you will still be paying for it when that great mountain scenery or week of Broadway plays is only a memory.
2. You buy something that depreciates: a car, a refrigerator, or a TV. You keep paying on the original cost while the value goes down and down. If you had an emergency and needed to pay the loan off, money received from selling the item would not cover the remainder of the loan.

3. You cannot afford to pay cash. In case you've forgotten this crucial concept from Chapter 1, let me repeat myself: *Do not spend more than you earn.* With very few exceptions (such as a house), if you do not have the cash to buy something today, you should not borrow to buy it.

4. You are buying on impulse. If you see a bargain and really need the item, that's fine. Don't go out and buy something because you're feeling blue. There's nothing wrong with rewarding yourself occasionally, but if you get in the habit of shopping for an emotional lift, you will have a debt problem. No matter how good a deal you get, don't buy something you really don't *need.*

5. You try to keep up with the Joneses (or the Rockefellers). Your neighbors may appear to be living "the good life" and yet be deeply in debt. That obstacle, ego, is keeping you from achieving financial independence. Set your priorities and stick to them.

6. You expect to get a raise, bonus, and so on. Never make financial plans on what might happen. Until you see the money in your paycheck, do not spend it.

7. You are going to speculate with the money. The October 1987 stock market was a good example of what can happen. What if you had borrowed so you could get on the bandwagon when the market was going up in early 1987? You could have easily lost it all and still owed the original loan amount.

If you are borrowing for any of these seven reasons, you have a problem with your liabilities, whether or not you want to admit it.

Ask your planner these questions:

- Is there a good reason to have debt?

- Is it a good idea to have a home mortgage?

- Should I buy or lease my car?

- How many credit cards should I have?

- What's the best way to consolidate my debt?

Types of Credit

Let's look at the types of credit available. Despite all the different names that are used, they break down into four types: consumer, mortgage, home equity, and business.

Consumer

This is the credit that most of us have used at one time or another. When you buy a car and finance it, take out a personal loan to fix up the house, or charge a new TV on your credit card, you are using consumer credit. Let's look briefly at car loans and credit cards.

Car

Have you noticed lately that most car ads no longer say how much the car costs (it would be too much of a shock), but how much the monthly payments are? As car costs have escalated, the monthly payments have become more than the average person can handle. So the banks and other sources of car loans have begun offering four-year and five-year car loans. Now your car can rust out from under you while you're still paying for it.

Most of us take out our first loan to get a car as we start our first job. Then we keep on borrowing to buy a new car to replace the old one. We never get out from under that car debt. Start saving for that next car. Pay cash for the car and you've saved all that interest you used to pay.

Instead of buying a car, some people lease a car. A lease is an agreement to rent a car for a certain number of months or years. Table 8.1 summarizes the differences between leasing and buying a car, as outlined in the Federal Reserve Board's free consumer publication, "Keys to Vehicle Leasing."

For more information on the buy/lease decision, the entire Federal Reserve Board's booklet on leasing is available by calling 202-452-3244; writing to Publications Services, MS-127, Board of Governors of the Federal Reserve System, Washington, DC 20551; or online (www.bog.frb.fed.us/pubs/leasing). Kiplinger's Personal Finance magazine usually has an article about leasing every year and has an online calculator to help in the lease/buy decision (www.kiplinger.com/calc). The Better Business Bureau also has leasing info at www.bbb.org/library/autolease.html.

Credit Cards

Credit cards come in two types: charge cards with a finance charge, and travel and entertainment cards. One of each should be enough for you. As long as you pay off the balance each month, these cards can be very useful. First, you get a detailed list of expenditures for business or personal recordkeeping. You will find them invaluable in a genuine emergency.

The main problem with credit cards of either type is when you don't handle them responsibly. Do you pay the full balance every month or do you always pay

TABLE 8.1   Shoud I Lease or Buy a Car?

Considerations	Leasing	Buying
Ownership	You do not own the vehicle.	You own the vehicle.
Up-front costs	May include first month's payment, refundable deposit, a down payment, taxes, registration, and other fees.	Cash price or a down payment, taxes, registration, and other fees.
Monthly payments	Payments may be lower than a loan payment.	Payments are higher because you pay everything up front.
Early termination	If you end the lease early, you may pay early termination charges.	If have a loan and pay it off early, you owe the pay-off amount.
Vehicle return	You may return the vehicle at lease end, pay any end-of-lease costs, and "walk away."	You may have to sell or trade this vehicle.
Future value	Whoever leased the vehicle to you has the risk of the future market value.	You have the risk of the vehicle's market value when you trade or sell it.
Mileage	Number of miles you can drive without added costs is limited; can negotiate higher limit.	Drive all you want; higher mileage lowers trade-in value.
Excess wear	Possible excess wear charges	No charges, but excess wear lowers trade-in value.
End of term	At the end of the lease, may have a new payment for this or another vehicle.	At end of loan, no other payments.

the minimum possible? Travel and entertainment cards must be paid off every month or your card will be canceled. However, charge card companies make their money from finance charges.

If you are always paying finance charges, if you have more than a few cards, if you use one to pay off another, you have a credit problem. Take a look at the debt ratios discussed later in this chapter under "How Much Debt Is Too Much?"

Mortgage

For most people, this is the largest loan they will ever have. Despite the different names the banker gives, there are only two types of mortgages: fixed and variable. Because choosing a mortgage depends so much on individual factors and the market, I can't tell you which one is right for you. Consult with your financial planner and read up-to-date books and articles to help you decide.

Before you even begin to look at houses, be sure to read Chapter 6. You need to understand that a home may not be the investment you thought it was. The points made in that chapter will give you a new perspective on home ownership.

Home Equity Loans

Are home equity loans deductible? Yes, but . . . . Go back and reread the good and bad reasons to borrow. These reasons are especially true when it comes to a home equity loan. They are deductible, up to a point. How much you can deduct depends on the "basis" of your home and its current value. Before you consider a home equity loan, talk it over with your financial planner and other advisors to be sure you know what the tax consequences will be.

Business

If you have a second business (and I believe everyone can benefit from a sideline business), you may need a business loan. If you're just starting out, you'll need to have a good business plan prepared to show you know what you're doing. If you're already in business, you'll need a current profit and loss statement as well as other details about your business. Don't let the terms "business plan" and "profit and loss" scare you if they are unfamiliar. Check with your local Small Business Administration office for information and assistance. Use your library as a information resource. There are many books on starting a second business and how to put together a business plan. A good accountant can help you prepare a profit and loss statement.

Get the Best Loan

Whether it's a business or personal loan you need, there are four ways to get the money:

1. Through an installment loan (the worst kind) which will cost you the most in interest charges. You pay almost all interest in the beginning and very little principal.
2. Through an interest and principal loan, in which you pay off the principal in approximately equal amounts each time you pay.
3. Through an interest-only loan, where you pay only the interest due and do not pay on the principal. If you already have large amounts in certificates of deposit or other investments at an institution, you can try to get an interest-only loan with them. A loan on the cash value of your life insurance may be an interest-only loan. See Chapter 7 for cautions about loans against your insurance.
4. Through yourself (the best kind of loan). Borrow from savings. Pay yourself back each month.

If you must get a loan, shop around for the best rate and terms. Try to get a simple (not compound) interest loan. If you can pay it off ahead of time, you won't get penalized. Avoid loans using the "rule of 78s" because you pay a penalty for prepaying the loan.

How Much Debt Is Too Much?

Check yourself on the following four debt ratios:

1. Percent of debt to income. Look at your balance sheet to determine this ratio.
2. Total debt payments. They should total no more than 36 percent of your gross income.
3. Consumer debt. It should be no more than 20 percent of your gross income.
4. Debt service charges (the interest you pay to have a loan). What is the ratio of take-home pay/debt service charges? Watch this ratio over time. It should go down, not up.

Establishing Credit

For most of us, the unsolicited credit card applications seem to arrive in the mailbox every day. However, if you are just out of school or just divorced or widowed, you may not have a credit history.

To establish credit, you need to have some collateral, usually a savings account. You take out a loan using the collateral. Then, you make sure that you pay off the loan before it is due. You have established that you are responsible and can handle debt. Depending on the type of credit you eventually want, say for a mortgage loan, you will need to demonstrate that you have the income, the stability, and the responsibility to pay off the loan. So you may have to take out several increasingly larger loans in order to get to your credit goal. Don't be afraid to ask the credit officer for a higher credit line.

A word to the wise married couple: establish your credit history *in both names* before you need it. Any of the family finance books (such as *Everyone's Money Book* by Jordan Goodman) have a detailed discussion of how to establish credit. I recommend you read them for more detail.

How to Get Out of Debt

What happens if you are so badly in debt that you think you can never get out? Or what if you're just beginning to exceed the debt ratios I mentioned? Unfortunately, a complete discussion of this subject is beyond this book. Books such as the *Credit Repair Kit* or *All About Credit* discuss this topic.

However, I do recommend these three steps.

1. Make it a priority to get out of debt. Commit to it. This is the hardest part psychologically.
2. Cancel your credit cards.
3. Go to a free credit counseling service. Most large cities have one. Look in the yellow pages under "credit counseling." These are professionals who know how to help you help yourself get out of debt. These counselors will help you deal with your creditors and set up a realistic repayment schedule. It will not be painless, but you must do it.

Conclusion

Don't kid yourself about your liabilities. That's why I keep reminding you that you must complete the worksheets in Chapter 3 so you will know where you stand. I'm not saying you should never have any debt. With proper financial planning, you can manage your liabilities. Be honest with yourself, and take action when it's needed. You can get out of debt.

Summary

A liability is anything you owe to someone else, whether it is money, property, or services. The worksheets you completed in Chapter 3 will give you a list of your liabilities.

Most Americans are saving less of their income but running up higher levels of debt. You must live on what you earn. When the demand for credit or loans exceeds the supply (funded from savings), rates will rise. When there is less demand, rates go down.

If you have no credit history at all, you need to establish it before you really need it. Use some money for collateral,

> **A**sk your planner for a financial planning software recommendation. It would be helpful if you and your planner had the same software, but it's not essential. Your planner should be aware of Quicken and Money, even if he or she doesn't have it. Having some expensive software does not make one a better planner. In fact, their professional software may not offer the "what if" capabilities that Quicken and Money now have.

take out a loan, and pay it back before it is due. Keep doing this until you reach your credit goal. For married couples, be sure both spouses have established credit, even if it's not needed now.

How do you get out of debt when you're in over your head? First, commit yourself to the goal of getting out of debt. Second, cut up your credit cards. Third, go to a free credit counseling service and let it help you. It won't be painless, but you can do it.

9

Taxes

One way to meet your financial goals is to reduce your income taxes. By reducing your taxes, you can accelerate your earnings and achieve your goals sooner. In this chapter, you will learn four different methods of tax reduction and specific tools to use in saving taxes. Reduce taxes and you have more money to invest or spend! I'll also briefly discuss the most recent tax law changes and how they affect you.

Keep in mind that in this chapter, I'm just going to point out the ways to reduce or save taxes. You will need to evaluate your situation to see if a particular strategy fits your total financial plan. Don't be an aggressive tax payer. Pay what is owed, but no more.

Four Methods for Reducing Taxes

There are four methods for reducing taxes:

1. Splitting
2. Deferring
3. Converting
4. Sheltering

I'll cover the basics of how each method works and then look at specific examples in the section "Tax Tools." Discuss each of these methods with your financial planner to see if they are suitable for your financial plan.

Splitting

What the government wants to do is to have one big pile of your money to tax. What you want to do is to split up your income into smaller piles so that you pay less tax. Taxes can be split by using family members, time, and tax tools (more on these later).

> **D**id you receive a large refund on your federal income tax? If so, you are paying too much in withholding tax. No matter what month it is, you still may be able to adjust the withholding on this year's taxes. Ask your financial professional to calculate what your withholding should be so you're within a few hundred dollars of what you owe. Likewise, if some unexpected financial event has occurred (a bonus, a new baby, loss of a job, etc.), you may want to adjust your withholding tax up or down accordingly.

To split your income with family members, have a sideline business (Appendix D) and employ your children. Usually they will be taxed at a lower rate than you will. Your ten-year-old can file papers or sweep floors—or maybe run your spreadsheets or payroll! Discuss this strategy with your financial advisor to be sure you understand what work your children can do, how many hours they can work, and any other restrictions.

Of course, you'll need to consider how much money you want your children to have and so on. Reread the chapter on education which covers the issue of control of money.

To split your income by time, use an installment sale to postpone income to later years. To split income with a tax tool, you could use a nonservice corporation to split income between yourself and the corporation.

Here's a very simple example to show how splitting can reduce your taxes. Let's say you expect $100,000 in income. You receive it all in one year, and the federal tax rate is 33 percent. (The tax rates used are for illustration only and I'm ignoring any other taxes, income, or deductions.) You would pay $20,381 in federal taxes. If the income can be split between yourself

> **M**eet with your accountant in the fall for a checkup meeting. You want to avoid tax surprises when you fill out the forms in January. If you don't use an accountant, the library has several tax planning books that will cover tax planning in the fall. Be sure to get the current year's book.

FIGURE 9.1   A Simple Splitting Example

	No Splitting Joint with 4 exemptions	With Splitting Joint with 4 exemptions	Single with 1 exemption
Adjusted gross income	$100,000	$60,000	$40,000
Standard deduction*	5,400	5,400	3,250
Personal exemptions*	8,200	8,200	2,050
Total deductions	13,600	13,600	5,350
Taxable income	86,400	46,400	34,700
Tax	$ 20,381	$ 8,781	$ 7,195
Tax bracket*	33%	28%	28%

*For illustration only

and a family member (let's say $60,000 to you and $40,000 to a child), then your tax rate would drop to 28 percent. You would pay federal taxes of $8,781. The child's tax rate (assuming she is over 14) would be 28 percent or $7,195 in taxes. The total federal tax bill for this second case is $15,976. You've saved $4,405 in federal taxes! Figure 9.1 summarizes this simple example. By using a corporation, your tax reduction can be even more dramatic. Don't forget that splitting is not assigning income. Check with your tax attorney or accountant on whether you can split income and how to do it correctly.

Deferring

If you had the choice of paying taxes today or paying taxes in 30 years, which would you choose? Figure 9.2 shows an example of what you could save by deferring the tax with a tool such as an IRA instead of paying it each year.

If you put money into a tool such as an IRA, you don't pay taxes on the interest earned until you withdraw it. Let's say you have $2,000 each year to invest and put it into a tool. If the investments are left in for 30 years at 12 percent (an after-tax return of 8.4 percent at a 30 percent tax bracket), you would have $482,665 from the tool. You have already paid tax on the original $60,000 you invested ($2,000 × 30 years) each year. At the end of 30 years, you would have to

FIGURE 9.2   Save Taxes by Deferring

In 30 Years at 12 Percent Interest and a 30 Percent Tax Bracket

	No Deferral	Defer Taxes with a Tool
Available to invest before taxes each year	$ 2,000	$ 2,000
Invest within tool	− 0	− 2,000
Available minus tool	2,000	0
Taxes paid each year	− 600	− 0
Available to invest after taxes each year	1,400	2,000
Value in 30 years	243,878	482,665
Taxable part of tool	NA	422,665
Taxes paid then	0	− 126,800
After-tax benefit	$243,878	$355,865
ADVANTAGE OF TOOL	($355,865 − $243,878) = $111,987	

pay $126,800 tax. Without the tool, your benefit would be $243,878. The advantage of using a tool is $111,987.

In addition to using a tool for deferral, taxes can be deferred through a variety of financial products. These are different from tools like 401(k) plans. These are investments that offer deferral in themselves without tools, such as:

- Series EE bonds or other bonds
- Annuities
- Installment sales
- Certificates of deposit
- Treasury bills
- Treasury notes and bonds
- Corporate coupon bonds

We'll discuss each product and how it can be used to defer taxes. For more information on the specifics of these investment choices, see Chapter 10.

Have your planner explain the difference between what your tax bracket is—15 percent, 28 percent, 36 percent—and the actual percentage you pay in taxes, including state and local taxes. Most people don't really know the total amount they pay in taxes.

Series EE bonds and HH bonds

You have a choice in the year you purchase the bonds to declare the interest that year on your income tax. This establishes your intent to declare the interest every year. If no declaration is made, then you will pay taxes on the interest earned when you redeem the bonds. Thus, you have deferred the taxes to a later date.

As an example, this deferral has obvious advantages for parents who wish to buy bonds for their children. Children under 14 are taxed at their parents' rate after the first $1,200 of unearned income. Holding these bonds until the child is 14 will not only defer taxes but allow the interest to be taxed at the child's rate: a double benefit, allowing you to save more. Remember that when you give the money to your children, it is their money to do with as they wish.

A Series HH bond can only be acquired by exchanging a Series EE (or the older Series E) bond. If you have a Series EE bond that is maturing and you do not want to cash it in, you may convert it into a Series HH bond, thus deferring the interest for an additional 20 years. You will have to declare the semiannual interest on a Series HH bond. Series I bonds are indexed for inflation.

Annuities

The plain annuity is for someone who lives beyond her or his life expectancy. It ensures that they won't run out of money. You do not pay taxes on annuity earnings until you receive the money.

How does an annuity work? There are three basic ways to buy one:

1. For a plain annuity, you give the insurance company a very large amount of money at retirement.
2. You can pay a premium over time. Each year, you pay a premium like any other insurance policy.
3. The single premium deferred annuity gives you the ability to buy an annuity in small amounts. You give the insurance company an amount of money now.

There are two ways to defer taxes with an annuity. The earnings from a plain annuity are not currently taxable. You pay taxes when you take the money out. There is no tax deduction when you buy the annuity.

If you work for a public, nonprofit institution such as a hospital, school, university, charity, etc., then you can set up a tax-deferred or 403(b) annuity. The amount you contribute reduces your salary because the IRS does not consider that amount as income until you receive it. Thus, the initial contribution and its earnings are not taxable until you receive a distribution. There is a limit on how much you can put away each year.

There are four ways to distribute the benefits of an annuity. Except for a refund, distributions can be fixed or variable amounts.

1. Straight life. Payments for the rest of your life.
2. Certain installments. Installments of the benefits to be paid at certain times.
3. Refund. A lump sum refund of the amount.
4. Joint and survivor. Payments over your life and your survivor's life. This choice would give you lower payments but extend the payments over your spouse or other beneficiary's life.

Be sure to discuss both the economic and the tax implications of these distributions with your accountant or tax attorney before you set up the annuity and before you sign any distribution agreement. You must balance what you need to live on versus the tax consequences.

Installment Sales

An installment sale can defer taxes for a short or long period. Remember the consideration here is how to reduce taxes by deferring income. Obviously, other factors must be taken into account when looking at a particular transaction. Is the income needed today? Will income be higher or lower in following years? Are there other financial events that might affect this sale? You will need to discuss this deferral strategy very carefully with your financial advisor.

Certificates of Deposit

Certificates of deposit (CDs) can be used to defer taxes. Let's say you have a 13-year-old child. You want to gift $10,000 to her towards her college fund. She already has some savings. The first $650 of unearned income is not taxed, and the next $650 is taxed at the child's rate. After this $1,300 (for 1999), the remainder of unearned income is taxed at your rate. So use a CD with a time period long enough so that it matures after the child turns 14.

Treasury Bills

You only pay federal taxes when the bill matures. No state or local taxes are paid.

Treasury Notes and Bonds

Notes and bonds only give you a short deferral because every six months interest is paid to you. When the note or bond matures, the principal is paid back to you. No state or local taxes are paid.

Corporate Coupon Bonds

Taxes are due on the interest earned when the coupon is paid on corporate coupon bonds. They are similar to T-bonds.

Converting

The technique of converting changes income or expenses from one status to another. Here are three ways to convert:

1. Convert nondeductible to deductible.
2. Convert ordinary income to capital gain.
3. Convert through an equity transfer.

I'll briefly outline each technique. You will need to discuss with your financial advisor whether converting techniques are appropriate for your situation.

Convert Nondeductible to Deductible

As I've mentioned already, I believe everyone should have a second business for either the extra income or the tax benefits. With a sideline business, you can convert nondeductible expenses such as travel, entertainment, and insurance to deductible expenses. You can end up with more cash to spend. Appendix D has a sample calculation showing how this works. There is more about a second business under the "Tools" section later in this chapter.

Convert Ordinary Income to Capital Gain

Capital gains can also be a form of tax deferral. Taxes are not due until the capital gain is realized. So even if capital gains are taxed at the same rate as ordinary income, it still makes sense to convert ordinary income to capital gain in order to defer taxes. One possible way is with real estate.

Convert through an Equity Transfer

Let's say you work for a school and can contribute to a tax-deferred annuity. You expect to receive $20,000 from the sale of some real estate. You can do an equity transfer by increasing your contribution to the TDA to the maximum allowed and using the $20,000 for living expenses. You have converted the $20,000 into a tax-deferred tool. Without doing this, you would have had to pay taxes on your pay and then take what's left and invest it. With an equity transfer you are able to invest the full $20,000.

Sheltering

A tax shelter is usually defined as any investment that you invest in for the main purpose of changing ordinary income which is taxable at a high rate into income which is taxed at a lower rate.

Too often I see people chasing questionable and risky tax shelters when good financial planning can easily reduce their taxes with a much lower risk. These people are being tripped up by two of those obstacles I talked about in Chapter 1: ego and lack of a plan. Without a good financial plan, you are easy prey for the "hot tips" that aren't really so hot. Remember, there are no great deals, just good planning.

One legitimate way to shelter income is through real estate (not your principal residence but a real estate investment). When it's in a down cycle, real estate is not a great investment. However, there are still ways to use real estate to shelter income from taxes. Real estate will be a better investment when the cycle turns back up.

One result of TRA 1986 with its categories of passive and active income and losses has been the appearance of reverse tax shelters. These are just as risky as the old tax shelters. They are supposed to be designed to offset passive losses. Avoid investments with the words "reverse tax shelter" or "PIG" (passive income generator) in the offering.

Tax Tools

There are a variety of "tools" available to you which will help reduce taxes. A *tool* is any technique which can be used to reduce taxes. Remember deals don't save taxes, *tools save taxes*. Investments don't save taxes, *tools save taxes*. Only the tax implications of these tools are discussed in this chapter.

Figure 9.3 and Figure 9.4 will illustrate a simple example of how a tool can save taxes. Without the tool, you pay taxes on your income and then you can save. With the tool, you save money in the tool, subtract that from your income and then pay taxes. Also, the taxes are deferred until you withdraw the money. I used a high return of 15 percent just to make the point of what a difference it makes over time as the interest compounds—$355,409!

Figure 9.5 shows that with a rate of 9 percent, the benefit to use the tool would be $74,126.

What is the tool? It's an IRA, available to most people. Specifics of using an IRA will be discussed a little bit later. For now, let's go back to the concept of a tool and look at how it should be used.

FIGURE 9.3   Saving Taxes with a Tool at 15 Percent

	Without Tool	With Tool Taxable Savings	Tool
Available to invest before taxes each year	$ 2,900	$ 2,900	$ 0
Invest within tool	− 0	− 0	− 2,000
Income minus tool	2,900	900	0
Taxes paid each year	− 870	− 270	− 0
Available to invest after taxes each year	2,030	630	2,000
Value in 30 years	367,189	113,955	869,490
Taxes paid then	− 0	− 0	− 260,847
After-tax benefit	367,189	$113,955	608,643
TOTAL BENEFIT	$367,189		$722,599
ADVANTAGE OF TOOL		$355,409	

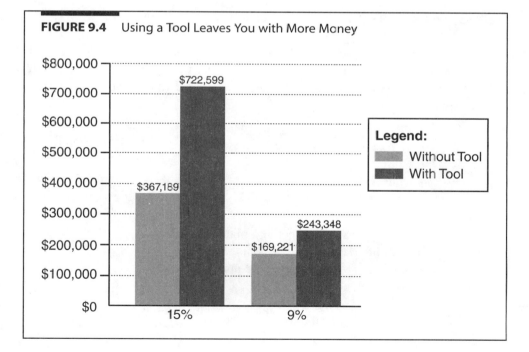

FIGURE 9.4   Using a Tool Leaves You with More Money

FIGURE 9.5   Saving Taxes with a Tool at 9 Percent

	Without Tool	With Tool Taxable Savings	Tool
Available to invest before taxes each year	$ 2,900	$ 2,900	$ 0
Invest within tool	− 0	− 0	− 2,000
Income minus tool	2,900	900	0
Taxes paid each year	− 870	− 270	− 0
Available to invest after taxes each year	2,030	630	2,000
Value in 30 years	169,221	52,517	272,615
Taxes paid then	− 0	− 0	− 81,785
After-tax benefit	169,221	$52,517	190,831
TOTAL BENEFIT	$169,221		$243,348
ADVANTAGE OF TOOL		$74,126	

Proper Use of Tax Tools

Be sure to use the tools that benefit you the most. The following list shows the most important tools to use first. If the first option is available and you can meet your goals with it, then there is no need to use the other tools. However, that's an unlikely scenario today.

- Pension and profit-sharing plans
- 401(k) or CODA plans
- Corporation
- Your own business
- Keogh
- IRA
- Employee stock ownership plans (ESOP)
- Simplified employment plans (SEP)
- Nonqualified deferred compensation plans
- 403(b) plans
- Thrift and savings plans
- Voluntary contributions

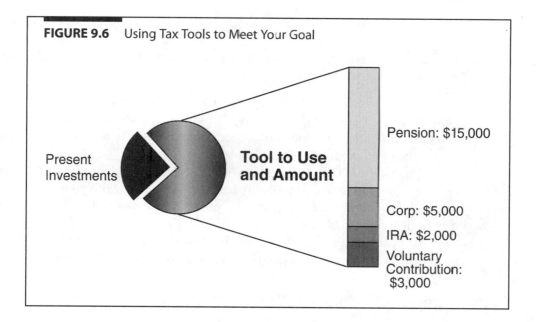

FIGURE 9.6   Using Tax Tools to Meet Your Goal

Present Investments

Tool to Use and Amount

Pension: $15,000

Corp: $5,000

IRA: $2,000

Voluntary Contribution: $3,000

Here's just one example of how you might use several tools to meet your goal. Your specific circumstances will be different. Let's say you want to save $25,000 each year for retirement. Figure 9.6 will show how, starting at the top of the list on the previous page, you might put $15,000 in your pension, $5,000 into your corporation's plan, $2,000 into an IRA, and the remaining $3,000 into a voluntary contribution plan.

Keep in mind that my goal is to cover the basic concepts of retirement planning tools. You owe it to yourself and your peace of mind to know what tools you are using now and how they work. Remember that your employer may already have a pension plan and/or other retirement plans available so you may not have to create a plan for yourself. Of course, if you are self-employed, then you should set up your own retirement plan(s).

In Chapter 12, I will discuss how to get the objective evaluation of your retirement plans that you need.

Defined-Benefit Retirement Plan Tools versus Defined-Contribution Tools

Before discussing each type of tool, you need to know the basis for the two types of retirement plans.

1. A defined-benefit plan provides you a certain amount of money per month when you retire.
2. A defined-contribution plan puts in a certain percentage of income while you are working.

Whether you put your money into a pension, profit-sharing plan, or Keogh, you will be using one of these two types. Which type you can choose or whether you have a choice may depend upon your employer's offering(s). If the employer is you, then you get to choose.

Which type is right for you? If you are self-employed and under 45, then the defined-contribution plan is probably best for you. Check with your tax advisor to see what the contribution limits are for you. If you are over 45, then the defined-benefit plan is probably best for you.

All plans have a penalty if you withdraw the money prior to age 59½. There is no penalty if you are 55 and take retirement with a lifetime annuity.

Pension and Profit-Sharing Plans

The pension is the very best tool you can use. If you can meet your retirement goal with a pension, you don't need to consider other tools. After a pension, look at profit-sharing plans.

What is the difference between a pension and a profit-sharing plan? You must contribute to the pension each year. The profit-sharing plan allows you to specify a percentage range for your contribution. I recommend the pension because it forces you to save for retirement instead of putting it off.

Most of these plans meet or are "qualified" under standards set by the Employee Retirement Income Security Act (ERISA).

401(k) or CODA Plans

The 401(k) or CODA plans are salary reduction plans. CODA stands for cash or deferred arrangements. They also may be called "pay conversion," "deferred pay," or other such names. This type of plan uses the tax deferral method discussed above. You can save up to the lesser of 25 percent of your salary or a specified amount adjusted for inflation each year. Your employer usually matches your contribution. You pay no taxes on either contribution until you withdraw it after age 59½. There are some provisions for hardship withdrawals and loans.

Corporation

Although the tax rates have changed due to recent tax laws, there are still advantages to having a corporation. For example, the corporation can hold stock and reduce the tax paid on the dividends. Family members can be shareholders in the corporation and receive dividends and/or they can be employees and participate in benefits such as a retirement plan, life insurance, and medical and dental coverage.

Appendix B discusses the advantages of incorporation.

Your Own Business

I believe you must have your own business. If you are an employee, you need a second business for the tax deductions. If you are making less than $50,000, you need a second business because you need the money. In 1996, 66 percent of the U.S. households were making less than $50,000, and over one-third (36 percent) had money income of less than $25,000, according to the U.S. Bureau of the Census *Statistical Abstract of the United States, 1998*. No wonder families need second and third incomes.

A second business will allow you to convert nondeductible expenses into deductible expenses, such as:

- Trips
- Car and transportation
- Entertainment
- Fringe benefits (medical insurance, car insurance, etc.)
- Home office

If you are making more than $50,000 per year, you need a second business because you need the tax deductions. For example, highly taxed income can be shifted to your children.

Business expenses are subtracted from business income and affect your adjusted gross income. Also, business expenses are not subject to the 2 percent threshold that applies to a miscellaneous itemized deduction. Refer to Appendix D for more advantages.

Keogh

If you have a business that is set up as a sole proprietorship or a partnership, you can set up a Keogh retirement plan. It can be either a pension or profit-sharing plan and is subject to the same limitations as corporate plans. The tax law changes in 1986 and later years set the theoretical amount for defined-contribution plans at the lesser of 25 percent of net earnings from self-employment or $30,000, but it never quite equals that much because of the calculations. On profit-sharing plans you can deduct up to 15 percent. Check with your accountant. The amount contributed is tax deductible.

IRA

Everyone should have an IRA unless they already have enough saved toward their goals with other tools. You have a choice between the traditional IRA and the Roth IRA. The traditional IRA is tax deductible (up to certain income limits). When you take money out at retirement, you pay according to your tax rate then. The Roth IRA is not tax deductible when you set it up, but you pay no tax when you withdraw it at retirement. If you believe that your tax rate will be the same or higher when you retire, then the Roth IRA is probably for you. Consult a financial advisor to see what's best for your specific situation.

Even if the traditional IRA is not tax deductible, it's still a good tool because the interest is tax deferred. If you save $2,000 per year for 30 years at 12 percent with a 30 percent tax rate, you will have $114,987 more at the end of 30 years than if you had put the money in an investment where the interest was taxed. Refer back to Figure 9.2 and Figure 9.3.

Employee Stock Ownership Plans (ESOP)

When you are part of an employee stock ownership plan or ESOP, your money is put mainly into your company's stock. There are a number of ways that ESOPs can be set up. Because there is always the risk that something could happen to the company, an ESOP should be only one part of your retirement plan.

Simplified Employment Plans (SEP)

A simplified employment plan is similar to an IRA except that your employer makes the contribution to the SEP. No taxes are paid on the SEP contribution.

SIMPLE Plans

The Savings Incentive Match Plan for Employees (SIMPLE) is a retirement plan designed for small businesses with 100 workers or fewer. Usually the employer matches up to 3 percent of employee contributions or contributes 2 percent of pay for each employee, even if the employee does not contribute. Self-employed business owners with no employees are allowed to contribute up to $6,000 of self-employment earnings.

Nonqualified Deferred Compensation Plans

These plans are an agreement between you and your employer. Your employer agrees to set aside money. If it's there when you retire, you get the money. If it's not, you don't. What can go wrong? The company may go out of business or it may get sued or sold. Because these plans are usually only available to executives, deferred compensation is probably only part of their retirement plan. So if something happens to the company, not all is lost.

403(b) Plans

These tax-deferred plans are available if you work for a public, nonprofit institution such as a university or public hospital. You pay no tax on the contribution and usually have some options as to how your money is invested. The investment limit is 20 percent or $9,500 of your earnings, whichever is less. There are provisions for "making up" contributions from years in which you were eligible but did not participate.

Thrift and Savings Plans

Generally, these plans are non–tax-deferred through your employer. A thrift plan can include a 401(k) which is tax deferred, plus the plan can include non–tax-deferred portions. Usually a variety of investments are available. Your employer may match your contribution to some extent.

Voluntary Contributions

Although voluntary contributions are not tax deductible, the earnings are tax deferred. When you withdraw some of the money, the IRS will consider the money to be part principal (not taxable) and part interest (taxable). Because there is no withdrawal penalty on the principal, the voluntary contribution is an excellent tool to use for an education fund.

If your employer has already contributed the maximum amount to your retirement plan, then you may not make any voluntary contribution.

Tax Law Changes

The Revenue Reconciliation Act Of 1993 and The Tax Reform Act Of 1986—along with subsequent "updates"—have changed the tax code more than any other tax laws in recent history. I've already mentioned in this chapter and in others some of the effects of these laws on your planning. There are many excellent books out now with all the details, sometimes more than you want or need to know. Don't be fooled into thinking these books can take the place of competent advisors. Tax law changes. Books about details can become out of date.

What you need to know is that a good financial plan makes more sense than ever in helping you reduce your taxes. Yes, some deductions have been reduced or eliminated, but there are still ways to reduce taxes, as you've seen in this chapter. Let's review just the basic tax rates and how the standard deduction and personal exemptions have changed.

> Have your planner review your paper gains and losses. Don't let the tax tail wag the economic dog.

Basic Tax Rates

Recent tax laws have changed the basic tax rates or brackets. Figure 9.7 shows 1999 rates. Check with your tax advisor to see what your current basic rate is.

FIGURE 9.7   Federal Income Tax Rates for 1999

| Single | | Joint | |
Income	Marginal Rate	Income	Marginal Rate
$0–$25,750	15%	$0–$43,050	15%
$25,751–$62,450	28%	$43,051–$104,050	28%
$62,451–$130,250	31%	$104,051–$158,550	31%
$130,251–$283,150	36%	$158,551–$283,150	36%
Greater than $283,150	39.6%	Greater than $283,150	39.6%

Standard Deduction

Since 1989 inflation has been taken into account in determining the amount of the standard deduction (shown in Figure 9.8).

Elderly and blind persons can add additional deductions if they do not itemize.

If you make too much money (according to the IRS), your itemized deductions are reduced by 3 percent of the amount by which your adjusted gross income (AGI) exceeds the $126,600 for married, filing joint return, or $126,600 for single filers. The maximum reduction is 80 percent of affected deductions. These amounts will change each year, so check with the IRS.

Personal Exemption

Personal exemptions are also adjusted for inflation. For 1999, the personal exemption was $2,800. Check in the IRS forms or with your tax advisor for the current exemption amount and the phaseout levels.

FIGURE 9.8   Standard Deductions for 1999

	Single	Married, Joint Return	Dependents
1999	$4,300	$7,200	$700

Of course there are many more changes in your taxes, but that's a whole book in itself. Look at several of the many books out which concentrate just on the tax law and choose one for study. For the most up-to-date advice, always consult with your tax advisor.

Use Your Spendable Cash Worksheet

Remember the Spendable Cash Worksheet you prepared back in Chapter 3? Here's another place where you can put it to work for you—evaluating how using a particular tool will affect your cash flow. Figure 9.9 shows how an IRA would affect cash flow.

FIGURE 9.9   How Using a Tool Affects Cash Flow

Spendable Cash Worksheet
Tax Calculation

Total income	$100,000	$100,000
IRA	− 0	− 4,000
Normal deductions	− 6,000	− 6,000
Exemptions	− 7,600	− 7,600
Taxable income	$ 86,400	$ 82,400
Taxes	$ 23,330	$ 21,930

Cash Flow Calculation

Total income	$100,000	$100,000
Taxes	− 23,330	− 21,930
Normal deductions	− 6,000	− 6,000
IRA	− 0	− 4,000
Save for retirement	− 25,000	− 21,000
Save for education	− 6,500	− 6.500
Certain living expenses	− 4,000	− 4,000
Spendable Cash	$ 35,170	$ 36,570
Increase in Cash Flow		$ 1,400

That's $1,400 of benefit, so the IRA for both of you ends up costing you only $2,600.

As I said earlier in this chapter, even if your IRA is not deductible, I believe you should have one. The advantages of compounding the interest tax deferred is too good to pass up.

> **B**e sure your financial planner checks that the right basis was used for calculating capital gains on your mutual funds. If you're not sure of the basis, call the mutual fund and ask.

Conclusion

We all should pay our fair share of taxes. But as far as I'm concerned, "fair" is negotiable. By using these tax tools and one or more of the tax reduction methods, you can legally reduce your taxes.

Summary

You can increase your savings and achieve your goals sooner by reducing your income taxes. However, be sure to evaluate any tax strategy as just one part of your financial plan.

Tools are techniques that help you reduce taxes. Remember, deals don't reduce taxes, investments don't reduce taxes, tools reduce taxes. Without a tool, you pay taxes on your income, then save. With a tool, you save part of your income in the tool, then pay taxes.

Here are twelve types of tax tools.

1. Pension and profit-sharing plans
2. 401(k) or CODA plans
3. Corporation
4. Your own business
5. Keogh
6. IRA
7. Employee stock ownership plans (ESOP)
8. Simplified employment plans (SEP)
9. Non-qualified deferred compensation plans
10. 403(b) plans

11. Thrift and savings plans
12. Voluntary contributions

If you can meet all of your goals with the first tool on the list, then you don't need to look at the other tools. Most retirement plan tools are either defined-benefit or defined-contribution. All plans have a penalty if you withdraw money before you reach 59½, except under some hardship circumstances.

Tax laws will continue to change. Let your financial advisors keep up on the details. Use the spendable cash worksheet to evaluate how a tool will help you.

10

Investments

This is the chapter you've been waiting for. If you're like most people, you may have even turned to this chapter first, before looking at the rest of the book or doing any of the worksheets. If so, read on. If you have worked through the rest of the book, then you can skip the rest of this paragraph. If you have not taken the time to do the worksheets and absorb the concepts from Chapter 1 especially, and do the work discussed in the other chapters, you will not get the full benefit of this book. Oh sure, if you go ahead and just read this chapter, you may do okay with your investments. But you won't have a financial plan. You'll just be going from investment to investment as so many people do, but you may never reach financial independence. If it's important to you to be financially independent (and I can't imagine anyone not wanting that), then please go back and read those chapters and do those worksheets. It's your money and your future; it's worth the time it will take. I've seen people turn their lives around once they finally developed a personal financial plan and stuck to it. You can do it, too.

In this chapter, I'll review the basics of saving and investing. You need to understand the foundation on which your investments will be based and how the financial cycles work. Then we'll look at risk and get into the details of a proven investment strategy that will let you beat inflation by two percent a year. I know that doesn't sound like much, but if you can do that, you should be able to meet your goals. I'll also cover investment mistakes to avoid and whether you should borrow to fund investments.

Financial Basics

Before I talk about how to invest and what to invest in, let's review the basics. The first basic fact is you have to have some money to invest before you can invest. Where does it come from? It comes from your savings.

Savings

Where do your savings come from? They come from your earnings (remember the income cycle from Chapter 1?). Save first from every paycheck, and you will have money to invest. Don't wait for your ship to come in before you start saving; your boat may never get out of dry dock. Don't wait for an inheritance; don't wait to hit it big in the lottery. Don't wait! You must take the initiative and make the commitment to save money from every single paycheck. I know it will take discipline. For some people it's harder than for others, but you must save first.

Most of us need to save more than we are now. According to the U.S. Department of Commerce, in 1996, the personal savings rate in the United States was 4.9 percent of disposable personal income. It has been going down since then and was 1.8 percent for the fourth quarter of 1999 (see Chapter 8). For comparison, in 1996 the Japanese were saving 13.2 percent, the West Germans 12.4 percent, and the French 12.5 percent. Today these countries are still above the U.S. rate. A high level of savings allows banks to loan more money back for businesses, mortgages, etc. Everyone benefits.

The Amazing Compound Interest Story

Besides saving more, you need to be an informed saver. Do you know how often the interest is compounded on your current savings accounts? Table 10.1 shows the difference among the compounding periods. How often the interest is compounded and when it is paid make a big difference over the long run. It may mean the difference between whether or not you can meet your goals.

Let's say you are saving $1,000 a year. Figure 10.1 shows you the comparison between annual, monthly, and daily compounding. Be sure to find out how quickly your interest compounds when shopping for a place to put your savings. Also ask when the interest is paid.

FIGURE 10.1   What Is the True Interest Rate?

The true interest rate varies depending upon the compounding period. If the stated rate of return is 5 percent, the real rate, based on how often dividends are paid, is as shown.

Annually	5.000%
Semi-annually	5.063%
Quarterly	5.094%
Monthly	5.120%
Weekly	5.125%
Continuously	5.127%

FIGURE 10.2   Comparison of Compounding Periods over Time

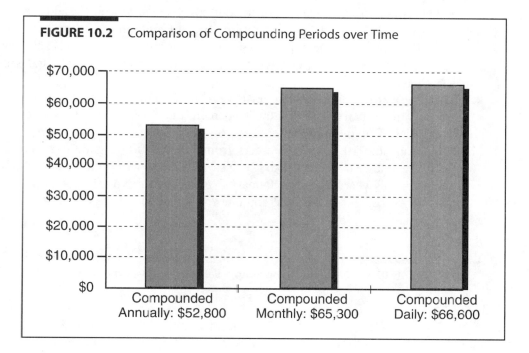

Save in January

Always save at the beginning—not the end—of the year so that you get the full benefit of a year of compound interest. Remember back in Chapter 1 when I talked about how, if you moved your funds from saving to spending one year too soon, you might not reach your goal? How can you figure out what a difference one year can make for you? Figure 10.3 shows how the basic calculation is done, using savings of $2,000 per year, an interest rate of 10 percent, and reinvestment of interest. I realize your goal may be higher or lower than $2,000 each year, and the rate you earn may be different, but this concept is valid regardless of the amounts and rates.

Figure 10.4 shows what the cost is to wait one year at various times during the life of your investment. Notice that between year one and year two the difference between the two years (cost to wait one year) is $2,160 for an 8 percent return and $2,200 for a 10 percent return. Two different interest rates are shown to dramatize how large the gap can be. Again, you *must* save $2,000 each year and not touch the earnings. Look what happens to the "cost to wait" figures as the years pass.

Look at the difference after 40 years—more than $40,000 at the 8 percent rate and more than $82,000 at the 10 percent rate! You can see how valuable that first dollar of savings can be.

Using the 10 percent numbers from Figure 10.4, Figure 10.5 shows how much that one year can be worth if you saved $2,000 per year at 10 percent on January 2 of this year instead of January 2 of next year. Notice what compounding does to the percent of the total amount you've saved. At the end of 40 years, the

---

FIGURE 10.3   Calculating the Simple Value of an Investment

Year	Amount Saved Each Year	Amount from Last Year	Amount to Invest for This Year	10% Interest Rate + 1	Value at End of Year
1	$2,000 +	0 =	$2,000 ×	1.10 =	$2,200
2	$2,000 +	$2,200 =	$4,200 ×	1.10 =	$4,620
and so on					

FIGURE 10.4   Will You Reach Your Goal? One Year Makes a Difference

| | 8% | | 10% | |
Year	Value at Start of Year	Cost to Wait One Year	Value at Start of Year	Cost to Wait One Year
1	$ 2,000		$ 2,000	
2	$ 4,160	$ 2,160	$ 4,200	$ 2,200
3	$ 6,493	$ 2,333	$ 6,620	$ 2,420
4	$ 9,012	$ 2,519	$ 9,282	$ 2,662
5	$ 10,733	$ 2,721	$ 12,210	$ 2,928
9	$ 24,975		$ 27,159	
10	$ 28,973	$ 3,998	$ 31,875	$ 4,716
14	$ 48,430		$ 55,950	
15	$ 54,304	$ 5,874	$ 63,545	$ 7,595
17			$ 81,089 (see Figure 10.2)	
19	$ 82,893		$102,318	
20	$ 91,524	$ 8,631	$114,550	$12,232
24	$133,530		$176,995	
25	$146,212	$12,682	$196,694	$19,699
29	$207,932		$297,262	
30	$226,566	$18,635	$328,938	$31,726
34	$317,253		$490,953	
35	$344,634	$27,380	$542,049	$51,095
39	$477,882		$802,896	
40	$518,113	$40,231	$885,185	$82,290

savings for the last year ($82,290) is 9.3 percent of the total amount saved ($885,185). That's more than the amount you had after the first 17 years of savings ($81,089)! That should make you run to the bank.

Now you can see in black and white the cost of waiting one year. One year can cost you 9 percent of the total amount saved!

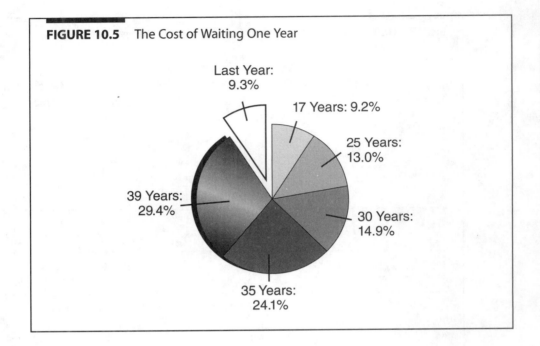

FIGURE 10.5   The Cost of Waiting One Year

Last Year: 9.3%

17 Years: 9.2%

25 Years: 13.0%

30 Years: 14.9%

35 Years: 24.1%

39 Years: 29.4%

Avoid Leakage

I mentioned leakage in Chapter 1 as an obstacle to becoming wealthy. It's worth repeating here. You can't meet your goals if you spend the profits. When you get a bonus, save it. When you earn interest, reinvest it. I know that $100 will seem like a small amount at the time. But if you don't stick with your plan and keep disciplining yourself to reinvest, you're going to slip further and further behind. Look again at the leakage example in Chapter 1.

How the Financial Cycle Works

Here's a basic outline of what a financial cycle is and how you can work with this cycle instead of against it. First, keep telling yourself you can understand how to invest. You probably already know the basics of the financial cycle and don't realize it. Let's look at a simple example. What if you could only put your money in money market funds or bonds? How would you decide which financial product to choose?

What happens when inflation goes up and interest rates go up? Businesses can't afford to borrow to finance growth. The stock market goes down. What to do? Use money market funds to keep up with rising rates.

What happens when interest rates go down? Businesses and individuals borrow, and the stock market goes up. You want to lock in higher rates through long-term bonds as the rates begin to fall. Figure 10.6 summarizes the points of this simple example.

Now I know someone is saying but what about such and such a year? There are as many variations—stagflation, disinflation, and so on—as there are pages in *The Wall Street Journal.* I just want you to know what happens during the very basic up and down cycle. Of course, it won't work this way every time, but you'll know what to watch for. A little later I'll show you how to use this knowledge to plan your investment strategy.

No matter where the financial cycle is on its roller coaster ride, you should always have a diversified portfolio. Even if you are absolutely sure that you know what the cycle will be doing next, be sure to have a mix of stocks, bonds, and cash.

FIGURE 10.6   How the Basic Financial Cycle Works

Inflation goes up; interest rates rise
- The stock market goes down
- Businesses can't afford to borrow
- Gold usually goes up
- Real estate—may go up or down

Your strategy?
- Keep more money in cash equivalents (money market funds)

Inflation goes down; interest rates go down
- The stock market goes up
- Businesses and individuals borrow
- Gold usually goes down
- Real estate—may go up or down

Your strategy?
- Lock in interest rates on the way down for a longer term (bonds)

Your Investment Goal

Your investment goal should always be to beat inflation by 2 percent per year after taxes. This is called the "real return." I know a 2 percent return doesn't sound like much, but if you can do that, you'll be a winner. You may not make a 2 percent real return every year. Some years you'll do better, some years worse. However, over the years you should aim for about a 2 percent average real return. In all my years as a financial planner, I've seen that people will reach their goal when they can beat inflation by just a modest amount.

When you prepare a good financial plan, you can take less risk and still meet your goal. This is good news. It means you don't have to dabble in pork bellies or exotic investments. Remember the game is not how much you make but did you reach your goal?

To review, you save from your earnings. From those savings, you have money to invest. However, maybe the word "investing" sounds risky to you. Let's look at what "risk" is and how you can deal with it.

Evaluating Risk

Did you know that even if you don't think you are investing, you are facing financial risk? The type of risk that everyone faces is inflation risk.

Inflation Risk

Even if you never buy a stock or bond, you must deal with inflation risk. If you have your savings in a savings account yielding 4 percent and inflation is 3 percent, you're only earning 1 percent on your money (your real return). Because of inflation, your money can lose some of its purchasing power over time. Go back and look at Figure 5.2 and see how the purchasing power of the dollar has been eroded by inflation. Over time, continuing inflation can compound into a very large loss of value. Inflation is your greatest enemy. Always has been, always will be—even at low rates.

Keep in mind that the government has to change the basis for the Consumer Price Index every decade or so because otherwise the numbers would go to negative dollars. There have been two changes since 1966.

Other Types of Risk

Some other types of financial risk besides inflation include:

- Principal or market risk. You can lose money if you sell an investment when the market value is less than you paid.
- Interest rate risk. Fixed income securities that pay a specified rate of interest lose some of their value if market interest rates rise.
- Reinvestment rate risk. Fixed income securities have a specific maturity date. If you are going to buy another bond, you have to be concerned with the price of bonds on that day.
- Credit risk (default risk). The bond issuer could fail to pay the principal or interest when due. This is referred to as default. To compensate investors for the increased risk, securities offered by issuers with poorer credit ratings generally pay a higher interest rate than the securities of more stable issuers.

There is always a risk in investing. You just have to decide which risk you want to take. In addition, if you don't plan well, by the time you pay taxes on your investment earnings, you may have no return because the taxes have eroded your return.

How do you determine your level of risk? You will need to look at risk within each financial choice you are considering. Figure 10.7 is a risk evaluation checklist to assist you. Be honest with yourself as you answer these ten questions.

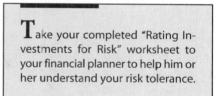

Take your completed "Rating Investments for Risk" worksheet to your financial planner to help him or her understand your risk tolerance.

While the final rating you calculate may help you compare different investments, this table is really meant as a caution light. I want you to think through the risks of an investment and look at your risk tolerance. If you are married, it is very helpful to see how you and your spouse answer these questions so you can discuss possible differences in your risk tolerance.

Investment Triangle

I developed the investment triangle in Figure 10.8 to help my clients choose investments based on the level of risk their situations would allow. You can use it to help plan your investment strategy and keep your risk down. You should be able to beat inflation by 2 percent per year after taxes.

FIGURE 10.7   Rating Investments for Risk

	Rate "5"	Rate "4"	Rate "3"	Rate "2"	Rate "1"	Score
What is the expected annual rate of return?	14%	12%	10%	8%	6%	_____
How liquid is the investment?	Immediate	6 mos.	1 yr.	2 yrs.	20 yrs.	_____
How much management time is required of you?	None	25%	50%	75%	100%	_____
How long for the investment to mature?	Immediate	6 mos.	1 yr.	5 yrs.	10 yrs. or more	_____
How inflation-proof is it?	Excellent	Good	Some	Almost None	None	_____
What tax advantages are there?	Excellent	Good	Some	Almost None	None	_____
How safe is your money?	Excellent	Good	Some	Almost None	None	_____
Is there low interest rate fluctuation?	Excellent	Good	Some	Almost None	None	_____
Can you tolerate this investment? (personal temperament)	Excellent	Good	Some	Almost None	None	_____
What is the potential for the income promised?	Excellent	Good	Some	Almost None	None	_____
Final Rating				TOTAL		_____

5 = Excellent
4 = Good
3 = Average
2 = Below average
1 = Poor

Divide by 10 = Final rating _____

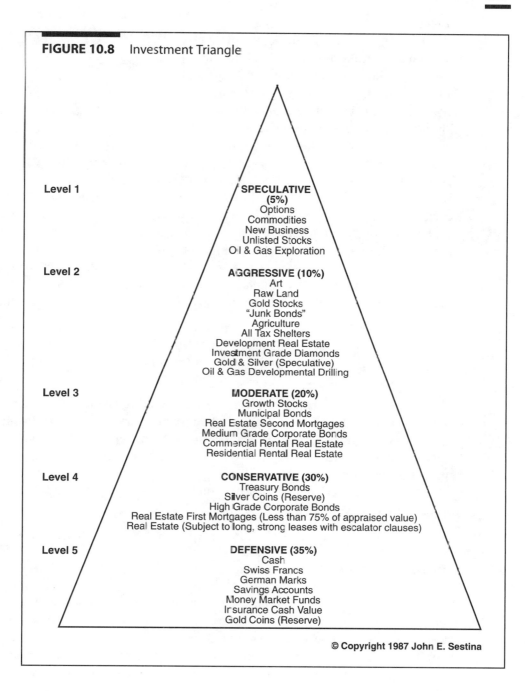

FIGURE 10.8 Investment Triangle

Level 1 — **SPECULATIVE** (5%)
Options
Commodities
New Business
Unlisted Stocks
Oil & Gas Exploration

Level 2 — **AGGRESSIVE (10%)**
Art
Raw Land
Gold Stocks
"Junk Bonds"
Agriculture
All Tax Shelters
Development Real Estate
Investment Grade Diamonds
Gold & Silver (Speculative)
Oil & Gas Developmental Drilling

Level 3 — **MODERATE (20%)**
Growth Stocks
Municipal Bonds
Real Estate Second Mortgages
Medium Grade Corporate Bonds
Commercial Rental Real Estate
Residential Rental Real Estate

Level 4 — **CONSERVATIVE (30%)**
Treasury Bonds
Silver Coins (Reserve)
High Grade Corporate Bonds
Real Estate First Mortgages (Less than 75% of appraised value)
Real Estate (Subject to long, strong leases with escalator clauses)

Level 5 — **DEFENSIVE (35%)**
Cash
Swiss Francs
German Marks
Savings Accounts
Money Market Funds
Insurance Cash Value
Gold Coins (Reserve)

How does it work? You only invest as much as your level of risk will allow. If you have *x* dollars, put *y* percent in the bottom level and work your way up the triangle until you run out of money. Using this method, the less money you have to

Is your planner sensitive to cost issues? Does he or she recommend following the investment triangle?

invest, the more conservative you must be. For example, if you only have $10,000 to invest, you might put $3,500 in the defensive level, $3,000 in the conservative level, $2,000 in the moderate level, $1,000 in the aggressive level and $500 in the speculative level. What can you get for $500? Nothing; so you are forced back one level. Now you have $1,500 ($1,000 + $500) to put in the aggressive level. Or you can back off one more level and have $3,500 to invest at the moderate level. Either way the amount you have to invest forces you to stay away from speculating.

Now I know that someone is saying, "Where did these percentages come from?" It doesn't matter if you don't agree with the exact percentages as long as you grasp these three concepts that can help you invest wisely and within your risk tolerance:

1. Have an investment plan and stick with it.
2. Diversify, but don't spread yourself too thin.
3. Determine the level of risk you can afford.

The investment triangle approach takes these three concepts and combines them into a workable method. Don't make investing more complicated than it is. Always ask yourself, "How does this investment fit my goal?" Always invest with a goal in mind. Make sure that your portfolio is structured for meeting your goal and not for performance.

After you've determined your risk tolerance, what strategy should you use to overcome risk in your investments?

Investment Strategy

You overcome risk with the investment strategy of diversification. How do you diversify? You don't buy just a little bit of everything. Some things you can't afford, for example, fine art that costs a million dollars. Some things do not provide consistent returns; therefore you don't get the value of compound interest.

The first step in diversification is to decide how much money you should have in growth investments, and how much in nongrowth, as shown in Figure 10.9.

FIGURE 10.9   Diversify Through Growth/Nongrowth Investments

Growth (appreciate over time)	Nongrowth (protect a certain amount of income)
Stocks	Money market mutual funds
Real estate	Bonds
Oil and gas	Savings accounts
Gold	CDs
	T-bills
	T-notes

Once you've determined how much you should put in growth and nongrowth investments, you need to decide what type of growth. Stocks or real estate? In nongrowth, should you invest in a money market fund or a bond?

> **I**s your planner suggesting investments that you're not comfortable with? Question the planner's reasons for recommending a particular investment. If the planner doesn't understand or accept your risk comfort level, find another advisor.

Your Decision Is Based on Time

You decide how much should be in growth and nongrowth investments based on time. How old are you? How long do you expect this portfolio to last (obviously to the end of your life)? So, if you are 45 and you expect to live until 85, there's a 40-year horizon. Of course, you're not going to put a dollar in today and leave it for 40 years. So we arbitrarily divide that by 2 and that gives us a 20-year investment horizon.

Nongrowth Investments Protect You from Volatility

Here's another way to look at how much should be in growth and how much should be in nongrowth investments. The nongrowth is simply there to protect you from volatility. For example, it's easy to see this principle in full-blown retirement. If you're fully retired, you take one year of cash flow and put it in money market funds. You take the next year's cash flow plus inflation, and put it in a one-year Treasury bill. Then place three year, four year, and five year's cash flow plus inflation in three-year, four-year, and five-year Treasury bills respectively. Now you have a five-year plan with your investments in a "ladder." You have five years to decide when to sell the funds.

However, you can use this approach even before retirement. How much nongrowth do you need, based on your safety needs? Do you want to have one year's worth of income? Two year's? Any answer can be correct; it depends on you and your specific situation.

Asset Allocation Is Based on History

You should prepare your financial plan, know the reasons why you are investing in a particular product (to meet your goals), and then take action. Asset allocation is a concept which looks at how much you should have in growth and how much in nongrowth based on past market history. Over a long-time horizon, stocks have performed better than any other investment.

Your broker has a record. Check it! The Securities and Exchange Commission (www.sec.gov), the New York Stock Exchange (www.nyse.com), and the National Association of Securities Dealers (www.nasdr.com; 800-289-9999) can provide you with information.

If it's clear that you ought to be in the stock market, then you ought to be totally in the market (100 percent allocated) if you can stand the volatility. The only issue is how you protect yourself against the volatility. That means you need to have enough cash so that you don't have to worry about the market for some period of time. What period of time? That depends on your horizon. A five-year to seven-year nongrowth amount should be more than adequate because market cycles tend to be in that five-year to seven-year period.

How Much Do You Need in Reserve?

Don't forget the issue of a "reserve" that I talked about in Chapter 3 when you were preparing your cash flow worksheet. Remember, a reserve is liquid cash you can get your hands on for emergencies, 24 hours a day. You need to have a reserve before you consider investing.

Timing the Market

A couple of words to those who think they can time the market: You can't. Several studies have been done showing that often people get out of the stock market in time, but they don't get back in in time. They miss the best day getting back, not getting out. That's why most people lose when they try to time the market. The number one thing about successful investing is time. Stop trying to time the market, it's more important to be properly allocated. That goes back to growth, nongrowth, and in what types of investments within those two areas.

Nongrowth Investments

In the nongrowth area, I would probably stay away from CDs and bank accounts because they tend not to be as successful for most of us as other types of investments. I don't want to buy a bond mutual fund because of volatility. Instead, I want to buy a bond that matures at my required date. Remember that the bond price fluctuates. Nonetheless, I want to know that in one year, x number of dollars will free up that I can put into my money market fund or somewhere where it's absolutely liquid. By "laddering" the maturity dates as discussed before, a specific amount of income can be planned for each time period that I want.

Growth Investments

In the area of growth, with all the information we have—Internet, *The Wall Street Journal,* etc.—by the time the investor finds out what's available, it's too late. What we want is a surrogate, somebody who's on the street, in the game, going into the boardrooms, inside these companies. Our surrogate is the mutual fund manager. For a small investor, mutual funds are a terrific way to get started.

Understanding the Investment Matrix

Review your investment strategy. First, you want some form of diversification: growth or nongrowth based on your time horizon. Within growth, you choose a type, for example, mutual funds or stocks. Within mutual funds, you look at the investment style of the mutual fund you should buy. Here's where the "investment matrix" is very helpful.

To evaluate investments, you can use a grid called an investment matrix. The matrix or grid is like a small checkerboard with labels across the top squares and down one side. Stocks are ranked according to their investment style, and the appropriate box in the grid is shaded. The labels vary among investment tracking firms. Morningstar uses "Large, Medium, Small" on the vertical side and "Value, Blend, and Growth" across the top for a total of nine investment style boxes. Value Line's grid has a rectangle of four boxes with four smaller boxes within each large one. Value Line's labels are "Large, Small" on the side and "Value, Growth" across the top. Both companies have sample reports on their Web sites which show how they use this investment matrix (www.morningstar.com and www.valueline. com). Or you can find their reports at most libraries.

Depending on your age and how much time you have, you can look at the matrix and say, "Okay, if I'm 70 years old, the majority of my stuff ought to be in the large value box." Or "If I'm 21 years old, the majority ought to be in the small growth box." As you get older, you just move up from the small to the large because there's less volatility in the large. It's just that simple. There's theoretically less volatility in the Value investment style as opposed to the Growth style.

As you build your portfolio, you may fill all of the boxes, but the percentages in the boxes will depend upon where you are in your financial time horizon. You might have six mutual funds that are Large Value and three mutual funds that are Small Growth.

In general, I suggest that you stay away from balanced funds because they generally have a large number of bonds in them. That's not why we're buying them. We're looking for growth investments and, of course, bonds are nongrowth investments.

One reliable indicator for mutual funds is the Sharpe ratio listed in the Morningstar reports on each mutual fund. This ratio shows whether the return you're getting is worth the risk you're taking. The higher the number the better, from the investor's point of view. A 1.0 is okay; the ratio goes up to about 3.

This concept of diversification should eliminate the problem that somebody has when their asset allocation gets out of line with their goals, as it can quickly do in a bull market. It doesn't matter how big your growth is; it matters what your nongrowth is.

Investment Choices

Now that you've learned about the financial cycle, risk, and diversifying to reduce risk, two of your choices should be obvious—bonds and cash. When I say cash, I mean money market funds, certificates of deposit, and even savings accounts. However, usually you can earn a better rate of interest on the first two than with a savings account.

The third choice that I recommend for your investment strategy is mutual funds. Let's look at bonds and mutual funds in more detail.

Bonds

What is a bond? You loan money to the bond issuer and it agrees to pay you a stated rate of return on your loan. There are many variations on this basic premise. The advantage to you is the ability to lock in a fixed rate of return for a fixed time period. This interest rate is the coupon rate. You receive the interest on a periodic basis. If you intend to keep the bond until maturity then you don't necessarily need to worry about this next part.

If you want to trade your bond before maturity, then market value is very important to you. What is market value, and how do you determine it? You know what the rate of return will be, but the value of the bond can still fluctuate with interest rates. What someone will give you today for the bond is its market value.

When you are evaluating whether to buy bonds or whether to hold on to the ones you have, you need to look at both the rate of return, its current value, and the income, if any. Figure 10.10 shows a simple example of how the value of a bond can change.

Notice that you still get the same amount of income, but when the market rate goes up, the value of the bond goes down to $500. This inverse or opposite response between rate and value occurs because an investor can buy a new bond paying a higher rate of return. So when they look at the value of your bond, they can pay you a lesser amount (half in the above example) to get the same rate of return.

FIGURE 10.10   What Is a Bond's Market Value?

	Rate Now	Rate Goes Up	Rate Goes Down
Market rate	10%	20%	5%
Value	$1,000	$500	$2,000
Income per year	$ 100	$100	$ 100
Interest	10%	20%	5%
Divide income by market rate			

When the rate goes down, the value goes up to $2,000 because an investor is willing to pay more.

There are many types of bonds: Treasury, Series EE, Series HH, agency, municipal, corporate, and zero coupon.

Treasury Bills

Treasury bills are sold by the U.S. government and are similar to EE savings bonds. T-bills are sold in amounts of $10,000 or more for periods of 13 weeks, 26 weeks, or 52 weeks. There are no state and local taxes. They can be purchased through any Federal Reserve Bank by mail or online. The general information Web site is www.frbservices.org/treasury/frTreasury.cfm. For details on purchasing directly from the Federal Reserve Bank (called "Treasury Direct"), use www.publicdebt.treas.gov/sec/sectrdir.htm. If you are an existing Treasury Direct customer, use www.publicdebt.tres.gov/sec/secinnsr.htm. Check with your local library or bank for the address of the nearest Federal Reserve Bank. You also can purchase T-bills through other financial institutions, but you will pay them a fee.

Treasury Bonds and Notes

Treasury bonds (T-bonds) are also considered safe because they are backed by the U.S. government. They are sold for lower minimum amounts than T-bills and are offered for longer periods of time. Treasury notes (T-notes) have a maturity of 1 to 10 years, T-bonds of 1 to 30 years. No state or local taxes are paid. Every six months, interest is paid to you. When the note or bond matures, the principal is paid back to you. They also can be purchased through any Federal Reserve Bank by mail or using the Web addresses shown above.

Series EE and Series HH Bonds

Series EE and Series HH bonds also are a safe investment because they are guaranteed by the U.S. government. Series EE are issued at 50 percent of face value and mature in 30 years. There are no state or local taxes on Series EE bonds. Unlike the old Series E bonds, these continue to pay interest past maturity. The rates fluctuate with the market, but there is a guaranteed minimum rate if you keep them for five years or more. EE bonds cashed before five years are assessed a three-month interest penalty. Rates are changed each May 1 and November 1 (1-800-872-6637 gives the current rate).

At maturity, you may exchange the EE bonds for HH bonds. The HH bonds pay interest every six months, which you must declare on your taxes. The online address is www.publicdebt.treas.gov/sav/savinvest.htm. You can purchase these bonds through a bank or at some companies through payroll deductions.

When you purchase the Series EE bonds, you can declare the interest that year on your income tax. This establishes your intent to declare the interest every year. If no declaration is made, then you will pay taxes on the interest earned when you redeem the bonds. Thus the EE bonds can be used to defer taxes. Check with your tax advisor on using EE bonds to fund your child's college education.

Be sensitive to the possible tax trap of savings bonds. If you have accumulated a lot and cash them all at once, it could push you into a higher tax bracket.

Series I Bonds

Series I bonds are issued at face value. Interest is calculated as an earning of a fixed rate of return and a semiannual inflation rate based on the Consumer Price Index. The first I bonds were issued September 1, 1998. They pay a fixed rate plus an inflation adjustment. I bonds cashed before five years are assessed a three-month interest penalty. Unlike EE bonds, there is no guaranteed level of earnings. I bonds cannot be exchanged for any other series of savings bonds. The online address is www.publicdebt.treas.gov/sav/savinvest.htm.

Agency Bonds

Agency bonds are not backed by the government, but they are reasonably safe. Examples include:

- Federal National Mortgage Association (FNMA or Fannie Mae) (www.fanniemae.com),
- Government National Mortgage Association (GNMA or Ginnie Mae) (www.ginniemae.gov),
- Federal Home Loan Mortgage Association (FHLMA or Freddie Mac) (www.freddiemac.com), and
- Student Loan Marketing Association (SLMA or Sallie Mae) (www.salliemae.com).

Municipal Bonds

State governments, local governments, and local development districts (for example, a water and sewer district) can issue municipal bonds to fund their projects. Unless you happen to live in the area, you won't know much about the project. You'll need to do some research at your library. There are two rating services, Moody's (www.moodys.com) and Standard and Poor's (www.standardandpoor.com), that you can check to evaluate the quality of these bonds.

Corporate Bonds

Corporations issue bonds when they want to raise more money. Before you buy a corporate bond, you will want to check out the company using the ratings given by Moody's or Standard & Poor's.

Zero Coupon Bonds or STRIPS

This is a bond which is stripped of interest. The return is based on the difference between the price you pay and the price when it matures. You must pay taxes on the interest even though you are not receiving the interest until the bond matures.

Mutual Funds

A mutual fund is a professionally managed corporation that invests in individual investments, such as stocks and bonds. What are the advantages of buying a mutual fund rather than the individual stocks?

- Professional management. Instead of you spending your time reading and researching the stock market in depth, you benefit (hopefully) from the professional managers and research staff's experience.
- Diversification. You can own more stocks at a lower cost because the fund buys in volume and gets better transaction costs than you could for the amount you have invested. The minimum to invest in an IRA is even lower than the usual minimum so you can diversify even within your first IRA.
- Liquidity. Because there is an open market with most funds, they may be bought and sold easily. You can usually make changes in your portfolio within a day by making a phone call or going online.
- Flexibility. If you own shares in a fund belonging to a "family" of funds, you can move back and forth more freely between funds with different styles. Usually there is no fee.

Types

There are three types of mutual funds. So you can look them up in Value Line or Morningstar, I list some examples, but *these are not recommendations.*

1. Open-end investment companies. You buy shares from the fund and sell them back to the fund. Some examples include Vanguard 500 Index and Fidelity Magellan.
2. Closed-end investment companies. These companies have a fixed number of shares. No new shares are issued. Some examples include Gabelli Equity and Black Rock Income.

3. Investment trusts. You purchase an interest in an unmanaged pool of investments. The trust agreement specifies the way in which the investments are held for safekeeping. There is no trading in these trusts. One type of investment trust is a Real Estate Investment Trust (REIT).

Charges

Some mutual funds levy a sales charge when you buy shares in the fund. This is called a front-end load. There may be other fees also. These are called load funds. No-load funds do not have an initial sales charge, but there may be charges when you sell your shares, such as exit fees, back-end loads, etc.

Evaluating Funds

Before you buy a mutual fund, you need to evaluate a fund on the following three points:

1. *Objectives.* Read the prospectus. In the first few pages, you will find a description of the objectives of the fund. Here are some examples of funds with different objectives.
   - Aggressive growth
   - Growth
   - Growth and income
   - Income
   - Balanced
   - Index
   - International
   - Bond
   - Money market

   In addition, some funds specialize in certain sectors such as utilities or technology.

2. *Performance.* Perhaps the next most important consideration is performance. Who is the fund's manager, how long has it been with the fund, and what is the track record? Keep in mind that the yield mentioned in the prospectus can be calculated on as little as five day's results. There are several mutual fund tracking reports available which will show the one-year, five-year, and ten-year performance of various funds. Two of them are offered by Morningstar (www.morningstar.com) and Value Line (www.valueline.com). In addition, most business magazines have monthly columns or annual reports on mutual fund performance. Once again, do your research before you pick a fund.

3. *Cost.* The selling price of the mutual fund is called the "Net Asset Value" or NAV. It is calculated by adding all the market closing prices of the mutual fund and dividing by the number of mutual fund shares that are outstanding. The "buy" price is also called the "Public Offering Price" or POP. This is the cost to the investor to buy one share of a mutual fund.

There are a variety of front-end and back-end loads, annual sales charges, fees, and so on that can be charged to you when you have a mutual fund. You will need to be persistent in discovering these because they are not always described in understandable terms in the prospectus. Avoid those funds with a 12b-1 charge. This fee can run up to 1.25 percent of your portfolio. This charge covers the selling and marketing costs of the fund.

The Securities and Exchange Commission requires that specific information on 12b-1 charges and other charges must be shown in a fund's prospectus. Use the worksheet in Figure 10.11 to compare the expenses of different mutual funds.

FIGURE 10.11   Worksheet for Comparing Mutual Fund Expenses

Possible Charges   **Fund Name**

_____   _____   _____

Actual Cost (in percent or dollars)

Possible Charges			
Front-end Load	_____	_____	_____
Back-end Load	_____	_____	_____
Re-load	_____	_____	_____
Exit Fee	_____	_____	_____
Management Fee	_____	_____	_____
12b-1 Fee	_____	_____	_____
Transfer Fee	_____	_____	_____
Total Expenses	_____	_____	_____

Aim for total expenses of less than 5 percent per year.

For more information on mutual funds, check our Web site (www.sestina. com), or the annual mutual fund issue of "Kiplinger's Personal Finance" (www. kiplinger.com).

Money Market Funds

A money market fund is a mutual fund that invests only in the "money market" (government securities, commercial paper, negotiable certificates of deposit). If you are conservative and have a very low risk tolerance, consider money market funds which invest only in U.S. government bills and bonds. Remember—the lower the risk, the lower your rate of return. Although you may feel secure investing in a money market fund which has a lower risk, are you accumulating enough dollars to meet your investment goals?

Evaluating Investments

How do you learn about investments and how to evaluate them? In Chapter 7, I explained the ABC approach to becoming an informed consumer on life insurance. Ask A, ask B, ask C; A looks at B, B looks at C, C at A. This approach will also work whether you're looking at stocks, bonds, mutual funds, or any investment.

Keep asking questions until you understand. Don't let the "trust me" attitude of some investment advisors bother you. It's your money they want to manage. If they're uncomfortable answering a lot of questions, go elsewhere.

What Is My Rate of Return?

A major part of the sales pitch for any investment is the "rate of return." One of your considerations should be the true rate of return for an investment, not what the salesperson says you will get. No one investment does well all the time so you need diversification in your investment plan.

To repeat myself, never be out of an investment you eventually want to be in. Your "crystal ball" on what's ahead in the business cycle just might be wrong. As I tell my seminar attendees: "Those who live by the crystal ball, must learn to eat ground glass."

Measuring and Defining Returns

When you invest, you need to measure and define what your return is so you'll know how you're doing. Here are five measures of how your investment is doing.

1. What is the cash flow? Is income needed? If so, what range is acceptable?
2. Is your investment appreciating? What balance do you want between income and appreciation?
3. Are you building up any equity?
4. Does the investment have advantages for your tax situation?
5. Consider the interaction between investments. Can one investment offset the taxable gains of another?

Common Investment Mistakes

No Plan

You must have a financial plan to meet your financial goals. Remember "successful investing" isn't measured by how many stocks you buy or sell or what percent return you make. You are successful when you meet *your* goals.

Excess Funds

Don't commit all your excess funds. Check your cash flow worksheet. You haven't done one yet? Go back and do it now. If you consistently have a surplus of $3,000 in your savings account every single month, then go ahead and invest it. But be sure you're not investing your cash reserve. How much do you need for your emergency fund? Financial folklore says six month's pay or some other figure. Don't rely on that. Figure out what's right for you with the help of your cash flow worksheet. You don't want to put all your excess funds in six-month T-bills, then find out two months later you need the money.

Avarice

Do you try to wring the last penny out of a winning investment? Don't be tight-fisted and hold onto an investment for fear you'll lose a dime, even when you've already made a dollar. Once you've doubled your money, you should sell half. If you have a plan, you decide before you make an investment when you should sell, instead of letting greed determine your actions. Another part of greed is letting the tax tail wag the economic dog. Don't buy an investment for tax reasons; buy it because it fits into your plan. Do the numbers. Is there any potential in the investment?

Gluttony

Financial gluttons are excessive with their investments. Their eyes are always bigger than their purses. Gluttons get so impatient that they trade too much. They think they will generate a higher return, but all they generate is more commission for their brokers. They lack discipline to make a plan and stick to it. Don't be distracted by the hope of making more.

Gullibility

Don't believe everything you hear about an investment and buy on hunches, tips, and rumors. Any "hot tip" you hear is just a rumor. Insider trading is illegal. The people who are insiders can't and shouldn't tell you what to buy. Anyone else is just guessing. Buy based on facts.

Sloth

Are you a lazy investor? Investing requires work. Some people spend more time buying a car than they do learning about the investment they're considering. Do your homework. Find out everything you can before you sign your name or put your money down. The most important factors are the people and their experiences. I'd rather be in a bad deal with good people than a good deal with bad people.

Once you've made an investment, you must supervise it. It is so easy to let someone else do things for you. Don't turn your financial affairs, investments or otherwise, over to someone else. At the very least, you need to keep in touch so that you know what is happening and your designated advisor knows that you are a concerned investor. No one cares more about your money than you do.

Pride

Don't let pride get in the way of your plan. When you make a mistake, admit it and move on. Stubborn pride makes you ride a loser all the way down. When your investment no longer fits your plan, get rid of the investment. Too many people worry if they made a good or bad decision or whether they sold too soon or too late. No financial plan is perfect.

Cowardice

Sometimes it's not pride, but fear of failure that trips you up. Remember that in financial planning, as in life, there is risk in everything you do. Driving a car is risky, but with defensive driving techniques, you can lower the risk. Even eating seems risky these days with our increased knowledge of the effects of different foods on our health. But you keep on driving and eating because you need to do them. You need to do a financial plan, too. If you do nothing, you face the risk that inflation will eat away at your purchasing power, that someone else will make the wrong decisions for you about your money, that changes in tax laws will take even more from your pocket.

Conformity

Don't follow the herd. When an investment is recommended in the media, wait a week or two until the price settles down. The institutions buy before the little guy has a chance to buy, then the institutions sell after the little guy buys in. You lose! Buy an investment only if it fits your plan, not because everyone else is doing it.

Overdiversify

It makes sense to diversify your investments. If one part of your investment portfolio has a loss, you stand a better chance that the other parts have not. The problem is that some people interpret this advice to mean that if a little bit of diversification is good, more is better. Don't own a little gold mining stock, a little real estate, some oil shares, a little in a money market fund, and a little in bonds. You'll be spread too thin and accomplish nothing.

Underdiversify

There is no investment for all seasons. How easy it would be if you could just park your money in one investment and come back in 30 years and take your profits. Unfortunately, there are a few financial advisors who seem to believe this myth. Or at least they want you to believe it and buy their advice. It just isn't true. The financial cycle causes fluctuations in the value of all investments at one time or another.

Speculate

Here's that obstacle, ego, again. We all keep trying to hit a financial home run. You can't afford the risk. I know some advisors will say speculate while you are young. Go back and look at that graph on the cost of one year. Do you really want to blow that much money on an ego trip? Why speculate when you can meet your goals without it? Why postpone your financial freedom even one year?

Bargains

Don't buy because the investment looks like a bargain. There are no bargains. Buy quality.

Fads

Don't buy fad investments. There will always be fads; leave them to someone else. They don't usually last long enough to be worth your time or money. Buy known financial products that will be here today and tomorrow.

Experts

Don't assume that an expert in X is an expert in Y. We're taught to respect authority. When you find someone who really is an expert in widgets, it's only human nature to ask their opinion on thingamajigs. They are flattered or egotistical so they tell you what they think. Just because they have an opinion doesn't mean they know what they're talking about.

Borrowing to Fund Investments

Should you borrow to fund your investments? You'll need to answer three basic questions before you consider this strategy:

1. Will you pay yourself back? Do you have the discipline to do it? If not, don't borrow.
2. Look at your cash flow. Can you afford to pay the interest?
3. Look at your liabilities. Check those debt/income ratios that I mentioned in Chapter 8.

If you answer no to any of these questions, then this strategy is not for you. But if you can meet these three tests, then read on.

Remember to always contribute at the beginning of the year. What if you don't have the money? Consider borrowing it. Figure 10.12 shows how you can come out ahead. Let's say you borrow $2,000 at the beginning of the year and put it into an IRA earning 10 percent. Even with an interest rate of 12 percent on an installment loan, you would still be ahead. The difference between starting your IRA on January 2, even with a loan, and waiting until you have the money at the end of the year is $9,822 in this example.

Even with nondeductible interest, it still may be better to borrow. Here's an example to illustrate the concept. Let's say your goal is to save $25,000 each year. If you could earn 10 percent interest on your savings through investments, it would

---

FIGURE 10.12   It Pays to Borrow for an IRA

Loan amount each year	$2,000
Loan rate	12%
Term (one-year loan every year for 30 years)	1 year
Loan monthly payment	$177.67
Interest paid for one year loan	$132
After-tax cost	$132
Total paid for one-year loan	$2,132
IRA earns	10%
Cost to wait one year (value of $2,000 in 30 years)	$31,726
Cost of interest paid for one year (the $132 could have grown to this amount)	$2,320
Benefit to borrow so you can invest at beginning of the year	$29,406

cost you $411,235 to wait one year. If you could borrow the money at 12 percent at the beginning of each year and pay it back in one year, the cost to borrow every year for 30 years would be $272,238. Your benefit to borrow ends up being $138,997. Figure 10.13 summarizes this example.

Don't worry about these specific numbers. Your goal for annual savings may be more or less. I want you to understand why it might be better to borrow. You'll have to evaluate your own situation to see if this technique is right for you.

Where should you borrow? Here's my order of preference for borrowing from lowest cost to highest cost:

1. Borrow from yourself and pay yourself interest. Take the money from your savings; let's say $2,000 as in Figure 10.12. Then each month pay yourself $177.67 (into your savings) from your income that month. This

---

FIGURE 10.13   It Pays to Borrow Rather Than Wait One Year to Save

SAVE NOW

Savings goal (per year)	$25,000
Interest earned	10%
Time period	30 years
If saved at beginning of year	$4,523,585
If saved at end of year	$4,112,350
COST TO WAIT ONE YEAR	$411,235

BORROW TO FUND SAVINGS

Borrow	$25,000
Interest rate	12%
Time period for loan	1 year
Total loan cost	$26,655
Interest paid	$1,665
Tax savings	$0
After-tax cost	$1,665
30-YEAR COST TO PAY OFF LOAN INSTEAD OF SAVING THAT MONEY (for a one-year loan each year for 30 years)	$272,238

COST/BENEFIT COMPARISON

Cost to wait one year	$411,235
Cost to borrow money	$272,238
BENEFIT TO BORROW	$138,997

payment includes an additional amount to cover the interest you lost on your savings that you took out initially.

2. If you have cash value in your life insurance, borrow against it. The interest rate on the loan probably will be lower than you could get elsewhere.

3. Get an interest-only loan against your certificates of deposit at your bank.

4. Get a simple interest loan.

5. If you can't do 1–4, then get an installment loan. This loan cost is usually higher than #4. Shop around for the best rate. Make sure there is no prepayment penalty.

Other Investments

I know some of you are saying, "But what about other investments? I can't make high returns with these products." Yes, you can. Yields on quality bonds and mutual funds have been in the double digits. Money market funds keep up with rising inflation rates. You don't need to invest in other products unless you have plenty of money to spare and a high risk tolerance.

"But how can I impress my friends? These investments are so dull, they'll laugh at me!" Ah, now we get down to the real problem, that obstacle I mentioned in Chapter 1, ego. Do you want to meet your goals or impress your friends? It's your money; no one cares more about it than you.

If you do have extra money to invest and have met your goals with my recommended investments, then I'll tell you this story about other investments. Several years ago I spent almost a year researching investment diamonds. I read everything I could get my hands on and asked lots of questions. I went to the diamond markets. I talked to the buyers and sellers. In talking one day with a diamond broker, I asked his opinion on some diamonds I was considering buying. Do you know what he told me? "Buy bonds; they're safer."

Know your investment. Buy what you know and do your research in that area.

Individual Stocks

Don't invest in individual stocks unless you have at least $100,000 to invest. Am I against stocks? Definitely not. However, if you buy individual stocks and have less than $100,000, the transaction costs will wipe out any profit you might make. Plus you won't be able to diversify enough.

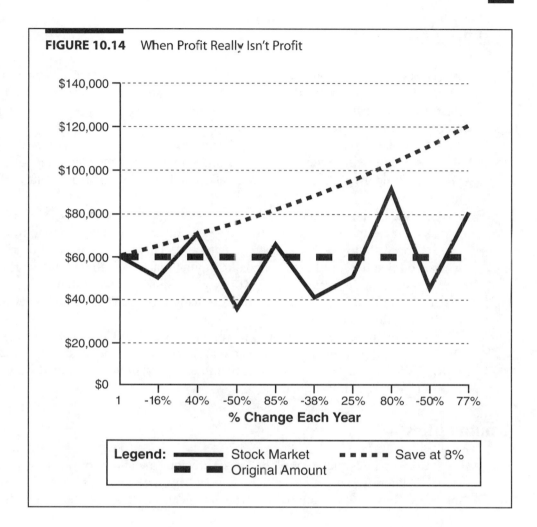

FIGURE 10.14   When Profit Really Isn't Profit

% Change Each Year

Legend: —— Stock Market   ▪ ▪ ▪ ▪ Save at 8%
         ▪ ▪ Original Amount

   Too many people get excited about the stock market because they hear others talking about the money they've made. What these people don't brag about is the money they've lost in the market. The October 1987 crash should have taught us all to view the stock market with more level heads. But in case you don't, Figure 10.14 shows a hypothetical example to make the point. In some years the returns were great, up to 85 percent. But the down years dipped as low as −50 percent. Did the investor in this example really make a profit? No. The real return is only 3.25 percent.

Real Estate

Real estate (not your residence) used to be a good investment. Its investment value depended on the fixed mortgage. Now with variable mortgages in as many flavors as ice cream, it's hard to get a good return on real estate without spending more time than you really need to spend.

If you are considering investing in real estate, compare the risk with CDs. What is a safe return with CDs? Can you get that same return with the property you are considering? Use the risk evaluation table to evaluate the risk factors for real estate.

As the business cycle and other factors change, the attractiveness of real estate as an investment changes. I use a 2½-hour rule. If you can't drive to it, don't buy it. You want to see it and keep an eye on it. This concept is valid no matter where you live because I assist clients in buying real estate all over the world.

If you consider real estate, don't buy glitz. Slick brochures don't necessarily mean a better deal. There are probably too many promotion costs and other overhead in big firms' deals.

When you buy real estate, buy a property, not a Real Estate Investment Trust (REIT). Again, you're buying real estate to diversify. In general, I'm not in favor of REITs for the same reason I don't recommend bond funds. You want to buy "the product," not a pool of products.

Commodities

Commodities such as pork bellies or precious metals are only for the professional. I know some people will be tempted by the "glamour" aspect of commodities. Don't trade commodities. You can meet your goals without them.

Gold

Buy gold itself, not paper. Take possession of the gold.

Collectibles

This category includes coins, art, and so on. Become an expert in whatever you plan to collect or don't bother. This can be a very risky area. Today's Beanie Babies can be tomorrow's Cabbage Patch dolls!

Annuities

You may expect to find annuities here. I don't care what the salespeople tell you, an annuity is not an investment. It should be a tool. Refer back to Chapter 9 for a discussion of annuities.

Conclusion

For the picky details on investing, refer to the reading list in Appendix F. Remember that there are many different "schools of thought" about how to invest. I've explained the concepts that I feel are time-tested and easy to use while keeping your time commitment and risk at a level where you can sleep at night. Some of you will choose a higher risk than others. Do what is right for you based on your finances and your temperament. You can still manage to be wealthy with conservative investments.

> Is your planner willing to provide you with a running total of commissions to date? If not, you may wish to find another planner who will provide this information. Less cost = more profits.

Summary

Save first from your income and always save from January. Don't wait until later in the year to "catch up" on your savings. You lose a substantial sum of compounded interest!

Avoid leakage by always reinvesting the interest.

Understand the basic financial cycle. When inflation goes up and interest rates go up, businesses can't afford to borrow and the stock market goes down. Use money market funds to keep up with the rising rates.

When interest rates go down, businesses and individuals borrow, and the stock market goes up. You want to lock in higher rates through long-term bonds. Never be totally out of a product that you may want at some time.

Try to beat inflation by 2 percent each year after taxes. That is your "real return."

Learn the different types of financial risk and evaluate your risk tolerance.

Manage risk through diversification into growth and nongrowth investments. Determine your investment time horizon. Within growth investments, choose an investment style that fits your personal situation.

There are lots of financial products to consider, but the three that I recommend are bonds, cash, and mutual funds.

Consider borrowing to invest *only* if you have the discipline to pay back the loan.

11

Estate Planning

Before you can plan what to do with your estate, you need to know what you have. Remember in Chapter 3 when you did a balance sheet? That balance sheet tells you what you are worth now. If you skipped over that part, please go back and complete a balance sheet now. It will be the cornerstone of your estate plan. You can't prepare an effective one unless you know exactly what you have.

Now is also the time to review the goals you set in Chapter 2. Because you have since worked on your retirement, education, and other goals, you may need to modify or change what you originally wrote down. Take the time to do that now. You want to end up with a written list of what you want your estate plan to accomplish. Be as specific as you can. Be sure to talk about these goals with your spouse and financial advisors.

Is Your Estate Adequate to Meet Your Goals?

The first question in planning your estate is: If you die today, how much money will be needed tomorrow? How much money will it take to pay off all your bills? Your balance sheet should tell you what that amount is. The leftover portion is your net worth.

Is your net worth enough? You'll need to compare what your goals for your estate are with how much money you have. If you are married and have young children and want their education covered, is there enough? If you are retired and want your spouse's expenses covered, is there enough? Only you can determine how much is enough to meet your individual goals.

Let your planner know how you would distribute your estate if you had no taxes to concern you. This provides them with insight into your overall goals.

Do you need insurance to fill in the gaps between what you want your estate to be worth and how much it is actually worth today? Many people need the most insurance when they have a young family. After you have completed your financial plan and begin to implement it, you will gradually need less insurance. Why? Because your investments will grow and replace the need for insurance.

We talked about this in Chapter 7, but it's worth repeating here. The cash flow worksheet from Chapter 3 will help you evaluate any life-changing event, including the effect of your death or your spouse's death on the family's cash flow. Redo the cash flow worksheet, but this time fill one out for each of the following three scenarios:

1. You have died.
2. Your spouse has died.
3. Both you and your spouse have died.

Do you see how your family's cash flow will change in each of these events? What changes do you need to make to your financial plan?

You Must Have a Will

If you don't like what the government has done with the recent tax changes, wait until you find out what they will do with your money if you don't have a will. The federal and state governments have laws that apply to people who die "intestate." "Intestate" means that you die without a will. Believe me, the government will get much of your money if you don't have a will, so please go do it now. The cost is not that much compared to the benefit that your heirs will receive. It's going to be hard enough for them dealing with all the details; don't make it worse for them. The benefit to you is peace of mind in knowing that your money will go to the people and institutions *you* choose.

A word of warning: please don't think you can do your will from a book. Or don't just write your will yourself and have it witnessed (this type of will is called a "holograph"). There are two important reasons why you need to have an attorney prepare your will:

1. You want to be sure your will is valid. If it's not, the government gets to decide where the money goes. There is a standard order in which your relatives are in line to get money from your estate. If you want to give certain percentages to different relatives or leave someone out entirely, you can only do that with a valid will.
2. You want to be sure the maximum amount of estate is preserved. The tax law changes have affected estate planning greatly. You need an attorney who knows all the current estate laws so that your hard-earned money will do what you want.

So find a competent attorney and get that will done now. Once you have a will, be sure to review it at least every two years, even if your circumstances have not changed. Based on what's happened in the past, the estate laws have been changing about every two years.

Property Transfers

During your lifetime, property may be transferred by gifts, loans, or by power of attorney. A "power of attorney" is a legal document assigning certain rights to another. After your death, property may be transferred by wills, trusts, life insurance policies, beneficiary designations, or jointly held property.

Different rules apply for federal and state tax laws. It is important to have a competent advisor help you think about these property transfers ahead of time to minimize expenses.

> If you have a family-owned business, talk to your planner about planning the transition. Should it be immediate or done in steps? Should the business be sold rather than have negative consequences for your family?

Terms You Need to Know

You've already learned that *intestate* means to die without a will. Here are just a few of the other words and phrases that have special meaning in the language of estate law.

- *Testator (male) or testatrix (female):* You, the person who dies with a will.
- *Executor (male) or executrix (female):* A person appointed by you in your will to "execute" your estate. Some of his or her duties will include: being recognized by the court as the executor, getting bonded, doing an inventory of the estate, distributing the estate to the beneficiaries, getting receipts from the beneficiaries for what they received, and filing a final report on the estate. You may appoint a friend or relative, your attorney, or your bank. The executor usually receives a fee for services (more about this issue later). You will want to list more than one executor in your will in case your first choice dies before you do or decides not to serve.
- *Administrator (male) or administratrix (female):* A person appointed by the court to "administer" your estate. If you have not appointed an executor in your will or you die without a will, the court will appoint an administrator. His or her duties are the same as those of the executor.
- *Guardian of the estate:* The person or entity, for example, a bank trust department, that is responsible for managing your estate by distributing money over time for minor children.
- *Guardian of the person:* The person who is responsible for actually taking care of your minor children. You may designate the same person as guardian of the estate and of the person. However, there may be very good reasons to designate different people. If you have a complex estate, you will probably want a professional to be the guardian of the estate. Even with a small estate, you may want to split these duties.
- *Joint tenancy:* Property held by you and another person, for example, your spouse. Such property does not go through probate but goes to the other owner upon your death. It is generally inflexible, and there is a possibility of unintended inheritance. It is a poor tax shelter and has other disadvantages. It is recognized by most states.
- *Tenancy by the entirety (only by a married couple):* Similar to joint tenancy but affords greater protection from creditors. Has some disadvantages. It is not recognized by all states.
- *Tenancy in common:* Property held by you and other persons. The shares may or may not be equal. Anyone may dispose of his or her share without the other person's consent. Most often used by business partners.

Must everything you own go into your estate? No, depending on when the ownership is determined.

When Is Joint Ownership Determined?

It is possible to have an estate which has no money and yet leave plenty of money to your heirs. How? By having ownership of the money determined not by your will but by a contract, a trust, or by joint tenancy. Each of these legal agreements takes precedence over anything your will may say. However, this doesn't mean that you avoid estate taxes.

Here are some examples of how some investments you may have would be handled.

- *Savings bonds.* Ownership is determined at contribution. Series EE and Series HH bonds go to the beneficiary or co-owner named on the bond and do not go through probate.
- *Bank accounts.* Ownership is determined at withdrawal. If the bank account is set up as a "payable on death" account, the money goes directly to the person named. The account does not go through probate.
- *Registered securities you hold.* Ownership is determined at purchase.
- *Securities held by broker.* Ownership is determined at termination. If the securities are held jointly and you sell them and take all the money, your spouse just gave you a gift.
- *Real estate.* Ownership is determined at inception. Refer back to the "terms you need to know" section above for a discussion of joint tenancy, tenancy in common, and tenancy by the entirety.

Letter of Last Instructions

Even with a will, you should have a letter of last instructions. Remember that the will is not always opened and read immediately after you die. The letter will cover all those details of who should do what and where that your family will need right away.

I know these are difficult subjects to talk about. However, if you have ever had a loved one die without this information readily available, you know firsthand how tough it is to make the decisions then. Please sit down with your family now and talk about these matters for you and your spouse and, if you have older children, with your children. If your children are older, discuss what they would want to have done for them if they die before you.

Here's a list of the minimum information you should put into a letter of last instructions.

- Write out your burial wishes. Do you want burial or cremation? Do you want an open casket or a closed one? Do you want a big funeral, a small one, or a memorial service? Where do you want to be buried or have your ashes placed? What family or religious customs do you want or not want to be observed?
- List in the letter what your important papers are and where each one is located. Be sure to give a specific location, for example, the top right-hand desk drawer, and always keep them there. If they are elsewhere for changes or updating, either update your letter or put a note in the drawer. Be sure to list the name and address of the bank where your safe deposit box is located. Say where you keep the key to the box.
- Include a list of important people, why they are important, and their phone numbers. Examples are your attorney, executor, and guardians of the estate and person.

Finally, don't forget to tell your family where the letter is located so it can be found.

Where to Keep Important Papers

Besides having a letter of last instructions readily available, your family will need to be able to find your important papers. Some of them will be needed almost immediately. I recommend buying a fireproof box in which to keep your important papers at home.

- *Will.* Never keep the original will in your safe deposit box. The box may be sealed upon your death. If the box is jointly owned, it may be sealed upon your spouse's death also. Have your attorney keep your original will in his or her office safe. Keep a copy at home with your other important papers.
- *Insurance policies.* Keep these at home in one place. Keep a list of the policy names, addresses, and numbers in a different location, perhaps your safe deposit box. If you have a trust, the bank may have these papers.
- *Birth and death certificates, marriage license, military discharge papers, Social Security cards, passports, divorce papers.* Keep these in your safe deposit box with a copy of each at home.

There are many other personal and financial papers that your family will need to have accessible when you die. There are useful worksheets in Appendix B.

Durable Power of Attorney

A "durable power of attorney" is different than the power of attorney mentioned earlier under Property Transfers. Designating a "durable power of attorney" is important even if you do none of the other estate planning that I've recommended. You need to select someone to act as your "agent" in case you are not able to sign papers or carry out other duties. As an example, let's say you are in an accident and are unconscious for days or longer. Who would write checks to pay your bills? Who would be able to cash your paycheck? Who would be able to sign important papers on your behalf? You may designate your spouse, your attorney, or anyone you want, but give it careful thought. Have your attorney help you prepare this. You may wish to have a backup person listed.

Administration and Other Costs

Administering an estate takes time, so the executor receives a fee for his or her services. If you have named a friend or relative as your executor, you may not expect to pay a fee. However, stop and think how you would feel in that position.

If you have named your attorney as executor, then you will need to plan for attorney's fees. Attorneys prefer a percentage of the estate. Try to arrange for a fixed fee. Even an hourly fee may save money for your estate.

Other costs that your estate will have to pay include bonding for your executor, probate costs, and so on. Ask your attorney to estimate these costs so that you can plan for them.

Is Your Family Wealth Threatened?

Probate and taxes are expenses that can dramatically reduce the actual amount that your family receives. Probate costs might cover administration fees, accountant fees, attorney fees, appraisals, and court costs. The larger and more complex the estate is, the higher the costs.

Taxes fall into two groups: inheritance and estate taxes. Someone who inherits something may pay an inheritance tax to the state. Your estate pays an estate tax to the federal government and perhaps to the state. Each state has different death taxes; some have none.

Tax Considerations

No, you don't escape taxes even when you die. You may not be around to see it, but be assured that the government will want its share of your estate. One of the important questions will be: did you have control over a specific piece of property when you died? If so, its value gets taxed. Let's look briefly at the federal and state estate taxes.

Federal Taxes

The United States has a uniform transfer tax that applies to gifts made while you are alive and to your estate when you die.

Even though there is a marital deduction, you probably do not want to take maximum advantage of it. Instead you want to take maximum advantage of the unified tax credit (currently at $650,000). As you'll see in the sample estate calculations in Figure 11.1 and Figure 11.2, this credit will make a big difference in how much your family will get.

> **Y**ou don't want Uncle Sam to be the relative to gain the most from your estate. Your goal should be to minimize estate taxes and consequences to heirs. Ask your planner if there's anything else you can do to meet this goal.

Any taxable gift you made after December 31, 1976, will be added to your estate. There is a credit for the taxes paid.

State Taxes

Even if you plan your estate so that it will not owe federal taxes, it may still owe state estate taxes. These vary from state to state. Check with a qualified attorney for the specifics in your state.

Probate Considerations

Your will goes through probate court. If you don't have a will, then the court distributes your estate according to the laws covering people without wills (intestate). The first question to be decided by the probate process will be: Is the will valid? So the first benefit of good estate planning is having a valid will. The next major question will be: Can the property in your estate be transferred by your will? As mentioned before, contracts, trusts, and joint tenancy supersede a will.

Trusts

Trusts are set up to distribute your estate assets for the amount of time you pick. Unlike a guardianship which ends when children become of age, a trust can go on for a long time.

Why have a trust?

- You want someone else to manage your estate during your lifetime.
- You want to have minor children protected in case of your death.
- You want to save on estate taxes.

If you have less than $650,000 in your estate, you probably don't need a trust. If your trust is more than three years old, you need to redo it.

If you are just starting out to set up a trust, call a bank trust department and have them send information to you. They will have useful brochures which describe what a trust is and what services the bank can offer.

The trustee you designate in your trust to run it has complete control of the funds from your estate. Make sure you choose someone who is capable and trustworthy. Many people name a bank for two reasons:

1. One individual may not be alive, but the bank trust department will always be there.
2. A bank trust department will provide professional, conservative management.

When you set up a trust, you want your beneficiaries to have certain rights:

- They should be able to change trustees.
- They should be able to influence investments.

- Your spouse should be able to get money from the children's trust once a year. The trustee must give permission above a certain amount or percentage. Permission is usually given.
- They should be able to get income from the children's trust.

For a children's trust, you should specify when they get the money. Do you want them to have it all at once or use some formula for periodic distribution (for example, an amount or percentage at various ages)?

Fees for a trust are usually about .25% of the estate value. I feel anything over 1 percent is excessive. Have someone keep an eye on the bank to make sure it is doing its job.

Don't forget that the estate tax laws usually change about every two years. Review your trust arrangements at least that often.

Types of Trusts

Let's look at the terms you'll need to know when setting up a trust and some of the basic forms of a trust. Obviously, this is such an important and complex matter that you will need to consult with qualified advisors to be sure your trust is set up to do exactly what you want.

Two terms that are crucial when setting up a trust are *revocable* and *irrevocable*. If a trust can be revoked, then you can at some time or under some conditions once again control the money. If a trust is irrevocable, then you have no further control of the money. These distinctions are important in determining ownership and thus taxation.

I'll only mention the three general types of trusts. There are many variations of these and other trusts which your attorney can describe for you, depending on your needs.

Inter Vivos (Living) Trust

The inter vivos (from Latin, meaning "among the living") trust is not included in the probate process so, theoretically, the cost of probate will be reduced. This trust is created separately and not by your will.

Other names for this trust include "shelter," "bypass," "credit," or "pocketbook" trust. If you have more than $1 million in your estate, you probably need one of these. The example cases I give later in this chapter will show the advantages of this type of trust.

Testamentary Trust

The testamentary trust is created in your will and is included in the probate process and in estate tax assessment. Thus, it is eroded by taxes. If your estate is under $1 million, this is probably the trust you want. Most likely, the surviving spouse will use up the remaining estate so that the actual value left when he or she dies will be under the current exemption amount.

Parents of minor children can use this trust to protect their children by providing a guardian of the estate and a guardian of the person for the children.

Charitable Trust

There are several types of charitable trusts. The charitable remainder trust is used to serve a charity and reduce taxes. The charity or charities named in this type of trust get the remainder of the estate after all the beneficiaries die. This trust is only useful if the estate is worth several million dollars or you have few beneficiaries.

In a charitable lead trust, you place income-producing assets into the trust. The income from the trust goes to the charity while you are alive. At your death, the principal goes to your heirs provided for by your will.

Sample Estate Plan

As you can see, estate planning is a very complex subject, one I can't completely cover in just one chapter. Let me give you one example to pull all of these ideas together. This example will show you the difference that good estate planning can make. Remember that you must use an attorney to be sure your estate plan does what you want.

Case 1 and Case 2 are two different calculations for the same husband and wife with the husband dying first. In Case 1, the full marital deduction is taken for the husband. Leaving everything to the surviving spouse is a frequent mistake. In Case 2, the husband takes advantage of his own individual exemption through a shelter trust. Figures 11.1 and 11.2 summarize the importance of proper estate planning.

Figures 11.1 through 11.3 show more detail on how just this one simple change in estate planning can greatly affect the benefit to your family.

As I mentioned before, with the help of your attorney or accountant, your family or someone else will need to file an IRS Form 706 after your death. Let's assume for this example that we know the amounts for each of the nine schedules

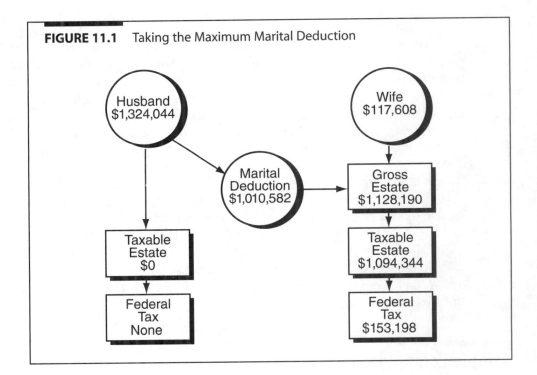

FIGURE 11.1 Taking the Maximum Marital Deduction

that go with Form 706. Figure 11.3 shows a summary of each of the schedules with the total of all nine making up the gross estate. Cases 1 and 2 end up with the same gross estate.

In Figure 11.4 adjustments are made to the gross estate. Notice that again the husband's calculations are the same for Cases 1 and 2. The adjusted gross estate is $1,010,582 for both.

The next step is crucial to sound estate planning. You and your advisors will need to evaluate carefully whether you want to take the full marital deduction. That used to be good planning. In many cases, doing that now will cost your family money.

In Case 2, the full marital deduction is not taken for the husband. Only $368,158 is taken. Notice that the wife in Case 1 has to add in the full marital deduction from the husband. The adjusted gross estate for Case 1 ends up being $623,151 more than in Case 2.

The future value computations at the bottom of Figure 11.2 show what the future value of the estate is worth to the family. Don't worry if you aren't sure

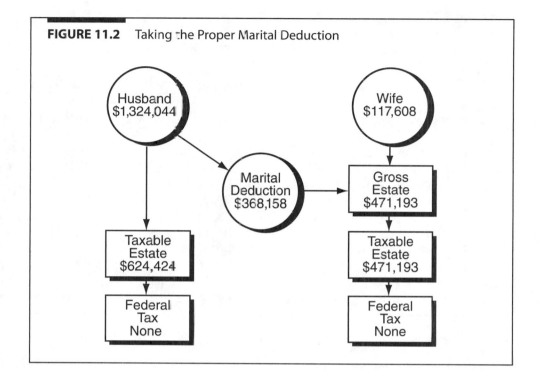

FIGURE 11.2   Taking the Proper Marital Deduction

FIGURE 11.3   Gross Estate Calculations—IRS Form 706 Schedules

		Case 1		Case 2	
		Husband	**Wife**	**Husband**	**Wife**
Schedule A:	Real estate	$251,398	$0	$251,398	$0
Schedule B:	Stocks & bonds	61,327	2,008	61,327	2,008
Schedule C:	Mortgages, notes & cash	104,379	9,274	104,379	9,274
Schedule D:	Life insurance	520,000	85,000	520,000	85,000
Schedule E:	Jointly owned property	4,322	4,322	4,322	4,322
Schedule F:	Other miscellaneous property	382,618	17,004	382,618	17,004
Schedule G:	Lifetime transfers	0	0	0	0
Schedule H:	Powers of appointment.	0	0	0	0
Schedule I:	Annuities	0	0	0	0
Gross estate		$1,324,044	$117,608	$1,324,044	$117,608

FIGURE 11.4   Adjusted Gross Estate Calculations

	Case 1		Case 2	
	Husband	Wife	Husband	Wife
Separate gross estate	$1,324,044	$117,608	$1,324,044	$117,608
Family—marital deduction from deceased spouse	0	1,010,582	0	368,158
Gross estate	1,324,044	1,128,190	1,324,044	485,766
Total funeral and administration expenses	39,721	33,846	39,721	14,573
Schedules K & L—debts and losses	273,741	0	273,741	0
Debts plus expenses	313,462	33,846	313,462	14,573
Adjusted gross estate	1,010,582	1,094,344	1,010,582	471,193
Family share for decedent 1	0	0	609,354	0
Family share for decedent 2	0	876,442	0	449,821
Future value both spouses	$0	$876,442	$0	$1,059,175

where these numbers came from. I want to show you the whole picture of what happens, not turn you into an estate planner in one chapter.

Figure 11.5 pulls everything together in a main worksheet. Notice again the difference in marital deductions for the husband. This results in the actual total taxable estate for Case 2 being $1,113,617 as compared with $1,094,344 for Case 1. Already you have a difference of $19,273 more for the family.

Now look at what happens when the unified tax credit is used. This is a tax credit allowed for each person's estate; for 1999 it was $650,000. The credit is lost for the husband in Case 1 because the full marital deduction was taken. Even with the credit, the wife in Case 1 pays $153,198 in federal estate taxes. However, in Case 2, by taking a lower marital deduction through a shelter trust, the combined benefit is $182,733 more to the family. Which estate plan would you rather have?

Increases in the Unified Credit

As shown in Figure 11.6, over the next few years the unified credit will increase. As I said before, estate law seems to change every two years or so. You need an advisor who keeps up-to-date.

FIGURE 11.5 Main Worksheet for Estate Planning

	Case 1		Case 2	
	Husband	Wife	Husband	Wife
Year of death	1987	1987	1987	1987
Adjusted gross estate	$1,010,582	$1,094,344	$1,010,582	$471,193
Marital deduction	1,010,582	0	368,158	0
Taxable estate	0	1,094,344	642,424	471,193
Federal estate	0	1,094,344	642,424	471,193
Federal estate per schedule	0	384,481	208,497	146,006
Unified credit	192,800	192,800	192,800	192,800
Federal tax + maximum credit	0	191,681	15,697	0
State death taxes – maximum credit	0	38,483	15,697	0
Federal tax special credits	0	153,198	0	0
Federal tax	0	153,198	0	0
Ohio death taxes – state schedule	23,470	64,704	33,070	21,372
Total death taxes	23,470	217,902	33,070	21,372
Remaining for family	0	876,442	609,354	449,821
Remaining for family, both spouses	$0	$876,442	$0	$1,059,175

Benefit from Proper Estate Planning = $182,733 more to the family

---

FIGURE 11.6 Unified Credit Changes

1999	$650,000
2000 and 2001	$675,000
2002 and 2003	$700,000
2004	$850,000
2005	$950,000
2006 and thereafter	$1,000,000

Conclusion

Estate planning is one of the most complex and least talked about parts of financial planning. I've tried to make it a little less mysterious and show you how important it is to get competent, reliable advisors to help you plan.

Go back now and revise your goals for your estate plan. Resolve to get a will drawn up now or amend your current one if needed. Write out your letter of last instructions, organize your important papers, and put them in a secure place. Sit down and discuss these matters with your family now while you can. It may be unpleasant to do so, but you will be providing them peace of mind for later.

Summary

Review your estate goals to see if they need modifying.

How much do you need in your estate if you were to die today? Use your balance sheet to see how much money would be needed to pay off all the bills. Do you need insurance to fill in the gap?

You must have a will. If you die without one, the federal and state government will use their rules to decide who gets what. Review your will at least every two years. Like tax laws, estate laws keep changing.

Even with a valid will, you should write a letter of last instructions. A will is not always read immediately after death. This letter covers all the details of your burial wishes, the "what and where" of your important papers, and a list of important people to contact. Some important papers should be kept at home, some in your attorney's safe. Do this organization now for peace of mind.

Have your attorney prepare a "durable power of attorney" for you. If you are ill or unable to carry out day-to-day matters, your "agent" will be able to handle these things for you.

Choose an executor for your estate.

Trusts are set up to distribute the assets of your estate for the length of time you pick. Have your financial advisor and attorney assist you in setting up a trust.

12

Seeking Professional Assistance

Are you self-employed? Do you have a large estate? Do you have a complex tax situation? Or do you simply need objective advice in managing your financial matters? If you answered yes to one or more of these questions, then you should seek the help of a professional financial advisor.

If your financial situation is more complex, this book will help you prepare the groundwork. After completing this book, you will have your financial goals in writing, you will have your financial data in order, and you will know and understand the terminology. You will then be better prepared for a productive meeting with your financial advisor.

Most people benefit from the advice of a financial advisor simply because the marketplace for investments, insurance, trusts, and so on, is constantly changing and expanding.

Then there are the new tax laws. Just when you almost had the old tax forms figured out, along comes a change. Even if you do your financial plan yourself with the help of this book, you may still need to consult a qualified financial advisor who keeps up-to-date with financial markets and the tax code.

Most people turn to a financial advisor as a guide through the maze of rules, exceptions to rules, and sales pitches. However, there are definite differences in the kind and quality of advice available.

Who Is a Financial Planner?

I've used the term financial advisor often. It's time to define it. "Financial advisor" means a stockbroker, an accountant, an attorney, or someone else who gives you financial advice. Don't misunderstand! You need competent specialists to help you, each in their own area of expertise. However, they are not financial planners.

A *financial planner* is a trained professional who assists you in performing the six steps of the financial planning process, provides unbiased advice, and works for a fee that you pay. You should use a planner who is not selling any other service or investment so there is no conflict of interest between the advice and what's best for you.

Everybody Says They Can Help You

Today, you only have to open up a business magazine or the business section of your newspaper to know that everyone from CPAs to your local department store are offering "financial services." What are they really selling you?

As a financial planner I'm not out to displace these financial advisors. However, you need to inform yourself so that when you're dealing with financial advisors you can't be fooled. The problem is that up to now, everyone has confused you. You need an unbiased financial planner to sort through all the claims and counterclaims of the sales pitches and to pull together all the different aspects of your financial plan. Don't expect your stockbroker to give you advice on estate planning or your insurance agent to tell you the best way to lower your taxes. Those are not their specialties.

How Do You Choose a Financial Planner?

Here are the three choices you have:

1. Fee-based (formerly called commission-based) advisors
2. Fee-basis advisors
3. Fee-only financial planners

"Fee-based" or "commission-based" means just that—the "advisor" is advising you to buy the product he or she is selling, whether or not it will help you meet your financial plan. They make their living by selling products such as life insurance or stocks. Because you do not pay their salary, their objectivity can be open to question.

"Fee-basis" means that the advisor will charge you a fee but will also make a commission or receive some other direct or indirect compensation for recommending certain products to you. If you purchase something they recommend, they receive money. This allows them to charge lower up-front fees because their commissions provide the majority of their income. These advisors appear to be a good deal because their fees are low. However, remember that they receive a commission (usually 15 percent) each time you buy a product they recommend. The overall cost will be more even though part of it is hidden.

> **P**art of your evaluation of the planner is based on the questions that he or she asks you and the data requested of you. Sometimes knowing the proper questions to ask is more important than knowing the answers.

"Fee-only" financial planners receive fees for the services they provide their clients. That is the only source of their income. They do not receive commissions or kickbacks or recommend a product that someone else in their family may sell. You pay their salary, generally a percentage of the assets they manage.

Which type of advisor is best? Of course, I believe the fee-only financial planner will give you the best value for your money in the long run because that's what I am. Here are the factors you should consider in making your decision: qualifications, objectivity, savings, service, investment focus, cost, actual rate of return, and implementation.

Qualifications

A financial planner should be certified as such by one or more national groups. There are two designations and several groups with which you should be familiar.

- Chartered Financial Consultant (ChFC). This is a two-year program, much like studying for a CPA exam. It has the most stringent requirements and is from the American College, Bryn Mawr, Pennsylvania.
- Certified Financial Planner (CFP). The College of Financial Planning, Englewood, Colorado, administers this program. The college is an independent, nonprofit educational institution incorporated in 1972. Approved by the American Council on Education, the CFP program is offered at numerous colleges and universities.

- Society of Independent Financial Advisors. This is a small group of financial planners. Membership is by invitation only. SIFA created NAPFA, the following group.
- National Association of Personal Financial Advisors. NAPFA was founded in 1983 by James Schwartz, Robert Underwood, and yours truly, John Sestina. It is the largest U.S. organization of fee-only financial planners. The planner must send in proof that they only do fee-only financial planning and send in a sample plan that they have done. Members are not allowed to receive any commissions nor do they sell products to their clients. They only recommend investments that are best for their clients. NAPFA members may not own more than a 5% interest in any organization which might benefit from their recommendations.
- Institute of Certified Financial Planners. The ICFP is a professional association whose members must have the CFP designation, must currently and continuously provide financial planning assistance, and must meet the ICFP's continuing education requirements. There is a Code of Ethics and a Standards of Practice that the members must follow.

Remember that just because someone earns one of these designations doesn't mean she or he is competent! Get referrals, choose a couple to interview, then visit their offices and interview them. They shouldn't come to your house at night and sit at your kitchen table unless you want them to do that.

Anyone serious about financial planning should have a master's degree. An accredited master's degree, the Master of Science in Financial Services (MSFS), is offered at the American College, Bryn Mawr, Pennsylvania. To earn the degree, one must earn 36 credits of which 30 must be in graduate courses. The program emphasizes how to conduct the complete financial planning process for both simple and very complex situations.

Bachelor's degrees are available at many schools. There is also the International Association for Financial Planning, a trade association that anyone can join by paying dues.

> You can never give too much information to your planner. If the planner doesn't have accurate information, you may receive good advice based on bad information.

Objectivity

Many professionals, for example CPAs and stockbrokers, may tell you they can do financial planning. They are not professional financial planners and don't have the training to provide you with a comprehensive financial plan.

Have you ever tried to reach your CPA for non–tax-related advice around April 15? CPAs are professional accountants. Use them for that purpose, but don't expect them to provide objective financial planning advice.

Stockbrokers *sell* stocks, bonds, and other financial products. They are paid depending on how many products they *sell*.

You need an unbiased third party, a professional financial planner, to evaluate financial proposals and to look at your financial documents and catch errors.

Savings

The commission-based and fee-basis advisors have no incentive to save you money. So they may recommend a "load" investment (one with a sales charge) because that's how they receive a commission. A "no-load" (one without a sales charge) may perform just as well for you, but there is no incentive for a commission-based or fee-basis advisor to recommend it. They make no money off that advice. You don't save.

When a fee-only financial planner is able to find a no-load investment for you, you get 100 percent of your money working for you instead of 2 percent to 8.5 percent of it going to the load or sales charge. In addition, fees paid for tax advice may be deductible; commissions are not.

Fee-only financial planners will charge in one of three ways:

1. An hourly rate
2. A contracted price
3. A percentage of income or investments or both.

You pay only this fee. There are no hidden charges so you should save more in the long run.

Service

Commission-based or fee-basis advisors earn their income from a commission on the products they recommend or sell to you. Thus, there is less incentive to provide the best service for your needs. They need to sell products every year in order to earn their livings.

The fee-only financial planners need to give you good service because they earn their living from fees and only fees. Customer service and continued customer goodwill are very important to them.

Investment Focus

Fee-only financial planners will look at the entire range of products available to fit your plan. Instead of being limited to a few products, they search to find the investments best for your particular needs.

Commission-based or fee-basis advisors are narrowly focused on the products they are selling now. For example, they may push you towards whole life insurance when term is probably better for you.

Cost

Although a fee-basis advisor may appear less costly initially, many clients are unaware that the advisor receives a commission, usually 15 percent, on the products that the client buys. It is not always clear on the sales form how much the advisor is making because they do not want you to know. Ask them to tell you in dollars how much their service will cost you.

Actual Rate of Return

If a commission is taken out of your investment money, you have less to invest, so you get a lower rate of return over time. This adds up. Using the previous example of a load and no-load investment, if the commission is 8.5 percent and you have $10,000 to invest, you would lose $2,204 in ten years at an annual rate of 10 percent. Multiply this times the number of different investments a commission-based or fee-basis advisor may recommend. The total amount can be considerable, and it lowers your actual rate of return.

Implementation

Finally, you want a financial planner who will help you implement your plan. Some people think *implement* means selling you a product. It really means that your financial planner helps you put together your plan and then sees that you follow it. Fee-basis or commission-based advisors

Your planner ought to be a professional nag. An important part of financial planning is the process: meeting on a regular basis, gathering the data, and asking for the information. Your planner keeps the process moving so you don't get lost in procrastination or delay.

need to keep selling you products. There is no incentive for them to follow up on your plan with you.

Evaluating Advisors

To help you in evaluating potential financial planners, ask each potential planner to fill out the Financial Planner Interview form in Figure 12-1. It was developed by NAPFA and will help you in evaluating which person to choose.

FIGURE 12.1   Financial Planner Interview

How to Choose a Financial Planner

This form was created by the National Association of Personal Financial Advisors (NAPFA) to assist consumers in selecting a personal financial planner. It can be used as a checklist during an interview or sent to prospective planners as a part of a preliminary screening. NAPFA recommends that individuals from at least two different firms be interviewed.

BACKGROUND & EXPERIENCE

The backgrounds of financial planners can vary as much as the services offered. The planner's education and experience should demonstrate a solid foundation in financial planning and a commitment to keeping current. In addition to the following questions, ask the planner to describe his or her specific financial planning work experience.

1. What is your educational background?

_____ College degree   Area of study: _____

_____ Graduate degree   Area of study: _____

Financial planning education and designations:

_____ Certified Financial Planner (CFP)

_____ Chartered Financial Consultant (ChFC)

_____ CPA/PFS

_____ Other: _____

(Continued)

FIGURE 12.1 Financial Planner Interview (Continued)

2. How long have you been offering financial planning services?

_____ Less than 2 years

_____ 2–5 years

_____ More than 5 years

3. What continuing education in financial planning do you pursue?

_____ 1–14 hours of professional education each year

_____ 15–30 hours of professional education each year

_____ At least 30 hours of professional education each year

4. Are you a member of any professional financial planning associations?

_____ Institute of Certified Financial Planners (ICFP)

_____ National Association of Personal Financial Advisors (NAPFA)

_____ International Association for Financial Planning (IAFP)

_____ Other: _____

5. Will you provide me with references from clients?

_____ Yes   _____ No

6. Have you ever been cited by a professional or regulatory governing body for disciplinary reasons?

_____ Yes   _____ No

7. Will you or an associate work for me?

8. If an associate will work with me or assist you, please complete questions 1–6 for the associate as well.

SERVICES

Financial planners provide a range of services. It is important to match client needs with services provided.

1. Does your financial planning service include:

_____ A review of my goals

FIGURE 12.1   Financial Planner Interview (Continued)

Advice on:

_____ Cash management and budgeting

_____ Tax planning

_____ Investment review and planning

_____ Estate planning

_____ Insurance needs in the area of life, disability, health, and property/casualty

_____ Retirement planning

_____ Other

2. Do you provide a written analysis of my financial situation and recommendations?

    _____ Yes   _____ No

    Is the analysis tailored to my personal needs and goals?

    _____ Yes   _____ No

3. Does your financial planning service include recommendations for specific investments or investment products?

    _____ Yes   _____ No

    Do you offer assistance with implementation?

    _____ Yes   _____ No

4. Do you offer continuous, ongoing advice regarding my financial affairs, including advice on non-investment financial issues?

    _____ Yes   _____ No

5. Do you take possession of, or have access to, my assets?

    _____ Yes   _____ No

(Continued)

FIGURE 12.1   Financial Planner Interview (Continued)

COMPENSATION

Financial planning costs include what a consumer pays in fees and commissions. Comparison between planners requires full information about potential total costs. It is important to have this information before entering into any agreement.

1. How is your firm compensated?

   _____ Fee only

   _____ Commission only

   _____ Fee and commissions

   _____ Fee offset

   How is your compensation calculated?

   _____ Fee only (as calculated below)

   Based on hourly rate of $ _____

   Flat fee or fee range of _____

   Percentage (_____ %) of _____

   Are fees capped?   _____ Yes   _____ No

   _____ Commission only (from securities, insurance, etc.) that clients buy from a firm with which you are associated.

   _____ Fee and commission ("Fee based")

   _____ Fee offset. You charge a flat fee against which commissions are offset. If the commissions exceed the fee, is the balance credited to me?

   _____ Yes   _____ No

2. If you earn commissions, approximately what percentage of your firm's commission income comes from:

   _____ % Insurance products   _____ % Stocks and bonds

   _____ % Annuities   _____ % Coins, tangibles, collectibles

   _____ % Mutual funds   _____ % Other (explain) _____

   _____ % Limited Partnerships   100   %

FIGURE 12.1   Financial Planner Interview (Continued)

3. Does any member of your firm act as a general partner, participate in or receive compensation from investments you may recommend to me?

_____ Yes   _____ No

[Note: the Securities and Exchange Commission (SEC) requires that this information be disclosed.]

REGULATORY COMPLIANCE

The SEC requires if an individual or firm hold out to the public as providing financial planning services, that under most circumstances, they are required to be registered with either the SEC or the state in which the individual practices.

1. Are you or your firm registered as an Investment Advisor with the U.S. Securities and Exchange Commission and/or with the appropriate regulatory authorities in this state?

_____ Yes   _____ No

If *NO*, please indicate the allowable reason for nonregistration:

_____

_____

_____

Please provide a copy of your registration with the Securities and Exchange Commission (Form ADV Part II) and/or your state, as required by the SEC under the Investment Advisors Act of 1940 and subsequent changes.

_____

Signature of Planner

_____

Firm Name

_____

Date

COPYRIGHT © 1999 THE NATIONAL ASSOCIATION OF PERSONAL FINANCIAL ADVISORS
355 West Dundee Road, Suite 200
Buffalo Grove, IL 60089
1-888-FEE-ONLY
www.napfa.org

Conclusion

If you earn more than $50,000 per year or have complicated items such as trusts, you probably will need to work with a financial planner. Why? Most people benefit from the advice of a financial planner simply because the marketplace for investments, insurance, trusts, and so on, is constantly changing and expanding.

Whether you are choosing a financial planner or getting expert advice on a specific part of your financial plan such as insurance, remember *you* are in charge. It's your money and you want the best advice you can get. Because you took the time to prepare your financial plan with the help of this book, you will be well prepared to discuss your needs with financial experts.

> **D**o not try to keep some information from your planner because you think it is embarrassing or irrelevant. As a financial planner I wear many hats: my psychologist hat, my marriage counselor hat, my preacher hat, and my financial professional hat. If the emotional connection is not there to trust this particular planner, then you have selected the wrong one.

Summary

A *financial planner* is a trained professional who assists you in performing the six steps of the financial planning process, provides unbiased advice, and works for a fee that you pay. There are three types of financial planners today: fee-based (or commission-based) advisors, fee-basis advisors, and fee-only financial planners. *Financial advisors* can be a stockbroker, an accountant, an attorney, or someone else.

Fee-based means the advisors make their living by selling products such as life insurance or stocks. Fee-basis means that the advisor will charge you a fee but will also make a commission or receive some other direct or indirect compensation for recommending certain products to you. Fee-only financial planners receive fees for the services they provide to their clients. That is the only source of their income.

13

Congratulations!

Congratulations! You've learned a lot about yourself, your goals, and your financial situation since you first picked up this book. Depending on your personal circumstances, you should have completed your own financial plan or be better equipped to meet with your financial advisors to set up your financial plan.

What's that? You didn't bother to do any of the worksheets in the book because:

- "It looked like too much work."
- "I don't have the time."
- "I already know my financial situation."

Let me repeat my message: *If you have truly understood Chapter 1 of this book, then you know that you must have a financial plan if you want to become financially independent.* Yes, it is work. But it's your money. Who cares more about it than you? Yes, it takes time, but not as much time as you fear once you set up your plan.

Do you really, honestly know your net worth? How much must you save each year in order to retire when you want with the resources you want? Are you adequately covered by life and disability insurance until your investments will cover

Is your planner following up with you on a timely basis? You should meet at least once a year, or more if you have some life-changing event occur. Is your planner reminding you to update your records every month?

the gap between what you want and what you have? What will happen to your family if you die today? These are only a few of the important questions that you need to know the answers to for your and your family's peace of mind.

In my almost 30 years experience as a financial planner, I've found that most people do not know the answers to these kinds of questions unless they have done a financial plan and review and update it annually.

The Myth of the "Great Deal"

One final word to those who may still think that all they have to do to "get ahead" is get a "hot tip," make a "big deal," or score a financial "home run." Let's suppose that you have come up with a great business idea—a product or service that everyone needs. All you need is some financial backing to get your idea into production. Where would you go to get the money? You'd probably ask your friends and relatives first if they would give you support. After all, they know you best. Next you'd probably go to your banker, who's loaned you money before. If those two sources didn't raise enough money, you might consider approaching the "big money" in your town. You know, the movers and shakers who are always looking to get in on the ground floor.

What if you still needed more financial backing? Who could you turn to? There are brokers, venture capitalist types who look for businesses to invest in. Where do they get their money? Well, if your business looked like a really good opportunity, they would sell it to their best clients first.

Who gets the last shot at this great business deal you've cooked up? You guessed it, the turkeys, those at the bottom of the list (Figure 13.1).

When you get a call from someone you don't know trying to sell you a great deal, stop and think. By the time a deal gets to you, it has been rejected by every thinking mind in the business community.

Stick with your financial plan. You can manage to be wealthy if you prepare a well-thought out financial plan, make a commitment to the plan, and then take action. Your financial planner can help you do this, but remember it is *your* plan. You must take action. The best financial plan is useless if it sits on the shelf.

Is your planner using financial software to run "what if" scenarios for you? Should you buy a financial software package for yourself?

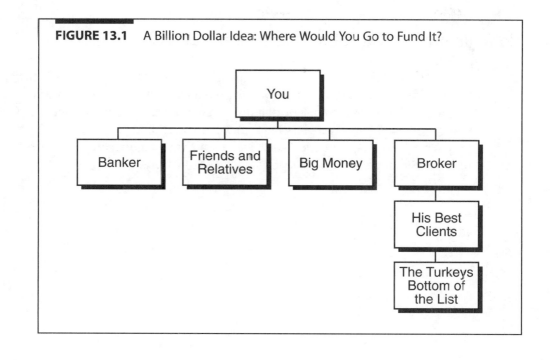

FIGURE 13.1   A Billion Dollar Idea: Where Would You Go to Fund It?

Additional Resources

Let me just remind you again that there is a wealth of financial information available. Sometimes it seems like there is too much to absorb. You must develop discernment as to what is useful and what is a sales pitch, what will help you reach your goals, and what will sidetrack you. Your financial planner can guide you to the right resources.

If you have a computer, find out which financial software might help in recordkeeping and analysis of your plan. This area changes so rapidly that rather than make recommendations, I invite you to visit our web site at www.sestina.com to learn about financial software and other resources. In addition, we have several different areas that will help you with your plan, whether you're just starting out or need more complex questions answered.

Don't forget the resources available at your public library. Larger city libraries have business sections that are very helpful, and interlibrary loans can bring almost any publication to you. If you don't have a computer or access to the Internet, your library probably does.

Conclusion: It's Your Money and Your Future!

I know you can do this. I've seen people turn their lives around after they put together financial plans. Any time you feel yourself tempted by what everyone else is doing—that is, reacting, not planning—go back and reread Chapter 1. Once you've followed your financial plan for a year, you should be able to see the results on your balance sheet and net worth statement. You can manage to be wealthy by following your personal financial plan.

Appendix A:
Reference Tables

These reference tables are used in the financial service industry to provide answers to questions like: How much will this investment be worth in 10 years at 8 percent? If I have X dollars when I retire and spend Y dollars every year, how long will my money last?

Refer to Chapters 2, 4, and 5 for the specifics of when and where to use each table in your financial planning.

TABLE A.1 Inflation Adjustment Factor

To have the same one dollar, you will need:						
IF INFLATION IS:						
Years	**4%**	**5%**	**6%**	**7%**	**8%**	**9%**	**10%**
1	1.0400	1.0500	1.0600	1.0700	1.0800	1.0900	1.1000
2	1.0816	1.1025	1.1236	1.1449	1.1664	1.1881	1.2100
3	1.1249	1.1576	1.1910	1.2250	1.2597	1.2950	1.3310
4	1.1699	1.2155	1.2625	1.3108	1.3605	1.4116	1.4641
5	1.2167	1.2763	1.3382	1.4026	1.4693	1.5386	1.6105
6	1.2653	1.3401	1.4185	1.5007	1.5869	1.6771	1.7716
7	1.3159	1.4071	1.5036	1.6058	1.7138	1.8280	1.9487
8	1.3686	1.4775	1.5938	1.7182	1.8509	1.9926	2.1436
9	1.4233	1.5513	1.6895	1.8385	1.9990	2.1719	2.3579
10	1.4802	1.6289	1.7908	1.9672	2.1589	2.3674	2.5937
11	1.5395	1.7103	1.8983	2.1049	2.3316	2.5804	2.8531
12	1.6010	1.7959	2.0122	2.2522	2.5182	2.8127	3.1384
13	1.6651	1.8856	2.1329	2.4098	2.7196	3.0658	3.4523
14	1.7317	1.9799	2.2609	2.5785	2.9372	3.3417	3.7975
15	1.8009	2.0789	2.3966	2.7590	3.1722	3.6425	4.1772
16	1.8730	2.1829	2.5404	2.9522	3.4259	3.9703	4.5950
17	1.9479	2.2920	2.6928	3.1588	3.7000	4.3276	5.0545
18	2.0258	2.4066	2.8543	3.3799	3.9960	4.7171	5.5599
19	2.1068	2.5270	3.0256	3.6165	4.3157	5.1417	6.1159
20	2.1911	2.6533	3.2071	3.8697	4.6610	5.6044	6.7275
21	2.2788	2.7860	3.3996	4.1406	5.0338	6.1088	7.4002
22	2.3699	2.9253	3.6035	4.4304	5.4365	6.6586	8.1403
23	2.4647	3.0715	3.8197	4.7405	5.8715	7.2579	8.9543
24	2.5633	3.2251	4.0489	5.0724	6.3412	7.9111	9.8497
25	2.6658	3.3864	4.2919	5.4274	6.8485	8.6231	10.8347
26	2.7725	3.5557	4.5494	5.8074	7.3964	9.3992	11.9182
27	2.8834	3.7335	4.8223	6.2139	7.9881	10.2451	13.1100
28	2.9987	3.9201	5.1117	6.6488	8.6271	11.1671	14.4210
29	3.1187	4.1161	5.4184	7.1143	9.3173	12.1722	15.8631
30	3.2434	4.3219	5.7435	7.6123	10.0627	13.2677	17.4494
31	3.3731	4.5380	6.0881	8.1451	10.8677	14.4618	19.1943
32	3.5081	4.7649	6.4534	8.7153	11.7371	15.7633	21.1138
33	3.6484	5.0032	6.8406	9.3253	12.6760	17.1820	23.2252

TABLE A.1 Inflation Adjustment Factor (Continued)

	To have the same one dollar, you will need:						
	IF INFLATION IS:						
Years	**4%**	**5%**	**6%**	**7%**	**8%**	**9%**	**10%**
34	3.7943	5.2533	7.2510	9.9781	13.6901	18.7284	25.5477
35	3.9461	5.5160	7.6861	10.6766	14.7853	20.4140	28.1024
36	4.1039	5.7918	8.1473	11.4239	15.9682	22.2512	30.9127
37	4.2681	6.0814	8.6361	12.2236	17.2456	24.2538	34.0039
38	4.4388	6.3855	9.1543	13.0793	18.6253	26.4367	37.4043
39	4.6164	6.7043	9.7035	13.9948	20.1153	28.8160	41.1448
40	4.8010	7.0400	10.2857	14.9745	21.7245	31.4094	45.2593

Formula for Table A.1 Inflation Adjustment Factor

To get the factor for a different inflation rate, use this formula.

$$Factor = (1 + i)^N$$ where i = the inflation rate you want, and
N = the number of years you want

For example, to find the factor for 0.056 (5.6 percent) for three years, the calculation would be:

$$Factor = (1 + 0.056)^3$$
$$= (1.056)^3$$
$$= 1.178$$

TABLE A.2 Compound Interest Factor

Your present investments will be worth:						
IF THEY ARE GROWING AT:						
Years	**4%**	**5%**	**6%**	**7%**	**8%**	**9%**	**10%**
1	1.0400	1.0500	1.0600	1.0700	1.0800	1.0900	1.1000
2	1.0816	1.1025	1.1236	1.1449	1.1664	1.1881	1.2100
3	1.1249	1.1576	1.1910	1.2250	1.2597	1.2950	1.3310
4	1.1699	1.2155	1.2625	1.3108	1.3605	1.4116	1.4641
5	1.2167	1.2763	1.3382	1.4026	1.4693	1.5386	1.6105
6	1.2653	1.3401	1.4185	1.5007	1.5869	1.6771	1.7716
7	1.3159	1.4071	1.5036	1.6058	1.7138	1.8280	1.9487
8	1.3686	1.4775	1.5938	1.7182	1.8509	1.9926	2.1436
9	1.4233	1.5513	1.6895	1.8385	1.9990	2.1719	2.3579
10	1.4802	1.6289	1.7908	1.9672	2.1589	2.3674	2.5937
11	1.5395	1.7103	1.8983	2.1049	2.3316	2.5804	2.8531
12	1.6010	1.7959	2.0122	2.2522	2.5182	2.8127	3.1384
13	1.6651	1.8856	2.1329	2.4098	2.7196	3.0658	3.4523
14	1.7317	1.9799	2.2609	2.5785	2.9372	3.3417	3.7975
15	1.8009	2.0789	2.3966	2.7590	3.1722	3.6425	4.1772
16	1.8730	2.1829	2.5404	2.9522	3.4259	3.9703	4.5950
17	1.9479	2.2920	2.6928	3.1588	3.7000	4.3276	5.0545
18	2.0258	2.4066	2.8543	3.3799	3.9960	4.7171	5.5599
19	2.1068	2.5270	3.0256	3.6165	4.3157	5.1417	6.1159
20	2.1911	2.6533	3.2071	3.8697	4.6610	5.6044	6.7275
21	2.2788	2.7860	3.3996	4.1406	5.0338	6.1088	7.4002
22	2.3699	2.9253	3.6035	4.4304	5.4365	6.6586	8.1403
23	2.4647	3.0715	3.8197	4.7405	5.8715	7.2579	8.9543
24	2.5633	3.2251	4.0489	5.0724	6.3412	7.9111	9.8497
25	2.6658	3.3864	4.2919	5.4274	6.8485	8.6231	10.8347
26	2.7725	3.5557	4.5494	5.8074	7.3964	9.3992	11.9182
27	2.8834	3.7335	4.8223	6.2139	7.9881	10.2451	13.1100
28	2.9987	3.9201	5.1117	6.6488	8.6271	11.1671	14.4210
29	3.1187	4.1161	5.4184	7.1143	9.3173	12.1722	15.8631
30	3.2434	4.3219	5.7435	7.6123	10.0627	13.2677	17.4494
31	3.3731	4.5380	6.0881	8.1451	10.8677	14.4618	19.1943
32	3.5081	4.7649	6.4534	8.7153	11.7371	15.7633	21.1138
33	3.6484	5.0032	6.8406	9.3253	12.6760	17.1820	23.2252

TABLE A.2 Compound Interest Factor (Continued)

	Your present investments will be worth:						
	IF THEY ARE GROWING AT:						
Years	**4%**	**5%**	**6%**	**7%**	**8%**	**9%**	**10%**
34	3.7943	5.2533	7.2510	9.9781	13.6901	18.7284	25.5477
35	3.9461	5.5160	7.6861	10.6766	14.7853	20.4140	28.1024
36	4.1039	5.7918	8.1473	11.4239	15.9682	22.2512	30.9127
37	4.2681	6.0814	8.6361	12.2236	17.2456	24.2538	34.0039
38	4.4388	6.3855	9.1543	13.0793	18.6253	26.4367	37.4043
39	4.6164	6.7048	9.7035	13.9948	20.1153	28.8160	41.1448
40	4.8010	7.0400	10.2857	14.9745	21.7245	31.4094	45.2593

Formula for Table A.2 Compound Interest Factor

To get the factor for a different interest rate, use this formula.

Factor = $(1 + i)^N$ where i = the interest rate you want, and
N = the number of years you want

For example, to find the factor for 0.056 (5.6 percent) for three years, the calculation would be:

Factor = $(1 + 0.056)^3$
= $(1.056)^3$
= 1.178

TABLE A.3 Annual Investment Factor

If you need one dollar in the future, you will need to invest each year:

Years	IF YOU CAN EARN: 4%	5%	6%	7%	8%	9%	10%
1	1.0000	1.0000	1.0000	1.0000	1.0000	1.0000	1.0000
2	0.4902	0.4878	0.4854	0.4831	0.4808	0.4785	0.4762
3	0.3203	0.3172	0.3141	0.3111	0.3080	0.3051	0.3021
4	0.2355	0.2320	0.2286	0.2252	0.2219	0.2187	0.2155
5	0.1846	0.1810	0.1774	0.1739	0.1705	0.1671	0.1638
6	0.1508	0.1470	0.1434	0.1398	0.1363	0.1329	0.1296
7	0.1266	0.1228	0.1191	0.1156	0.1121	0.1087	0.1054
8	0.1085	0.1047	0.1010	0.0975	0.0940	0.0907	0.0874
9	0.0945	0.0907	0.0870	0.0835	0.0801	0.0768	0.0736
10	0.0833	0.0795	0.0759	0.0724	0.0690	0.0658	0.0627
11	0.0741	0.0704	0.0668	0.0634	0.0601	0.0569	0.0540
12	0.0666	0.0628	0.0593	0.0559	0.0527	0.0497	0.0468
13	0.0601	0.0565	0.0530	0.0497	0.0465	0.0436	0.0408
14	0.0547	0.0510	0.0476	0.0443	0.0413	0.0384	0.0357
15	0.0499	0.0463	0.0430	0.0398	0.0368	0.0341	0.0315
16	0.0458	0.0423	0.0390	0.0359	0.0330	0.0303	0.0278
17	0.0422	0.0387	0.0354	0.0324	0.0296	0.0270	0.0247
18	0.0390	0.0355	0.0324	0.0294	0.0267	0.0242	0.0219
19	0.0361	0.0327	0.0296	0.0268	0.0241	0.0217	0.0195
20	0.0336	0.0302	0.0272	0.0244	0.0219	0.0195	0.0175
21	0.0313	0.0280	0.0250	0.0223	0.0198	0.0176	0.0156
22	0.0292	0.0260	0.0230	0.0204	0.0180	0.0159	0.0140
23	0.0273	0.0241	0.0213	0.0187	0.0164	0.0144	0.0126
24	0.0256	0.0225	0.0197	0.0172	0.0150	0.0130	0.0113
25	0.0240	0.0210	0.0182	0.0158	0.0137	0.0118	0.0102
26	0.0226	0.0196	0.0169	0.0146	0.0125	0.0107	0.0092
27	0.0212	0.0183	0.0157	0.0134	0.0114	0.0097	0.0083
28	0.0200	0.0171	0.0146	0.0124	0.0105	0.0089	0.0075
29	0.0189	0.0160	0.0136	0.0114	0.0096	0.0081	0.0067
30	0.0178	0.0151	0.0126	0.0106	0.0088	0.0073	0.0061
31	0.0169	0.0141	0.0118	0.0098	0.0081	0.0067	0.0055
32	0.0159	0.0133	0.0110	0.0091	0.0075	0.0061	0.0050
33	0.0151	0.0125	0.0103	0.0084	0.0069	0.0056	0.0045

TABLE A.3 Annual Investment Factor (Continued)

	If you need one dollar in the future, you will need to invest each year:						
	IF YOU CAN EARN:						
Years	**4%**	**5%**	**6%**	**7%**	**8%**	**9%**	**10%**
34	0.0143	0.0118	0.0096	0.0078	0.0063	0.0051	0.0041
35	0.0136	0.0111	0.0090	0.0072	0.0058	0.0046	0.0037
36	0.0129	0.0104	0.0084	0.0067	0.0053	0.0042	0.0033
37	0.0122	0.0098	0.0079	0.0062	0.0049	0.0039	0.0030
38	0.0116	0.0093	0.0074	0.0058	0.0045	0.0035	0.0027
39	0.0111	0.0088	0.0069	0.0054	0.0042	0.0032	0.0025
40	0.0105	0.0083	0.0065	0.0050	0.0039	0.0030	0.0023

Formula for Table A.3 Annual Investment Factor

To get the factor for a different interest rate, use this formula.

$$\text{Factor} = FV/(((1 + i)^N - 1)/i)$$ where FV = the future value you want,
i = the interest rate you want, and
N = the number of years you want

For example, to find the factor for $1 at an interest rate of 0.056 (5.6%) for three years, the calculation would be:

$$
\begin{aligned}
\text{Factor} &= 1/(((1 + 0.056)^3 - 1)/0.056) \\
&= 1/(((1.056)^3 - 1)/0.056) \\
&= 1/((1.178 - 1)/0.056) \\
&= 1/(0.178/0.056) \\
&= 1/3.179 \\
&= 0.3146
\end{aligned}
$$

TABLE A.4 Lump Sum Factor

If you need one dollar in the future, you need to have this lump sum today:						
IF YOU CAN EARN:						
Years	**4%**	**5%**	**6%**	**7%**	**8%**	**9%**	**10%**
1	0.9615	0.9524	0.9434	0.9346	0.9259	0.9174	0.9091
2	0.9246	0.9070	0.8900	0.8734	0.8573	0.8417	0.8264
3	0.8890	0.8638	0.8396	0.8163	0.7938	0.7722	0.7513
4	0.8548	0.8227	0.7921	0.7629	0.7350	0.7084	0.6830
5	0.8219	0.7835	0.7473	0.7130	0.6806	0.6499	0.6209
6	0.7903	0.7462	0.7050	0.6663	0.6302	0.5963	0.5645
7	0.7599	0.7107	0.6651	0.6227	0.5835	0.5470	0.5132
8	0.7307	0.6768	0.6274	0.5820	0.5403	0.5019	0.4665
9	0.7026	0.6446	0.5919	0.5439	0.5002	0.4604	0.4241
10	0.6756	0.6139	0.5584	0.5083	0.4632	0.4224	0.3855
11	0.6496	0.5847	0.5268	0.4751	0.4289	0.3875	0.3505
12	0.6246	0.5568	0.4970	0.4440	0.3971	0.3555	0.3186
13	0.6006	0.5303	0.4688	0.4150	0.3677	0.3262	0.2897
14	0.5775	0.5051	0.4423	0.3878	0.3405	0.2992	0.2633
15	0.5553	0.4810	0.4173	0.3624	0.3152	0.2745	0.2394
16	0.5339	0.4581	0.3936	0.3387	0.2919	0.2519	0.2176
17	0.5134	0.4363	0.3714	0.3166	0.2703	0.2311	0.1978
18	0.4936	0.4155	0.3503	0.2959	0.2502	0.2120	0.1799
19	0.4746	0.3957	0.3305	0.2765	0.2317	0.1945	0.1635
20	0.4564	0.3769	0.3118	0.2584	0.2145	0.1784	0.1486
21	0.4388	0.3589	0.2942	0.2415	0.1987	0.1637	0.1351
22	0.4220	0.3418	0.2775	0.2257	0.1839	0.1502	0.1228
23	0.4057	0.3256	0.2618	0.2109	0.1703	0.1378	0.1117
24	0.3901	0.3101	0.2470	0.1971	0.1577	0.1264	0.1015
25	0.3751	0.2953	0.2330	0.1842	0.1460	0.1160	0.0923
26	0.3607	0.2812	0.2198	0.1722	0.1352	0.1064	0.0839
27	0.3468	0.2678	0.2074	0.1609	0.1252	0.0976	0.0763
28	0.3335	0.2551	0.1956	0.1504	0.1159	0.0895	0.0693
29	0.3207	0.2429	0.1846	0.1406	0.1073	0.0822	0.0630
30	0.3083	0.2314	0.1741	0.1314	0.0994	0.0754	0.0573
31	0.2965	0.2204	0.1643	0.1228	0.0920	0.0691	0.0521
32	0.2851	0.2099	0.1550	0.1147	0.0852	0.0634	0.0474
33	0.2741	0.1999	0.1462	0.1072	0.0789	0.0582	0.0431

TABLE A.4 Lump Sum Factor (Continued)

If you need one dollar in the future, you need to have this lump sum today:						
	IF YOU CAN EARN:					
Years	**4%**	**5%**	**6%**	**7%**	**8%**	**9%**	**10%**
34	0.2636	0.1904	0.1379	0.1002	0.0730	0.0534	0.0391
35	0.2534	0.1813	0.1301	0.0937	0.0676	0.0490	0.0356
36	0.2437	0.1727	0.1227	0.0875	0.0626	0.0449	0.0323
37	0.2343	0.1644	0.1158	0.0818	0.0580	0.0412	0.0294
38	0.2253	0.1566	0.1092	0.0765	0.0537	0.0378	0.0267
39	0.2166	0.1491	0.1031	0.0715	0.0497	0.0347	0.0243
40	0.2083	0.1420	0.0972	0.0668	0.0460	0.0318	0.0221

Formula for Table A.4 Lump Sum Factor

To get the factor for a different interest rate, use this formula.

Factor = $FV/(1 + i)^N$ where FV = the future value you want,

$\qquad\qquad\qquad\qquad$ i = the interest rate you want, and

$\qquad\qquad\qquad\qquad$ N = the number of years you want

For example, to find the factor for $1 at an interest rate of 0.056 (5.6%) for three years, the calculation would be:

$$\text{Factor} = 1/(1 + 0.056)^3$$
$$= 1/(1 .056)^3$$
$$= 1/1.178$$
$$= 0.85$$

TABLE A.5 Payout Factor

If you take one dollar each year, you will need to have this lump sum today:

Years	IF YOU CAN EARN: 4%	5%	6%	7%	8%	9%	10%
1	0.9615	0.9524	0.9434	0.9346	0.9259	0.9174	0.9091
2	1.8861	1.8594	1.8334	1.8080	1.7833	1.7591	1.7355
3	2.7751	2.7232	2.6730	2.6243	2.5771	2.5313	2.4869
4	3.6299	3.5460	3.4651	3.3872	3.3121	3.2397	3.1699
5	4.4518	4.3295	4.2124	4.1002	3.9927	3.8897	3.7908
6	5.2421	5.0757	4.9173	4.7665	4.6229	4.4859	4.3553
7	6.0021	5.7864	5.5824	5.3893	5.2064	5.0330	4.8684
8	6.7327	6.4632	6.2098	5.9713	5.7466	5.5348	5.3349
9	7.4353	7.1078	6.8017	6.5152	6.2469	5.9952	5.7590
10	8.1109	7.7217	7.3601	7.0236	6.7101	6.4177	6.1446
11	8.7605	8.3064	7.8869	7.4987	7.1390	6.8052	6.4951
12	9.3851	8.8633	8.3838	7.9427	7.5361	7.1607	6.8137
13	9.9856	9.3936	8.8527	8.3577	7.9038	7.4869	7.1034
14	10.5631	9.8986	9.2950	8.7455	8.2442	7.7862	7.3667
15	11.1184	10.3797	9.7122	9.1079	8.5595	8.0607	7.6061
16	11.6523	10.8378	10.1059	9.4466	8.8514	8.3126	7.8237
17	12.1657	11.2741	10.4773	9.7632	9.1216	8.5436	8.0216
18	12.6593	11.6896	10.8276	10.0591	9.3719	8.7556	8.2014
19	13.1339	12.0853	11.1581	10.3356	9.6036	8.9501	8.3649
20	13.5903	12.4622	11.4699	10.5940	9.8181	9.1285	8.5136
21	14.0292	12.8212	11.7641	10.8355	10.0168	9.2922	8.6487
22	14.4511	13.1630	12.0416	11.0612	10.2007	9.4424	8.7715
23	14.8568	13.4886	12.3034	11.2722	10.3711	9.5802	8.8832
24	15.2470	13.7986	12.5504	11.4693	10.5288	9.7066	8.9847
25	15.6221	14.0939	12.7834	11.6536	10.6748	9.8226	9.0770
26	15.9828	14.3752	13.0032	11.8258	10.8100	9.9290	9.1609
27	16.3296	14.6430	13.2105	11.9867	10.9352	10.0266	9.2372
28	16.6631	14.8981	13.4062	12.1371	11.0511	10.1161	9.3066
29	16.9837	15.1411	13.5907	12.2777	11.1584	10.1983	9.3696
30	17.2920	15.3725	13.7648	12.4090	11.2578	10.2737	9.4269
31	17.5885	15.5928	13.9291	12.5318	11.3498	10.3428	9.4790
32	17.8736	15.8027	14.0840	12.6466	11.4350	10.4062	9.5264
33	18.1476	16.0025	14.2302	12.7538	11.5139	10.4644	9.5694

TABLE A.5 Payout Factor (Continued)

	If you take one dollar each year, you will need to have this lump sum today:						
	IF YOU CAN EARN:						
Years	**4%**	**5%**	**6%**	**7%**	**8%**	**9%**	**10%**
34	18.4112	16.1929	14.3681	12.8540	11.5869	10.5178	9.6086
35	18.6646	16.3742	14.4982	12.9477	11.6546	10.5668	9.6442
36	18.9083	16.5469	14.6210	13.0352	11.7172	10.6118	9.6765
37	19.1426	16.7113	14.7363	13.1170	11.7752	10.6530	9.7059
38	19.3679	16.8679	14.8460	13.1935	11.8289	10.6908	9.7327
39	19.5845	17.0170	14.9491	13.2649	11.8786	10.7255	9.7570
40	19.7928	17.1591	15.0463	13.3317	11.9246	10.7574	9.7791

Formula for Table A.5 Payout Factor

To get the factor for a different interest rate, use this formula.

Factor = PMT × $((1 − (1 / (1+i)^N)) / i)$ where PMT = payment you want,

$\qquad\qquad\qquad\qquad\qquad\qquad$ i = the interest rate you want, and

$\qquad\qquad\qquad\qquad\qquad\qquad$ N = the number of years you want

For example, to find the factor for taking out $1 each year for three years at an interest rate of 0.056 (5.6 percent), the calculation would be:

$$Factor = 1 \times ((1 − (1 / (1 + 0.056)^3)) / 0.056)$$
$$= 1 \times ((1 − (1 / (1.056)^3)) / 0.056)$$
$$= 1 \times ((1 − (1 / 1.178)) / 0.056)$$
$$= 1 \times ((1 − 0.849) / 0.056)$$
$$= 1 \times (0.151 / 0.056)$$
$$= 1 \times 2.696$$
$$= 2.696$$

TABLE A.6 Future Value Factor

If you invest one dollar each year it will be worth:						

| | IF YOU CAN EARN: | | | | | | |
Years	4%	5%	6%	7%	8%	9%	10%
1	1.0000	1.0000	1.0000	1.0000	1.0000	1.0000	1.0000
2	2.0400	2.0500	2.0600	2.0700	2.0800	2.0900	2.1000
3	3.1216	3.1525	3.1836	3.2149	3.2464	3.2781	3.3100
4	4.2465	4.3101	4.3746	4.4399	4.5061	4.5731	4.6410
5	5.4163	5.5256	5.6371	5.7507	5.8666	5.9847	6.1051
6	6.6330	6.8019	6.9753	7.1533	7.3359	7.5233	7.7156
7	7.8983	8.1420	8.3938	8.6540	8.9228	9.2004	9.4872
8	9.2142	9.5491	9.8975	10.2598	10.6366	11.0285	11.4359
9	10.5828	11.0266	11.4913	11.9780	12.4876	13.0210	13.5795
10	12.0061	12.5779	13.1808	13.8164	14.4866	15.1929	15.9374
11	13.4864	14.2068	14.9716	15.7836	16.6455	17.5603	18.5312
12	15.0258	15.9171	16.8699	17.8885	18.9771	20.1407	21.3843
13	16.6268	17.7130	18.8821	20.1406	21.4953	22.9534	24.5227
14	18.2919	19.5986	21.0151	22.5505	24.2149	26.0192	27.9750
15	20.0236	21.5786	23.2760	25.1290	27.1521	29.3609	31.7725
16	21.8245	23.6575	25.6725	27.8881	30.3243	33.0034	35.9497
17	23.6975	25.8404	28.2129	30.8402	33.7502	36.9737	40.5447
18	25.6454	28.1324	30.9057	33.9990	37.4502	41.3013	45.5992
19	27.6712	30.5390	33.7600	37.3790	41.4463	46.0185	51.1591
20	29.7781	33.0660	36.7856	40.9955	45.7620	51.1601	57.2750
21	31.9692	35.7193	39.9927	44.8652	50.4229	56.7645	64.0025
22	34.2480	38.5052	43.3923	49.0057	55.4568	62.8733	71.4027
23	36.6179	41.4305	46.9958	53.4361	60.8933	69.5319	79.5430
24	39.0826	44.5020	50.8156	58.1767	66.7648	76.7898	88.4973
25	41.6459	47.7271	54.8645	63.2490	73.1059	84.7009	98.3471
26	44.3117	51.1135	59.1564	68.6765	79.9544	93.3240	109.1818
27	47.0842	54.6691	63.7058	74.4838	87.3508	102.7231	121.0999
28	49.9676	58.4026	68.5281	80.6977	95.3388	112.9682	134.2099
29	52.9663	62.3227	73.6398	87.3465	103.9659	124.1354	148.6309
30	56.0849	66.4388	79.0582	94.4608	113.2832	136.3075	164.4940
31	59.3283	70.7608	84.8017	102.0730	123.3459	149.5752	181.9434
32	62.7015	75.2988	90.8898	110.2182	134.2135	164.0370	201.1378
33	66.2095	80.0638	97.3432	118.9334	145.9506	179.8003	222.2515

TABLE A.6 Future Value Factor (Continued)

	If you invest one dollar each year it will be worth:						
	IF YOU CAN EARN:						
Years	**4%**	**5%**	**6%**	**7%**	**8%**	**9%**	**10%**
34	69.8579	85.0670	104.1838	128.2588	158.6267	196.9823	245.4767
35	73.6522	90.3203	111.4348	138.2369	172.3168	215.7108	271.0244
36	77.5983	95.8363	119.1209	148.9135	187.1021	236.1247	299.1268
37	81.7022	101.6281	127.2681	160.3374	203.0703	258.3759	330.0395
38	85.9703	107.7095	135.9042	172.5610	220.3159	282.6298	364.0434
39	90.4091	114.0950	145.0585	185.6403	238.9412	309.0665	401.4478
40	95.0255	120.7998	154.7620	199.6351	259.0565	337.8824	442.5926

Formula for Table A.6 Future Value Factor

To get the factor for a different interest rate, use this formula.

Factor = PMT × (((1 + i)^N − 1) / i) where PMT = payment you want to invest each year,

i = the interest rate you want, and

N = the number of years you want

For example, to find the factor for the future value of $1 in three years at an interest rate of 0.056 (5.6 percent), the calculation would be:

Factor = 1 × (((1 + 0.056)^3 − 1) / 0.056)

= 1 × (((1.056)^3 − 1) / 0.056)

= 1 × ((1.178 − 1) / 0.056)

= 1 × (0.178 / 0.056)

= 1 × 3.179

= 3.179

TABLE A.7 Life Expectancy Table

1980 Commissioners Standard Ordinary Mortality Table				
Age	Male Mortality Rate Per 1,000	Male Expectancy, Years	Female Mortality Rate Per 1,000	Female Expectancy, Years
0	4.18	70.83	2.89	75.83
1	1.07	70.13	0.87	75.04
2	0.99	69.20	0.81	74.11
3	0.98	68.27	0.79	73.17
4	0.95	67.34	0.77	72.23
5	0.90	66.40	0.76	71.28
6	0.85	65.46	0.73	70.34
7	0.80	64.52	0.72	69.39
8	0.76	63.57	0.70	68.44
9	0.74	62.62	0.69	67.48
10	0.73	61.66	0.68	66.53
11	0.77	60.71	0.69	65.58
12	0.85	59.75	0.72	64.62
13	0.99	58.80	0.75	63.67
14	1.15	57.86	0.80	62.71
15	1.33	56.93	0.85	61.76
16	1.51	56.00	0.90	60.82
17	1.67	55.09	0.95	59.87
18	1.78	54.18	0.98	58.93
19	1.86	53.27	1.02	57.98
20	1.90	52.37	1.05	57.04
21	1.91	51.47	1.07	56.10
22	1.89	50.57	1.09	55.16
23	1.86	49.66	1.11	54.22
24	1.82	48.75	1.14	53.28
25	1.77	47.84	1.16	52.34
26	1.73	46.93	1.19	51.40
27	1.71	46.01	1.22	50.46
28	1.70	45.09	1.26	49.52
29	1.71	44.16	1.30	48.59
30	1.73	43.24	1.35	47.65
31	1.78	42.31	1.40	46.71
32	1.83	41.38	1.45	45.78
33	1.91	40.46	1.50	44.84

TABLE A.7 Life Expectancy Table (Continued)

1980 Commissioners Standard Ordinary Mortality Table			
Age	Male Mortality Rate Per 1,000	Male Expectancy, Years	Female Mortality Rate Per 1,000	Female Expectancy, Years
34	2.00	39.54	1.58	43.91
35	2.11	38.61	1.65	42.98
36	2.24	37.69	1.76	42.05
37	2.40	36.78	1.89	41.12
38	2.58	35.87	2.04	40.20
39	2.79	34.96	2.22	39.28
40	3.02	34.05	2.42	38.36
41	3.29	33.16	2.64	37.46
42	3.56	32.26	2.87	36.55
43	3.87	31.38	3.09	35.66
44	4.19	30.50	3.32	34.77
45	4.55	29.62	3.56	33.88
46	4.92	28.76	3.80	33.00
47	5.32	27.90	4.05	32.12
48	5.74	27.04	4.33	31.25
49	6.21	26.20	4.63	30.39
50	6.71	25.36	4.96	29.53
51	7.30	24.52	5.31	28.67
52	7.96	23.70	5.70	27.82
53	8.71	22.89	6.15	26.98
54	9.56	22.08	6.61	26.14
55	10.47	21.29	7.09	25.13
56	11.46	20.51	7.57	24.49
57	12.49	19.74	8.03	23.67
58	13.59	18.99	8.47	22.86
59	14.77	18.24	8.94	22.05
60	16.08	17.51	8.47	21.25
61	17.54	16.79	9.47	20.44
62	19.19	16.08	10.13	19.65
63	21.06	15.38	10.96	18.86
64	23.14	14.70	12.02	18.08
65	25.42	14.04	13.25	17.32
66	27.85	13.39	14.59	16.57
67	30.44	12.76	16.00	15.83

TABLE A.7 Life Expectancy Table (Continued)

	1980 Commissioners Standard Ordinary Mortality Table			
Age	**Male Mortality Rate Per 1,000**	**Male Expectancy, Years**	**Female Mortality Rate Per 1,000**	**Female Expectancy, Years**
68	33.19	12.14	17.43	15.10
69	36.17	11.54	18.84	14.38
70	39.51	10.96	20.36	13.67
71	43.30	10.39	22.11	12.97
72	47.65	9.84	24.23	12.28
73	52.64	9.30	26.87	11.60
74	58.19	8.79	30.11	10.95
75	64.19	8.31	33.93	10.32
76	70.53	7.84	42.97	9.71
77	77.12	7.40	48.04	9.12
78	83.90	6.97	53.45	8.55
79	91.05	6.57	49.53	8.01
80	98.84	6.18	65.99	7.48
81	107.48	5.80	73.60	6.98
82	117.25	5.44	82.40	6.49
83	128.26	5.09	92.53	6.03
84	140.25	4.77	103.81	5.59
85	152.95	4.46	116.10	5.18
86	166.09	4.18	129.29	4.80
87	179.55	3.91	143.32	4.43
88	193.27	3.66	158.18	4.09
89	207.29	3.41	173.94	3.77
90	221.77	3.18	190.75	3.45
91	236.98	2.94	208.87	3.15
92	253.45	2.70	228.81	2.85
93	272.11	2.44	251.51	2.55
94	295.90	2.17	279.31	2.24
95	329.96	1.87	317.32	1.91
96	384.55	1.54	375.74	1.56
97	480.20	1.20	474.97	1.21
98	657.98	0.84	655.85	0.84
99	1000.00	0.50	1000.00	0.50

TABLE A.8 Federal Estate and Gift Taxes

Unified Tax Rate Schedule				
If the Amount Is:		**Tentative Tax Is:**		
From	**To**	**Tax**	**+ %**	**On Excess Over**
$0	$10,000	$0	18	$0
10,000	20,000	1,800	20	10,000
20,000	40,000	3,800	22	20,000
40,000	60,000	8,200	24	40,000
60,000	80,000	13,000	26	60,000
80,000	100,000	18,200	28	80,000
100,000	150,000	23,800	30	100,000
150,000	250,000	38,800	32	150,000
250,000	500,000	70,800	34	250,000
500,000	750,000	155,800	37	500,000
750,000	1,000,000	248,300	39	750,000
1,000,000	1,250,000	345,800	41	1,000,000
1,250,000	1,500,000	448,300	43	1,250,000
1,500,000	2,000,000	555,800	45	1,500,000
2,000,000	2,500,000	780,800	49	2,000,000
2,500,000	3,000,000	1,025,800	53	2,500,000
3,000,000	3,500,000	1,290,800	57	3,000,000
3,500,000	4,000,000	1,575,800	61	3,500,000
4,000,000	4,500,000	1,880,800	65	4,000,000
4,500,000	5,000,000	2,205,800	69	4,500,000
5,000,000	——	2,550,800	70	5,000,000

Appendix B:
Personal Inventory

Personal Information

Legal Name	Birth Date	Social Security Number
Name 1 _____	_____	_____
Name 2 _____	_____	_____

Maiden Name _____

Street Address _____

City _____ State _____ Zip _____ Phone _____

NAME 1	NAME 2
Occupation_____	Occupation_____
Employer_____	Employer _____
Street Address _____	Street Address _____
City, State, Zip_____	City, State, Zip_____
Phone _____	Phone _____
Title or Specialty_____	Title or Specialty _____
Employment Date_____	Employment Date _____

CHILDREN

Name	Sex	Birth Date	Social Security Number	Marital Status	Number of Children
_____	____	_____	_____	_____	_____
_____	____	_____	_____	_____	_____
_____	____	_____	_____	_____	_____
_____	____	_____	_____	_____	_____
_____	____	_____	_____	_____	_____
_____	____	_____	_____	_____	_____

PARENTS AND/OR DEPENDENTS

Name_____

Birth Date _____   Relationship _____

Street Address _____

City _____   State _____   Zip _____   Phone _____

Name_____

Birth Date _____   Relationship _____

Street Address _____

City _____   State _____   Zip _____   Phone _____

Name_____

Birth Date _____   Relationship _____

Street Address _____

City _____   State _____   Zip _____   Phone _____

Date

SAFE DEPOSIT BOX INFORMATION

Name of Bank _____

Bank Address _____

Box in Name of _____

Box Number _____

Location of Box Keys _____

CURRENT MARRIAGE

Date _____ City _____ State _____

PREVIOUS MARRIAGES

Dissolution Agreement _____

Date _____ City _____ State _____

Property settlements and/or premarital agreements. _____

POTENTIAL INHERITANCE

Name _____ Amount _____

PERSONAL ADVISORS

Name(s) _____ Date _____

Personal Accountant Name _____

Address _____ Phone _____

Business Accountant Name _____

Address _____ Phone _____

Personal Attorney Name _____

Address _____ Phone _____

Business Attorney Name _____

Address _____ Phone _____

Banker Name _____

Address _____ Phone _____

Clergy Name _____

Address _____ Phone _____

Financial Planner Name _____

Address _____ Phone _____

Insurance Agent—Automobile _____

Address _____ Phone _____

Insurance Agent—Disability _____

Address _____ Phone _____

Insurance Agent—Homeowners _____

Address _____ Phone _____

Insurance Agent—Life _____

Address _____ Phone _____

Insurance Agent—Medical _____

Address _____ Phone _____

Physician Name _____

Address _____ Phone _____

Stockbroker Name _____

Address _____ Phone _____

Trust Officer Name _____

Address _____ Phone _____

Other Name _____

Address _____ Phone _____

Asset/Lifestyle Accounts

Name 1 _____ Date _____

Name 2 _____

Checking

Name(s) on Account_____

Name of Institution _____ Account Number _____

Contact Person _____ Phone _____

Savings

Name(s) on Account_____

Name of Institution _____ Account Number _____

Contact Person _____ Phone _____

Fixed Assets

Vehicles

Description _____

Vehicle Identification Number _____ Registered Owner _____

Title Location _____ Purchase Date _____ Fair Market Value _____

Real Estate Interests

Property Number	1	2
Description		
Address		
Owner(s) and % Ownership		
Current Market Value		
Acquired From		
How Acquired (purchased, gift, inheritance, etc.)		
Date Acquired		
Original Cost		
Cash Down Payment		
Amount Borrowed		
Cost of Improvements		
Second Mortgage		
Amount Borrowed		
Rental Properties		
Tenant Name		

Date Leased _____

Terms of Lease, Sq. Ft. Leased _____

Monthly Rental _____

Operating Expense_____

Depreciation _____

Basis _____

Method _____

Life_____

Liabilities

CONSUMER DEBT—CAR LOANS

Date _____ Creditor Address _____

Account Number _____ Phone _____ Monthly Payment _____

Original Amount _____ Payment Date _____ Interest Rate _____

Date _____ Creditor Address _____

Account Number _____ Phone _____ Monthly Payment _____

Original Amount _____ Payment Date _____ Interest Rate _____

Date _____ Creditor Address _____

Account Number _____ Phone _____ Monthly Payment _____

Original Amount _____ Payment Date _____ Interest Rate _____

Totals_____

EQUITY DEBT—HOME EQUITY LOANS

Date _____ Creditor Address _____

Account Number _____ Phone _____ Monthly Payment _____

Original Amount _____ Payment Date _____ Interest Rate _____

Totals_____

EQUITY DEBT—MORTGAGES AND LAND CONTRACTS

Date _____ Creditor Address _____

Account Number _____ Phone _____ Monthly Payment _____

Original Amount _____ Payment Date _____ Interest Rate _____

Date _____ Creditor Address _____

Account Number _____ Phone _____ Monthly Payment _____

Original Amount _____ Payment Date _____ Interest Rate _____

Totals_____

LEASES

Lessee _____

Lessor _____

Date of Lease _____

Lease Number _____

Item(s) Leased _____

FMV of Items Leased _____

Terms of Lease _____

Lease Payment _____

Taxes _____

License Fees _____

Security Deposit _____

Renewal Option _____

Buy-out Option_____

Annual Mileage Limit_____

Maintenance_____

Insurance _____

Payment _____

Credit Card Summary

Creditor	Balance	Account Number	Current Name on Card *	Paid Off Monthly (Yes/No)	Interest Rate	Phone
_____	_____	_____	_____	_____	_____	_____
_____	_____	_____	_____	_____	_____	_____
_____	_____	_____	_____	_____	_____	_____
_____	_____	_____	_____	_____	_____	_____
_____	_____	_____	_____	_____	_____	_____
_____	_____	_____	_____	_____	_____	_____
_____	_____	_____	_____	_____	_____	_____
_____	_____	_____	_____	_____	_____	_____
_____	_____	_____	_____	_____	_____	_____
_____	_____	_____	_____	_____	_____	_____

*H = husband, W = wife, B = business, C = corporation

Investment Accounts

Date _____

TAX DEFERRED

401(k)

Name on Account _____   Name of Institution _____

Account Number _____   Beneficiary _____

Phone _____   Contact Person _____

IRA

Name on Account _____   Name of Institution _____

Account Number _____   Beneficiary _____

Phone _____   Contact Person _____

TAXABLE

Name on Account _____   Name of Institution _____

Account Number _____

Phone _____   Contact Person _____

BROKERAGE ACCOUNTS

Name on Account _____   Name of Institution _____

Account Number _____

Phone _____   Contact Person _____

CERTIFICATES OF DEPOSIT

Name on Account _____   Name of Institution _____

Account Number _____   Phone _____

Due Date _____   Interest Rate _____

401(k) Summary

Employee _____

Company _____

Investment Advisor _____

Phone Number _____

Current Allocation _____

As Of _____

Other Investment Options _____

Investment Changes _____

Current Contribution _____

Company Match _____

Loans Available _____

As Of _____

Business Interests Summary

Business Name _____

Address _____

Description of Business _____

Federal ED No. _____ Effective Date _____

Fiscal Year End _____

Business Type _____

Sole Proprietorship _____ Regular Corporation _____

General Partnership _____ Subchapter S Corporation _____

Limited Partnership _____

Accounting Method _____

Cash Basis _____ Accrual Basis _____ Hybrid Basis _____

Amount Invested $ _____ Amount Loaned $ _____

Number of Shares or Units Authorized _____

Shareholders or Partners _____

Number _____ % of _____

Name _____ of Shares/Units Ownership _____

Total Shares/Units Outstanding _____ 100

Directors _____

　　Officers_____

President _____

Vice President _____

Secretary _____

Treasurer _____

1. Do you have an employment agreement?   ☐ Yes ☐ No

2. Do you have a buy-sell agreement?   ☐ Yes ☐ No

3. Have you established any goals for your business? If so, please discuss.

4. What is your estimate of a fair market value for your business? _____

5. How did you arrive at this figure? _____

6. Fringe Benefits: Automobile _____   Company loans available at _____%

   Stock Options _____   Other _____

PARTNERSHIP INTEREST SUMMARY

	1	2
Business Name		
Owner		
Ownership %		
Units		
General Partner		
Description		
Federal ID #		
Effective Date		
Fiscal Year End		
Business Type		
Accounting Method		
Investment		
Date		
Amount		

Life Insurance Summary

Insured _____   TOTALS _____

Company _____

    Address _____

    City, State, Zip _____

    Phone _____

Policy Number _____

Policy Type _____

Term Riders _____

Face Value _____

Policy Date _____

Age at Issue _____

Premium _____

    Annualized _____

    Payable _____

Dividend Option_____

    Reduce Premium _____

    Pay Cash _____

    Paid Up Additions _____

    Accumulate _____

Additional Benefits_____

    Waiver of Premium _____

    Accidental Death _____

    Automatic Premium Loan _____

Owner _____

Beneficiary _____

    Primary _____

Secondary _____

Loan Interest_____

Purpose_____

Agent Name _____

Agency _____

Address _____

City, State, Zip _____

Phone _____

Medical Insurance

Insured _____

Policy Holder _____

Insuring Co._____

Policy No. _____

Policy Date _____

Annualized Premium _____

Payable _____

Additional Insureds _____

Agent _____

HOSPITAL/SURGICAL _____ Daily _____ Maximum _____

Hospital_____

Intensive Care _____

Miscellaneous Medical Expense_____

Physicians—In Hospital _____

Ambulance _____

Surgical Expenses Schedule _____

MAJOR MEDICAL _____

    Maximum Lifetime Medical Expenses _____

    Deductible Amount _____

        Accumulation Period _____

        Family Maximum Deductible _____

    Co-Insurance Percentage _____

        Amount Insured Pays Before Co-insurance % Goes to 100% _____

        Individual _____

        Family _____

SPECIAL LIMITS AND ADDITIONS _____

    Preexisting Conditions _____

    Nervous and Mental _____

        In-Hospital _____

        Out of Hospital _____

    Alcoholism and Drug Addiction_____

    X-Ray and Lab _____

    Maternity _____

    Preadmission Review Required _____

    Phone Number _____

    Private Duty Nursing_____

Medigap Policy Plan_____

Insured _____

Policy Holder _____

Insuring Co._____

Policy No. _____

Policy Date _____

Annualized Premium _____

    Payable _____

Additional Insureds _____

Agent _____

Phone Number _____

Plan Letter A–J _____

Basic Benefit _____

Skilled Nursing Care Coinsurance _____

Part A Deductible _____

Part B Deductible _____

Part B Excess (100%)_____

Foreign Travel Emergency _____

At-Home Recovery _____

Extended Drug Benefit 1250 or 3000 _____

Preventive Care _____

Dental-Vision Insurance

Insured _____

Policy Holder _____

Insuring Co._____

Policy No. _____

Policy Date _____

Annualized Premium _____

    Payable _____

Additional Insureds _____

Agent _____

Phone Number _____

Dental/Vision _____ Coverage Amount _____ Maximum _____

Preventive Care _____

Basic _____

Endodontics _____

Periodontics _____

Oral Surgery _____

Major Restorative _____

Prosthetic Repairs_____

Prosthetics _____

Orthodontics _____

Deductible _____

Long-Term Care

Insured _____

Policy Holder _____

Insuring Co._____

Policy No. _____

Policy Date _____

Annualized Premium _____

    Payable _____

    Premiums will increase as benefits increase _____

    Premiums will increase only if rates go up for all policyholders _____

Additional Insureds _____

Agent _____

Phone _____

Daily Benefit Limits _____ Daily _____ Maximum _____

    Nursing Home (Company Approved) _____

    Nursing Home (Other Nursing Homes) _____

    Home Health Care _____

    Adult Day Care _____

Inflation Protection _____

Benefit Period Years _____

    Nursing Home _____

    Home Health Care _____

Elimination Period _____

    Nursing Home _____

    Home Health Care _____

Home Health Care Coverage _____

    Custodial _____

    Intermediate _____

    Skilled _____

    Care Provided by Relatives _____

Qualification for Benefits _____

    Your Doctor's Certification _____

    Company Doctor's Certification _____

    Inability to Perform ADLs _____

    Prior Hospital Stay (Home Care) _____

    Prior Hospital Stay (Nursing Home) _____

Preexisting Condition Waiting Period (Months) _____

Exclusions _____

    Alzheimers _____

    Mental or Nervous Disorders _____

    Other _____

Miscellaneous Benefits _____

    Respite Care (Pays for Temporary Substitute) _____

    Nonforfeiture _____

    Death Benefit _____

    Restoration of Benefits _____

    Discount When Both Spouses Buy _____

    Other _____

PRESENT COST Of LONG-TERM CARE IN AREA _____

    Nursing Home Daily Charge _____

    NAME _____

    NAME _____

    Home Health Care Agency Daily Charge_____

    NAME _____

    NAME _____

Property Casualty Insurance

Type_____

Name of Insured_____

Insuring Company _____

Company Address _____

Agent Name _____

Agency _____

Agent Address _____

Agent Phone _____

Policy Number _____

Property Description _____

Date of Issue _____

Expiration _____

Annualized Premium _____

Premium Payable _____

Co-insurance Clause_____

Deductible Amount _____

HOMEOWNERS _____

  1. Dwelling _____

2. Appurtenant Structures _____

3. Scheduled Property _____

4. Unscheduled Personal Property_____

5. Additional Living Expenses _____

6. Liability _____

   a. Personal Injury _____

   b. Property Damage_____

   c. Medical Payments _____

7. Inflation Protection _____

8. Replacement Cost _____

9. Theft _____

10. Rider for Computer _____

11. Coverage for Business Pursuits _____

AUTOMOBILE/MARINE _____

1. Comprehensive _____

2. Collision _____

3. Liability _____

   a. Bodily Injury _____

   b. Property Damage _____

   c. Medical Payments _____

4. Uninsured Motorists _____

5. Underinsured Motorists _____

6. Towing and Labor _____

7. Rental Reimbursement _____

8. Multi-Car Discount _____

9. Automatic Safety Belts _____

Annual Premium _____

UMBRELLA _____

Limit of Liability _____

    a. Each Occurrence _____

    b. Annual Aggregate _____

    c. Retained Limit _____

Schedule of Underlying Insurance Per Person, Per Occurrence _____

    a. Homeowners _____

    b. Automobile _____

Bodily Injury _____

Property Damage _____

Annual Premium _____

Disability Insurance

Insured _____ TOTAL _____

Company _____

    Address _____

    State, City, Zip _____

    Phone _____

Policy Number _____

Monthly Benefits _____

Policy Type _____

    Individual _____

    Business Overhead _____

    Group _____

    Guaranteed Renewable _____

    Noncancellable _____

Policy Date _____

Age at Issue _____

Premium _____

    Annualized _____

    Payable _____

    Payor _____

Accident _____

    Elimination _____

    Benefit _____

Sickness _____

    Elimination _____

    Benefit _____

Partial Benefit _____

Waiver of Premium _____

Residual Benefit _____

Future Increase Option _____

Cost-of-Living Adjustment _____

Agent Name _____

    Agency _____

    Address _____

    City, State, Zip _____

    Phone _____

Will

Testator _____

Date Signed _____

Executor _____

    Address _____

    City, State, Zip _____

Contingent Executor

    Address _____

    City, State, Zip _____

Guardian

    Address _____

    City, State, Zip _____

Asset Distribution Provisions _____

Specific Assets _____

Remainder _____

Drafting Attorney _____

Address _____

Phone Number _____

Location of Document _____

Durable Power of Attorney

    Name _____

    Date_____

    Attorney _____

    Agent _____

    Successor Agent _____

    Provisions _____

Health Care Proxy

    Name _____

    Date_____

    Health Care Provisions _____

Appendix C:
Blank Worksheets

Annual Income Worksheet

EARNED INCOME

    Salary   _____

    Self-employment   _____

    Retirement   _____

    Other earned income   _____

INVESTMENT INCOME

    Interest—taxable   _____

    Interest—Federal & State exempt   _____

    Interest—Federal tax exempt   _____

    Interest—State tax exempt   _____

    Interest—money market fund   _____

    Dividends   _____

    Capital gains   _____

Annuity _____

Other _____

OTHER INCOME

Social Security _____

Alimony received _____

Unemployment compensation _____

Other—not taxable _____

State & local income tax refund _____

Other—taxable _____

BUSINESS INCOME

Sales _____

Gross receipts _____

Fees _____

Other _____

UNCLASSIFIED INCOME

_____   _____

_____   _____

_____   _____

_____   _____

_____   _____

_____   _____

_____   _____

_____   _____

_____   _____

Annual Expenses Worksheet

INCOME AND PAYROLL TAXES

    Federal Income Tax (FIT)—withheld   _____

    FIT—estimated payments   _____

    FIT—payment with return   _____

    State Income Tax (SIT)—withheld   _____

    SIT—estimated payment   _____

    SIT—payment with return   _____

    Local income tax   _____

    Social Security tax   _____

    State disability insurance   _____

    Income tax penalties   _____

HOUSEHOLD EXPENSES

    Fixed real estate   _____

    Maintenance and repairs   _____

    Real estate taxes   _____

    Home improvement   _____

    Furniture and decorating   _____

    Utilities   _____

    Personal property taxes   _____

    Vacation home expenses   _____

    Other   _____

PERSONAL EXPENSES

    Food   _____

    Personal allowances   _____

    Medical   _____

    Dental   _____

Clothing and personal   _____

Sales tax   _____

Charitable contributions   _____

Political contributions   _____

Other   _____

TRANSPORTATION EXPENSES

Automobile   _____

Other vehicles and equipment   _____

Other transportation   _____

INVESTMENT/PROFESSIONAL EXPENSES

Investment management fees   _____

Accounting fees   _____

Legal fees—deductible   _____

Legal fees—not deductible   _____

Notary fees   _____

Rental investment expense   _____

Other   _____

INTEREST

Interest—home mortgage   _____

Interest—consumer loans   _____

Interest—credit cards   _____

Penalty—early withdrawal   _____

Bank service charge   _____

JOB RELATED EXPENSES

Unreimbursed business   _____

Business education   _____

Membership   _____

Professional subscriptions   _____

Moving   _____

Child care   _____

Other   _____

OTHER EXPENSES

Education   _____

Alimony paid   _____

Child support   _____

Casualty losses   _____

Other   _____

BUSINESS EXPENSES

Cost of goods   _____

Advertising   _____

Bad debts   _____

Bank service charges   _____

Transportation   _____

Commission   _____

Dues and publications   _____

Employee wages   _____

Employee benefits   _____

Freight   _____

Insurance   _____

Interest   _____

Laundry and cleaning   _____

Legal and professional   _____

Office   _____

Pension and profit sharing   _____

Rent   _____

Repairs   _____

Supplies and materials   _____

Taxes   _____

Travel and entertainment _____

Utilities and telephone _____

Other _____

Spendable Cash Worksheet

	Scenario A	Scenario B
ADD INCOME:		
1. Business	_____	_____
2. Salary or salaries	_____	_____
3. Investment	_____	_____
4. Other	_____	_____
5. TOTAL INCOME	_____	_____
LESS:		
6. IRA	_____	_____
7. Keogh	_____	_____
8. Corporation retirement plans	_____	_____
9. 401(k)	_____	_____
10. Public employee retirement system	_____	_____
11. State teacher retirement system	_____	_____
12. 403(b) tax-deferred annuity	_____	_____
13. Medical/dental plans	_____	_____
14. Disability plans	_____	_____
15. Business expenses	_____	_____
16. Depreciation	_____	_____
17. Normal deductions	_____	_____
18. Exemptions	_____	_____

19. TAXABLE INCOME   _____   _____

LESS:

20. Taxes (for illustration only)   _____   _____

ADD BACK FROM ABOVE:

21. Depreciation   _____   _____

22. Exemptions   _____   _____

23. Non-taxable income   _____   _____

LESS:

24. Retirement savings   _____   _____

25. Medical/dental expenses   _____   _____

26. Disability insurance   _____   _____

27. Life insurance   _____   _____

28. Education   _____   _____

29. Certain living expenses   _____   _____

30. SPENDABLE CASH   _____   _____

31. CASH FLOW INCREASE   _____

Balance Sheet

ASSETS   **Date:** _____

CURRENT ASSETS

Cash on hand   _____

Checking accounts   _____

Money market accounts   _____

Savings accounts   _____

Treasury bills   _____

Life insurance cash value   _____

Escrow account _____

Other current assets _____

TOTAL CURRENT ASSETS _____

MARKETABLE INVESTMENTS

Common stocks _____

Preferred stocks _____

Treasury bonds _____

Corporate bonds _____

Municipal bonds _____

Unit investment trust _____

REIT (Real Estate Investment Trust) shares _____

Mutual funds _____

Traded stock options _____

Warrants _____

Futures contracts _____

Other marketable investments _____

TOTAL MARKETABLE INVESTMENTS

LONG-TERM INVESTMENTS

Real estate _____

Farming interests _____

Oil & gas investments _____

Tax shelters _____

Leasing investments _____

Research & development ventures _____

Venture capital investment _____

Annuities _____

Deposits _____

Long-term receivables _____

Mortgage receivables _____

Interest-free loan receivables   _____

Stock purchase plan   _____

Executive stock options   _____

Investment collections   _____

Precious metals   _____

Mineral royalties   _____

Closely-held businesses   _____

Other long-term assets   _____

TOTAL LONG-TERM ASSETS   _____

RETIREMENT/DEFERRED ASSETS

IRA   _____

Keogh account   _____

Retirement plan   _____

Deferred compensation plan   _____

Other retirement plans   _____

TOTAL RETIREMENT/DEFERRED ASSETS   _____

TRUST AND ESTATE ASSETS

Trust assets   _____

Estate assets   _____

TOTAL TRUST AND ESTATE ASSETS   _____

PERSONAL/NON-EARNING ASSETS

Residence   _____

Vacation property   _____

Automobiles   _____

Home furnishings   _____

Other personal property   _____

Noninvestment collection   _____

Other vehicles and equipment   _____

Other nonearning assets   _____

TOTAL PERSONAL/NON-EARNING ASSETS   _____

BUSINESS ASSETS

Cash account/business   _____

     Checking account/business   _____

     Accounts receivable/business   _____

     Short-term investments/business   _____

     Deposits/business   _____

     Inventory/business   _____

     Land/business   _____

     Buildings/business   _____

     Furniture and fixtures/business   _____

     Manufacturing equipment/business   _____

     Transportation equipment/business   _____

     Office equipment/business   _____

     Other fixed assets/business   _____

     Other assets/business   _____

TOTAL BUSINESS ASSETS   _____

UNCLASSIFIED ASSETS

     Unclassified assets   _____

TOTAL UNCLASSIFIED ASSETS   _____

TOTAL ASSETS   _____

LIABILITIES

CURRENT LIABILITIES

     Credit cards   _____

     Demand notes   _____

     Margin accounts   _____

     Other   _____

TOTAL CURRENT LIABILITIES   _____

LONG-TERM LIABILITIES

    Home mortgage   _____

    Home improvement loan   _____

    Other real estate mortgages   _____

    Automobile loans   _____

    Student loan   _____

    Loan on life insurance   _____

    Investment liabilities   _____

    Interest-free loan payable   _____

    Other long-term liabilities   _____

TOTAL LONG-TERM LIABILITIES   _____

BUSINESS LIABILITIES

    Accounts payable/business   _____

    Accrued expenses/business   _____

    Prepaid orders/business   _____

    Employment taxes/business   _____

    Accredited FICA tax/business _____

    Other payroll taxes/business _____

    Long-term loans/business   _____

    Other liabilities/business   _____

TOTAL BUSINESS LIABILITIES   _____

UNCLASSIFIED LIABILITIES

    Unclassified liabilities   _____

TOTAL UNCLASSIFIED LIABILITIES   _____

TOTAL LIABILITIES   _____

NET WORTH

(TOTAL ASSETS – TOTAL LIABILITIES)   _____

Baseline Data for Estimating College Costs

Child's name   _____   _____

Current age   _____   _____

Number of years until entry   _____   _____

Number of years in school   _____   _____

Current cost of college   _____   _____

Rate of increase of costs   _____   _____

CALCULATING THE FUTURE COST OF SCHOOL

Year	(name)'s Current Cost	(name)'s Current Cost	Total Cost	Inflation Adjustment Factor (8%) (Table A.1)	Future Cost
0	_____	_____	_____	_____	_____
1	_____	_____	_____	_____	_____
2	_____	_____	_____	_____	_____
3	_____	_____	_____	_____	_____
4	_____	_____	_____	_____	_____
5	_____	_____	_____	_____	_____
6	_____	_____	_____	_____	_____
7	_____	_____	_____	_____	_____
8	_____	_____	_____	_____	_____
9	_____	_____	_____	_____	_____
10	_____	_____	_____	_____	_____
11	_____	_____	_____	_____	_____
12	_____	_____	_____	_____	_____
13	_____	_____	_____	_____	_____
TOTALS	_____	_____	_____	_____	_____

How Much to Save for Education Each Year

Year	Future Cost	Annual Investment Factor (8%) (Table A.3)	Need for a Specific Year	Save Each Year
0	$ _____	_____	$ _____	$ _____
1	_____	_____	_____	_____
2	_____	_____	_____	_____
3	_____	_____	_____	_____
4	_____	_____	_____	_____
5	_____	_____	_____	_____
6	_____	_____	_____	_____
7	_____	_____	_____	_____
8	_____	_____	_____	_____
9	_____	_____	_____	_____
10	_____	_____	_____	_____
11	_____	_____	_____	_____
12	_____	_____	_____	_____
13	_____	_____	_____	_____
TOTALS	_____	_____	_____	_____

Lump Sum Calculation

Year	Future Cost (8%)	Lump Sum Investment Factor (Table A.4)	Need Today to Fund
0	_____	_____	$ _____
1	_____	_____	_____
2	_____	_____	_____
3	_____	_____	_____
4	_____	_____	_____
5	_____	_____	_____
6	_____	_____	_____
7	_____	_____	_____
8	_____	_____	_____
9	_____	_____	_____
10	_____	_____	_____
11	_____	_____	_____
12	_____	_____	_____
13	_____	_____	_____
TOTALS	_____	_____	_____

Comparison of Alternatives for Funding Education

Year	Pay As You Go	Save Each Year	Deposit Lump Sum
0	$_____	$_____	$_____
1	_____	_____	_____
2	_____	_____	_____
3	_____	_____	_____
4	_____	_____	_____
5	_____	_____	_____
6	_____	_____	_____
7	_____	_____	_____
8	_____	_____	_____
9	_____	_____	_____
10	_____	_____	_____
11	_____	_____	_____
12	_____	_____	_____
13	_____	_____	_____
TOTALS (NET)	$_____	$_____	$_____

BEFORE TAXES

(GROSS)   (_____)_____   _____   _____

Retirement Fund Calculations: Basic Data

BASIC DATA

Retirement age   _____

Present age   _____

Years until retirement   _____

Life expectancy   _____

    (Table A.7)   _____

Annual living expenses needed for
    retirement (today's dollars)   _____

Inflation rate   _____

Inflation adjustment factor for 30 years
    at 6% (Table A.1)   _____

Gross rate of return   _____

Tax bracket   _____

CALCULATIONS

Living Expenses /(1 − tax rate) = Total living expenses plus taxes

_____

Total living expenses plus taxes   _____

Inflation adjustment factor for 30 years @ 6% (Table A-1)   _____

Inflated gross annual retirement cost   _____

(Inflated gross annual retirement cost)/(Gross rate of return) =
Inflated total retirement fund needed

_____

Net (After-Tax) Rate of Return Calculation

Gross (before taxes) rate of return × tax rate = Percentage lost to taxes

		Gross rate of return (_____%)
×	_____	Tax rate (_____%)
	_____	
	_____	Lost to taxes (_____%)

Gross rate of return − percentage lost to taxes = Net rate

		Gross rate of return (_____%)
×	_____	Lost to taxes (_____%)
	_____	
	_____	Net rate of return (_____%)

How Much Will Your Current Savings Be Worth?

Net (after-tax) rate of return	_____% or 0._____
Years until retirement	_____ years
Current retirement savings	$_____
Compound interest factor	×_____
for _____% (Table A.2)	
	_____
Future value	$_____

© 1988 by John E. Sestina

How Much to Save Each Year to Reach Retirement Goal

Still needed for retirement fund $_____

Annual investment factor for a net rate of _____%   × 0 ._____

(Table A.3)   _____

Net savings needed each year (taxes not included) $_____

Tax rate   0._____

Total gross savings per year
    (Net savings / (1 − tax rate)) $_____

Effect of Deferring Taxes on Your Savings Goal

	Not Deferred	Deferred
Gross rate of return	_____	_____
Net rate of return	_____	_____
Annual retirement living expenses including tax	_____	_____
Total lump sum for retirement fund (annual amount / gross rate)	_____	_____
In 30 years, $10,000 becomes	_____	_____
Still needed	_____	_____
Annual net savings needed	_____	_____
Annual gross savings needed	_____	_____

How Much Can Refinancing Save You?

Current monthly payment at _____%   _____

Proposed monthly payment at _____%   _____

1 − (tax bracket)   × _____

Monthly after-tax savings   _____

Lost investment return   _____

    (Total refinancing cost × net return = $ _____/12 months = Lost investment return)

Net monthly savings   _____

Total refinancing cost   _____

Net monthly savings   _____

Months to break even (Total refinancing cost = ____/ Net monthly savings = ___)
= ____months

Shifting Income by Employing Your Children

	Don't Employ	Do Employ
Your taxable income	_____	_____
Income to the child	_____	_____
Net taxable income	_____	_____
Your taxes (30%)	_____	_____
Your net income after taxes	_____	_____
Education fees you pay	_____	_____
YOUR CASH FLOW BENEFIT	_____	_____
Child's taxable income	_____	
Child's taxes (16.7%)	_____	
Child's net income after tax	_____	
CHILD PAYS EDUCATION FEES	_____	Net Cost _____

Saving Money with Business Deductions

Your income	_____	_____
Income from a second job	_____	_____
Second business income	_____	_____
TOTAL GROSS INCOME	_____	_____
Your expenses	Business Expenses versus Deductions	
Car	_____	_____
Travel	_____	_____
Entertainment	_____	_____
Home insurance	_____	_____
TOTAL EXPENSES	_____	_____
Net personal income	_____	_____
Net business income (from Schedule C)	_____	_____
TOTAL NET INCOME FOR YOU	_____	_____
TOTAL TAXABLE INCOME	_____	_____
Personal income taxes*	_____	_____
Self-employment tax on net business income (Schedule C)	_____	_____
TOTAL TAXES	_____	_____
CASH YOU HAVE LEFT	_____	_____
(Gross income minus taxes and expenses)		
GAIN FROM SECOND BUSINESS	_____	MORE CASH

© 1988 by John E. Sestina

Increasing Cash Flow with Business Deductions

Your income	_____	_____
Your gross business income	_____	_____
TOTAL GROSS INCOME	_____	_____

	Personal Expenses	Business Deductions
Your expenses		
Car	_____	_____
Travel	_____	_____
Entertainment	_____	_____
Home insurance	_____	_____
TOTAL EXPENSES	_____	_____
Net personal income	_____	_____
Net business income (from Schedule C)	_____	_____
TOTAL NET INCOME FOR YOU	_____	_____
TOTAL TAXABLE INCOME	_____	_____
Personal income taxes	_____	_____
Self-employment tax on net business income (Schedule C)	_____	_____
TOTAL TAXES	_____	_____
CASH YOU HAVE LEFT	_____	_____
(Gross income minus taxes and expenses)		
GAIN FROM SECOND BUSINESS	_____	Less tax

Rating Investments

	Rate "5"	Rate "4"	Rate "3"	Rate "2"	Rate "1"	Score
What is the expected annual rate of return?	14%	12%	10%	8%	6%	_____
How liquid is the investment?	Immed.	6 mos.	1 yr.	2 yrs.	20 yrs.	_____
How much management time is required of you?	None	25%	50%	75%	100%	_____
How long for the investment to mature?	Immed.	6 mos.	1 yr.	5 yrs.	10 yrs. or more	_____
How inflation-proof is it?	Excellent	Good	Some	Almost None	None	_____
What tax advantages are there?	Excellent	Good	Some	Almost None	None	_____
How safe is your money?	Excellent	Good	Some	Almost None	None	_____
Is there low interest rate fluctuation?	Excellent	Good	Some	Almost None	None	_____
Can you tolerate this investment? (personal temperament)	Excellent	Good	Some	Almost None	None	_____
What is the potential for the income promised?	Excellent	Good	Some	Almost None	None	_____

Final Rating   TOTAL   _____

5 = Excellent
4 = Good
3 = Average   Divide
2 = Below average   by 10 =
1 = Poor   Final
                                             rating   _____

Worksheet for Comparing Mutual Fund Expenses

Possible Charges   Fund Name

_____   _____   _____

Actual Cost (in percent or dollars)

Front-end Load	_____	_____	_____
Back-end Load	_____	_____	_____
Re-load	_____	_____	_____
Exit Fee	_____	_____	_____
Management Fee	_____	_____	_____
12b-1 Fee	_____	_____	_____
Transfer Fee	_____	_____	_____
Total Expenses	_____	_____	_____

Aim for total expenses of less than 5 percent per year.

Appendix D:
You Need a Second Business

W hy do you need a second (sideline) business? If you earn less than $50,000, you may need the money to help you meet your goals. If you earn more than $50,000, you need the tax deductions that a second business makes available.

I want to be very clear that I'm not talking about a "work trap" that ties up your time. You can start a second business that will only take ten hours a week to keep running after the initial startup time. Nor am I talking about a huge investment of your hard-earned money. You can start a second business for $100. Only you can decide

1. if you're disciplined enough to do this, and
2. if the benefits of additional income and more tax deductions balance the time, money, and emotional costs.

There are many books out now on how to start and run a second business. I'm just going to hit the highlights to get you thinking about the possibilities. Do your research and check with your attorney before you start!

Here are three specific reasons to get started:

1. You can shift highly taxed income to your children.
2. You can deduct expenses that would otherwise not be deductible. Some examples include: trips, car and transportation expenses, entertainment, fringe benefits, and a home office.
3. You can develop money-making interests and activities.

Before You Start

Before you begin dreaming about all the money you're going to make, take time to consider these seven points.

1. What is the purpose of the business? In order to succeed, you must be clear on exactly what you will be doing.
2. How much will it cost to set up? Estimate the expenses of organization and the legal work needed.
3. How much will it cost to run? Estimate the expenses and personnel needed to operate the business.
4. How much time are you willing to spend on this business?
5. When and how will you get out of the business? Before you get into a business, plan how to dissolve or dispose of it if needed or desirable.
6. What form of business is best from the tax, benefit, and liability standpoints?
7. Finally, is all the bother worth the benefit? After answering questions 1–6, are the benefits worth the costs?

Your Business Format

In setting up any business, you have four basic choices: a sole proprietorship, a partnership, a corporation, or a limited liability company. Within the corporation choice, you can choose a regular or an S corporation. Here are the advantages and disadvantages of each:

Sole Proprietorship

Advantages

1. The business is kept in the family. Remember, one of your goals is to make more money for your family.
2. You can have your child work for you, and you don't have to pay Social Security.
3. A sole proprietorship has less paperwork than a corporation.

Disadvantages

1. You have personal liability.
2. You must file a Schedule C and pay taxes.

Partnership

Advantages

The advantages are almost the same as for a sole proprietorship. The difference with a partnership is that you have others joining you in the business.

Disadvantages

1. Are you sure the partnership will last?
2. Unfortunately, you assume liability for mistakes your partners make.

Corporation

Advantages

1. You are generally protected from personal liability.
2. You can get fringe benefits paid for by the corporation, such as the ones discussed as tools in Chapter 9.
3. You can set up pension, profit-sharing, or other retirement plans that you would not be able to have as an individual.

Disadvantages

It will cost about $1,000 per year for attorney's fees and so on. You will need to save about $2,000 to $5,000 minimum on your taxes before it is worth it.

S Corporation

Advantages

You can put your children or parents in as shareholders and let the profits go to them. Although this may sound unusual, it is rather ordinary and a legitimate concept.

Disadvantages

There is only one class of stock.

Limited Liability Company

Advantages

1. You are generally protected from liability.
2. You show the LLC income on your tax return. You really benefit from the deductions. Also when there is income, it is not double taxed as with a regular corporation.
3. You have more choices in tax planning because of the flexibility of both corporate and partnership advantages in one vehicle: the LLC

Disadvantages

Each state has different laws regarding LLCs. You need expert advice if you conduct business in more than one state or some of your family lives in another state.

Resources to Help You

For more details on business formats, refer to the Small Business Administration's (SBA) publications (www.sbaonline.sba.gov) and the Service Corps of Retired Executives (SCORE) (www.score.org) courses offered through the SBA. These are great resources for the small business person.

Some states have one-stop offices for starting up a small business. At the very least each state will have some state department, agency, or office that handles some of the paperwork of setting up a business. Be sure to discuss your plans with an attorney so that you benefit from his or her up-to-date knowledge on setting up a business in your state.

Businesses to Avoid

I recommend avoiding the following businesses. *Remember you're setting up a second business to generate income, not to work yourself to death or tie up all your money.*

- Any food service business
- Any retail clothing business
- Any franchise business

- Any vending or customer-operated machine business
- Any business requiring expensive, complicated equipment or special personnel
- Any business requiring a large cash outlay or borrowing
- Any operation you cannot control by yourself
- Any business involving hair care or cosmetic applications (i.e., beauty salons, barber shops); sales are okay.
- Partners with neither money nor real expertise
- Work traps

How to Prepare

Before you start your second business, plan for success through research, talk, and work.

Research the Business

Twelve years ago, few financial advisors were recommending having a sideline business. Now there are many books and articles out that will help you. In addition, take the time to research the specific business that interests you.

You need to know all the pros and cons before you start. Find out what others have written about this particular business. Start with the local library and the SBA and explain what you are doing. They can save you hours of research time and steer you to books, magazine articles, newspaper stories, and other useful publications.

Talk to Successful People

Find people who have been successful in the business you're considering and talk to them.

1. What do they like and dislike?
2. How did they start out?
3. What were the big problems?
4. How much time does it really take?

Be considerate. Don't expect something for nothing. Take them out to eat, pay for an hour of consulting time, or in some way compensate them for the time they take in advising you. It will be time and money well spent. If you can't find anyone in your town in the same business, find someone in a nearby town and set up an appointment to visit.

Work for Someone in the Business

"Good grief," you say, "I'm just going into business, not studying for a Ph.D." Sure, it's only business. However, you'll find that all successful business people know their businesses inside and out. That's what you need to do before you start your own. The best way to find out what the business is really about is to work for someone else.

I'm not saying you must quit your current job and go to work full-time, although with a few businesses you might want to do that. Arrange to work part-time for several months so you can observe the operations. You'll see the customer complaints and the supply problems firsthand. You'll also pick up the tricks of the trade that are second nature to the owner. If you just interview the owner, she might overlook these tips because they have become commonplace.

During this research, you may find out this isn't for you. That's okay. Better to know it now than a year down the road with a full inventory and a payroll. The time you spend researching any business will not be wasted. You'll learn what you like and didn't like. That knowledge will help you refine your search for the second business that is right for you.

Businesses for Different Purposes

Second businesses can be set up for two different purposes: income shifting or deduction of expenses.

Income Shifting

Businesses which will help you shift income include these options:

1. Lab corporation
2. Office maintenance
3. Filing and administration
4. Collections
5. Other separate businesses that your spouse might set up

Let's say you employ your children in your second business. By shifting income to your children, you may be able to lower your taxes, provide for an education fund, and have more money to spend. Figure D.1 shows a simple example.

By shifting $6,000 of income to your child, you get $840 more cash to spend now instead of paying it to Uncle Sam. Check with your attorney to be sure you comply with the current laws regarding employing your child.

Deduction of Expenses

A second business allows you to deduct certain living expenses that you would be paying out of your own pocket anyway. We all have to eat, most everyone owns a car and has home insurance, and travel broadens your horizons. Why not have a second business so that these costs become business expenses?

Let's say you decide to set up an art appraisal service as a second business. With careful planning, the cost of visiting the art galleries in New York will be tax deductible. You could spend five days of vacation

As mentioned in Chapter 9, Taxes, taking a deduction from a home office probably makes sense only if you'll be in your home a long time or if you're renting. Check with your financial advisor.

FIGURE D.1   Shifting Income by Employing Your Children

	Don't Employ	Do Employ
Your taxable income	$7,200	$7,200
Income to the child	–0	–6,000
Net taxable income	7,200	1,200
Your taxes (30%) *	–2,200	–360
Your net income after taxes	5,000	840
Education fees you pay	–5,000	–0
YOUR CASH FLOW BENEFIT	$ 0	$ 840
Child's taxable income		$6,000
Child's taxes (16.7%) *		–1,000
Child's net income after tax		5,000
CHILD PAYS EDUCATION FEES		–5,000
		$0

*Numbers are rounded to the nearest $100 Tax rates are for illustration only.

from your first job doing business and the weekend going to Broadway plays. If the major purpose of the trip was for business and you can substantiate that with good records, then you would have to pay only for the personal part of the trip out of your own pocket.

Recent tax laws have changed the amount of these expenses that are deductible. Be sure to check with your tax advisor on the details of deducting business meals, travel, and entertainment. All of this recordkeeping may be more trouble than it's worth to you. Only you can decide that.

Here's a simple example of how business expense deductions can save you money. You can deduct the actual costs of using your car or use a standard mileage rate. You can take 50 percent of the cost of business meals as an expense. You can deduct a percentage of your home insurance if you have a home office. You can deduct travel costs. To keep the math simple, let's say these four items add up to

> **W**hat items are you paying for out of personal funds that should be second business deductions? Ask your accountant to go over allowable business deductions that you are currently taking. Are there other expenses you could deduct?

$8,000. If you don't have a second business, you have to pay for these expenses out of your own pocket. If your tax rate is 30 percent, then you would have to earn at least $11,429 in order to spend $8,000.

$$\text{Expenses} / (1 - \text{tax rate}) \text{ or } \$8,000 / (1 - 0.30) = \$11,429$$

But if you have a second business, then these expenses become business deductions. Table D.2 shows a basic example to make my point (personal exemptions, other deductions, credits, etc., are ignored here). Look at the difference it makes in your taxes and in how much cash you have to spend. As I said at the beginning of this chapter, if you make less than $50,000, you need the extra income. Let's say you're already working a second job now. Figure D.2 shows a very simple example of the difference between working at a second job earning $15,000 or having a second business grossing $15,000. You end up with $3,200 more cash after taxes!

If you make $50,000 now, you may need the tax deductions a second business can provide. Figure D.3 shows that if you could change some of your personal expenses into business deductions, you would be ahead by $2,500 more cash in your pocket. This simple example assumes that you can change some of your current income into second business income. Even if you can't, you will still benefit from the deductions that are available to you with a second business because they are business expenses on the business part of your tax return instead of personal expenses that are not deductible.

FIGURE D.2   Saving Money with Business Deductions

Your income	$35,000	$35,000
Income from a second job	15,000	15,000
TOTAL GROSS INCOME	50,000	50,000
	Personal	Business
Your expenses	Expenses	Deductions
Car	$ 2,000	$ 2,000
Travel	2,000	2,000
Entertainment	2,000	2,000
Home insurance	2,000	2,000
TOTAL EXPENSES	8,000	8,000
Net personal income	42,000	35,000
Net business income		
(from Schedule C)	0	7,000
TOTAL NET INCOME FOR YOU	42,000	42,000
TOTAL TAXABLE INCOME	50,000	42,000
Personal income taxes*	9,800	5,600
Self-employment tax on net		
business income (Schedule C)	0	1,000
TOTAL TAXES	$ 9,800	$ 6,600
CASH YOU HAVE LEFT	$32,200	$35,400
(Gross income minus		
taxes and expenses)		
GAIN FROM SECOND BUSINESS	$3,200	MORE CASH

*Tax rates for illustration only.

Remember these are very simple examples. Think what you can do with a good business plan and the right business.

Businesses that help in deducting expenses include these options.

- Interior decorating
- Art appraisal or dealing
- Antique appraisal and dealing
- Travel coordinator (not agency)
- International import/export
- Jewelry making/selling
- Photography (travel, not portrait)

FIGURE D.3   Increasing Cash Flow with Business Deductions

Your income	$50,000	$40,000
Your gross business income	0	10,000
TOTAL GROSS INCOME	$50,000	$50,000
	Personal	Business
Your expenses	Expenses	Deductions
Car	$2,000	$2,000
Travel	2,000	2,000
Entertainment	2,000	2,000
Home insurance	2,000	2,000
TOTAL EXPENSES	8,000	8,000
Net personal income	42,000	40,000
Net business income (from Schedule C)	0	2,000
TOTAL NET INCOME FOR YOU	42,000	42,000
TOTAL TAXABLE INCOME	50,000	42,000
Personal income taxes*	9,800	7,000
Self-employment tax on net business income (Schedule C)	0	300
TOTAL TAXES	9,800	7,300
CASH YOU HAVE LEFT (Gross income minus taxes and expenses)	$32,200	$34,700

GAIN FROM SECOND BUSINESS $2,500 Less tax

*Tax rates for illustration only.

- Real estate investment
- Presentations, speeches, conferences

Businesses for Different Skills

Many people set up second businesses which take advantage of skills they already have or can develop. If you're a professional musician, you can give music lessons on the side. If you're in sales, you can sell a different product in your spare time. If you love gourmet cooking, you can bake specialty items for restaurants, write a cookbook, or give cooking lessons. The possibilities are limited only by your imagination.

Selling Markets

Temporary agencies and clerical work
- Kelly Girl and other agencies
- Set up your own for small companies; do work on a per item basis
- At-home typing
- Research
- Telemarketing from home
- Help out at conventions
- Conduct surveys
- Mystery shopper
- Demonstrate products

After-hours work at businesses open late or round the clock

- Part-time, shift work
- Fast food restaurants
- Chain stores
- Supermarkets
- Regional centers of large corporations
- Airport passenger service (reservations, freight agent)

Driving

- School buses
- Chauffeur invalids and busy executives
- Haul trash to the dump
- Cab

Selling products (just a few of the many opportunities)

- Amway
- Avon
- Beeline Fashions
- Encyclopedia Britannica
- Home Interiors and Gifts
- Mary Kay Cosmetics
- Sara Coventry

- Shaklee
- Stanley Home Products
- Tupperware

Selling What You Make

- Wholesale baking and catering
- Hand-crafted articles
- Collectibles
- Operate a consignment shop
- Seamstress (everyday, special events—weddings, formal, swimsuits)

Hobbies

- Calligrapher (wedding invitations, menus)
- Videotape weddings, personal property, graduations
- Photography (movies of weddings)

Spin-Offs from Your Talents

- Personal resume preparation
- Telling stories (private parties, children's library events)
- Help foreigners
  - Translator and interpreter
  - Care for personal problems (forms, disputes)
  - Instruct in American culture (etiquette, and so on)
- Feasibility studies for employers
- Programs for convention spouses
- Deliver singing messages ("turkey gram")

Teaching

- Adult education classes
  - Home repair
  - Cooking

- Health and exercise
  - Martial arts
  - Aerobics
- Workshops at home
  - Painting
  - Cooking

What to Do with Your Business when You Retire

Depending upon your business format, you will have different options when you are ready to retire.

Pass the Business to Family Members

With a limited liability company, your heirs receive the business on a "stepped-up basis." The heirs' basis in the business is the current market value. Then, if they want to sell the business for the same amount, they will have no capital gains tax.

Sell the Business

You can sell the business if you can find a willing buyer. If the business depends heavily upon your particular skills, then you may be able to sell your client list and/or equipment but not the actual business.

Dissolve the Business

This is the simplest option. If you have to dispose of inventory and/or equipment, it can take time and money.

Change Its Purpose

If you set up your business as a corporation, then you can change its purpose. Check with your attorney to work out the details.

Conclusion

I truly believe everyone should have a second business for more income and for reducing taxes. This strategy may not be for you, but I wanted you to know that sideline businesses can be a viable option as part of your overall financial plan. Determine if you have the discipline to start and run a sideline business, then discuss the options with your financial planner and attorney.

Summary

Why do you need a second business? If you earn less than $50,000, you may need the money to help you meet your goals. If you earn more than $50,000, you may need the tax deductions that a second business makes available. With a second business, you may be able to

1. shift highly taxed income to your children.
2. deduct expenses that are not currently deductible.
3. develop money-making interests and activities.

In setting up your business, you have four basic choices:

1. Sole proprietorship
2. Partnership
3. Corporation
4. Limited liability company.

Remember you're setting up a second business to generate income, not to work yourself to death or tie up all your money. Before you start a second business, take time to research the kind of business you are considering.

Second businesses can be set up to shift income or to deduct expenses. You may already have a hobby or skill that you enjoy doing in your spare time. Could it be developed into a second business? A variety of businesses are listed using different skills.

Finally, be sure to plan what you want to do with the business when you retire. You may want to sell it, dissolve it, or change its purpose.

Appendix E: Glossary

accidental death benefits A provision that may be put into a life insurance policy calling for the payment of double benefits in the case of death by accidental means. See *double indemnity*.

accruals Continually recurring short-term liabilities. Examples are accrued wages, accrued taxes, and accrued interest.

accrued interest Interest accrued on a bond since the last interest payment was made. The buyer of the bond pays the market price plus accrued interest. Exceptions include bonds that are in default and income bonds.

actuary A person professionally trained in the mathematics and other technical aspects of life insurance who calculates premiums, reserves, and dividends.

aging schedule A report showing how long accounts receivable have been outstanding. It gives the percent of receivables not past due and the percent past due by, for example, one month, two months or other periods.

amortization A method of paying off a loan, such as a home mortgage.

annuitant The person who has a contract with a life insurance company to receive periodic payments for a specific number of years or for life.

annuity A series of payments of a fixed amount for a specific number of years.

asked price The price at which a dealer will sell a nonlisted or over-the-counter security.

assets Everything a corporation owns or is owed. Cash, investments, money due, materials and inventories = current assets. Buildings and machinery = fixed assets. Patents and goodwill = intangible assets.

balanced fund An investment company that holds varying proportions of bonds, preferred stocks, and common stocks from time to time in order to maintain relatively greater stability of both capital and income.

balance sheet A condensed statement showing the nature and amount of a company's assets, liabilities, and capital on a given date. In dollar amounts the balance sheet shows what the company owned, what it owed, and the ownership interest in the company of its stockholders.

balloon clause A clause in an installment loan contract calling for a final payment substantially larger than the other payments.

balloon payment The final payment larger than the preceding payments when a debt is not fully amortized.

bankruptcy A legal procedure for formally liquidating a business carried out under the jurisdiction of courts of law.

bear market Technical term for a long-run, downward-moving securities market.

bearer bond A bond that does not have the owner's name registered on the books of the issuing company and that is payable to the holder.

beneficiary The person who receives certain benefits as spelled out in a will or a life insurance contract.

bid price The price at which a dealer will buy nonlisted or over-the-counter securities.

blue chip stocks The common stock of large, well-known, financially strong corporations with good records of earnings and dividend payments over many years.

blue-sky laws The laws of the various states regulating the sale of securities and the activities of security salesmen, brokers, and dealers.

bond Basically, an IOU or promissory note of a corporation, usually issued in multiples of $1,000, although $100 and $50 denominations are not uncommon. A bond is evidence of a debt on which the issuing company usually promises to pay the bondholders a specified amount of interest for a specified length of time and to repay the loan on the expiration date. In every case a bond represents debt. Its holder is a creditor of the corporation and not a part owner like the shareholder.

book value An accounting term, book value of a stock is determined from a company's records by adding all assets (generally excluding such intangibles as goodwill), then deducting all debts and other liabilities, plus the liquidation price of any preferred issues. The resulting sum is divided by the number of common shares outstanding to determine the book value per common share. Book value of the assets of a company or a security may have little or no significant relationship to market value.

breakeven analysis An analytical technique for studying the relation between fixed cost, variable cost, and profits. A breakeven chart graphically depicts the nature of breakeven analysis. The breakeven point represents the volume of sale at which total costs equal total revenues (that is, profits equal zero).

broker A person in the business of buying and selling securities for another party for which a commission is received.

bull market Technical term for a long-run, upward-moving securities market.

callable A bond issue all or part of which may be redeemed by the issuing corporation under definite conditions before maturity. The term also applies to preferred shares that may be redeemed by the issuing corporation.

call option A contract giving the holder the privilege of purchasing a given security from the option dealer at a specific price for a specific period of time.

call price As applied to bonds, the price at which a corporation can prematurely retire bonds.

capital Total assets of a business.

capital gains The market appreciation in the value of securities or other assets.

capital gains tax A special tax that must be paid by those who receive capital gains.

capital loss The decline in the market value of securities or other assets.

capital stock All shares representing ownership of a business, including preferred and common.

capital structure The relative proportions of capital represented by bonds, preferred stock, and common stock.

capitalization Total amount of the various securities issued by a corporation. Capitalization may include bonds. debentures, and preferred and common stock. Bonds and debentures are usually carried on the books of the issuing company in terms of their par or face value. Preferred and common shares may be carried in terms of par or stated value. Stated value may be an arbitrary figure decided upon by the directors or may represent the amount received by the company from the sale of the securities at the time of issuance.

capitalization rate A discount rate used to find the present value of a series of future cash receipts; sometimes called discount rate.

cash budget A schedule showing cash flows (receipts, disbursements, and net cash) for a firm or individual over a specified period.

cash flow Reported net income of a corporation or individual, plus amounts charged off for depreciation, depletion, amortization, and extraordinary charges to reserves, which are bookkeeping deductions and not paid out in actual dollars. In recent years, cash flow has been used as a yardstick. Because of the larger noncash deductions, cash flow appears to offer a better indication of a company's ability to pay dividends and finance expansion from self-generated cash than the conventional reported net income figure.

cash surrender value The amount of cash a person may obtain by voluntarily surrendering a life insurance policy.

certificates of deposit Certificates given by banks to indicate the number of dollars in savings a person has in a special long-run account.

closed-end investment company A company that has a definite limit to the number of shares in itself which it may sell.

collateral Securities or other property pledged by a borrower to secure repayment of a loan.

collateral trust bond A bond secured by collateral deposited with a trustee. The collateral is often the stocks or bonds of companies controlled by the issuing company but may be other securities.

common stock equities Certificates of ownership in a corporation.

commission brokers Brokers who buy and sell securities for their customers, for which they receive a commission.

compensating balance A required minimum checking account balance that a firm must maintain with a commercial bank. The required balance is generally equal to 15 to 20 percent of the amount of loans outstanding. Compensating balances can raise the effective rate of interest on bank loans.

consolidated balance sheet A balance sheet showing the financial condition of a corporation and its subsidiaries.

consumer price index A statistical device that measures the increase in the cost of living for consumers. It is sometimes used to illustrate the extent that prices in general have risen or the amount of inflation that has taken place.

contact brokers Brokers who assist commission brokers unable to handle the entire volume of business by themselves. Contact brokers do not deal with the public.

convertible A bond or preferred stock that may be, under specific circumstances, exchanged for a certain number of shares of common stock.

credit life insurance Special term life insurance purchased when borrowing money on an installment loan basis. Credit life insurance is used to pay off the loan in the event of the borrower's death before it is paid off.

cumulative preferred A stock having a provision that if one or more dividends are omitted, those dividends must be paid before additional dividends may be paid on the company's common stock.

current assets Those assets of a company which are reasonably expected to be either realized in cash, sold, or consumed during the normal operating cycle of the business. These include cash, U.S. government bonds, receivables, money due (usually within one year), and inventories.

current liabilities Money owed and payable by a company, usually within one year.

dealer A person or firm that stands ready to buy or sell securities at a given price. Dealers differ from brokers in that the market is made in the given securities by a willingness to simultaneously either buy at a given price or sell at a different given price.

debenture A promissory note backed by the general credit of a company and usually not secured by a mortgage or lien on any specific property.

depletion Natural resources, such as metals, oils, and gas and timber (which conceivably can be reduced to zero over the years) that can present a special problem in capital management. Depletion is an accounting practice consisting of charges against earnings based upon the amount of the asset taken out of the total reserves in the period for which accounting is made. A bookkeeping entry, it does not represent any cash outlay, nor are any funds earmarked for the purpose.

depreciation Normally, charges against earnings to write off the cost, less salvage value, of an asset over its estimated useful life. It is a bookkeeping entry and does not represent any cash outlay, nor are any funds earmarked for the purpose.

director One of a number of people elected by shareholders at the annual meeting to establish company policies. The directors appoint the president, vice-presidents, and all other operating officers. Directors decide, among other matters, if and when dividends shall be paid.

discounting The process of finding the present value of a series of future cash flows. Discounting is the reverse of compounding.

diversification Investing in the securities of a number of different firms and a number of different industries in an attempt to spread the risk and lessen the likelihood of losses.

dividend The payment designated by the board of directors to be distributed pro rata among the shares outstanding. On preferred shares, it is generally a fixed amount. On common shares, the dividend varies with the fortunes of the company and the amount of cash on hand. It may be omitted if business is poor or if the directors decide to withhold earnings to invest in plant and equipment. Sometimes a company will pay a dividend out of past earnings even if it is not currently operating at a profit.

dollar cost averaging Buying securities at regular intervals with specific and equal dollar amounts regardless of the price level. This results in lowering the average price of securities because more are purchased when the prices are depressed than when they are high.

double taxation Short for "double taxation of dividends." The federal government taxes corporate profits as corporate income. Any part of the remaining profits distributed as dividends to stockholders is taxed again as income to the recipient stockholder.

Dow-Jones average A statistical device that shows the general level and movement of security prices.

earnings A corporation's income after all expenses, including preferred dividend payments.

equity The ownership interest of common and preferred stockholders in a company. Also refers to excess of value of securities over the debit balance in a margin account.

ex dividend "Without dividend." This means that when the stock is purchased, it does not include the most recent dividend that has been declared.

ex rights "Without the rights." Corporations raising additional money may do so by offering their stockholders the right to subscribe to new or additional stock, usually at a discount from the prevailing market price. The buyer of a stock selling ex rights is not entitled to the rights.

face value Sometimes referred to as par value, the value of a bond that appears on its face, unless that value is otherwise specified by the issuing company. Face value is ordinarily the amount the issuing company promises to pay at maturity. Face value is not an indication of market value.

fiduciary A person who has certain legal rights and powers relating to financial matters to be exercised for the benefit of another person.

financial leverage The ratio of total debt to total assets. There are other measures of financial leverage, especially ones that relate cash inflows to required cash outflows. The debt-total asset ratio is generally used to measure leverage.

fixed annuity A contract with a life insurance company that provides the periodic payment of a fixed number of dollars for a specific period of time or for life.

goodwill Intangible assets of a firm established by the excess of the price paid for the going concern over its book value.

government bonds Obligations of the U.S. government regarded as the highest grade issues in existence.

grace period The period, usually 30 days, following the premium due date of a life insurance policy during which an overdue premium may be paid without penalty.

growth stock Stock of a company with prospects for future growth—a company whose earnings are expected to increase at a relatively rapid rate.

hedge fund A mutual fund (or investment company) that hedges its market commitments by holding certain securities it believes are likely to increase in value and, at the same time, sells others short because it believes they are likely to decline in value. Its main objective is capital appreciation.

holding company A corporation that owns the securities of another, in most cases with voting control.

income bonds Bonds on which the interest is paid only if earned.

income stock Stock of a corporation that has a historical record of above-average earnings and dividends and that is likely to continue performing favorably.

insurance dividend The payment made to owners of mutual life insurance policies. Part of this must be looked upon as a return of premiums, part of it as earnings.

investment company A corporation that sells stock of itself to the public, and then uses the funds to buy the securities of many other firms. There is no limit to the number of shares an open-end investment company may sell of itself, whereas a closed-end investment company definitely has a limit in the number of shares it may sell.

investment trust A closed-end fund that has a set number of shares. Regulated by the Investment Company Act of 1940, many investment trusts specialize in a specific business sector, industry, country, etc., for example, a Real Estate Investment Trust.

Keogh bill The bill which allows most of the self-employed to set up their own retirement program with generous tax savings.

leverage The use of borrowed money to increase the earnings of the common stockholder. If money is borrowed at 6 percent and the corporation earns 12 percent with it, the extra 6 percent accrues to the common stockholder.

liabilities All the claims against a corporation. Liabilities include accounts and wages and salaries payable, dividends declared payable, accrued taxes payable, and fixed or long-term liabilities such as mortgage bonds, debentures, and bank loans.

limit order An order to a broker to buy a certain stock only if its price falls to a specified level or to sell a stock only if the price rises to a specified level.

line of credit An arrangement whereby a financial institution (bank or insurance company) commits itself to lend up to a specified maximum amount of funds during a specified period. Sometimes the interest rate on the loan is specified; at other times it is not. Sometimes a commitment fee is imposed for obtaining the line of credit.

liquid Anything that is easily and quickly convertible to cash without a substantial price concession. Liquidity is a relative term.

load The fees which must be paid when buying mutual funds. These generally range from 7 percent to 9 percent, but some are above and some are below this rate. There are even some no-load funds.

management fees The fees charged by the managers of investment companies for their services in managing the portfolio.

margin purchases Purchases of securities with money that is partially borrowed.

margin requirements The percentage of the price of a security which must be paid with the buyer's own money. The remainder may be borrowed.

monthly investment plan An arrangement for regular purchases of stock listed on the New York Stock Exchange. These arrangements can be made with most member firms.

mortality tables Tables indicating the number of deaths per thousand at various ages, developed from past experiences by life insurance companies.

mortgage bonds Bonds behind which specific assets of a corporation have been pledged as collateral.

municipal bond A bond issued by a state or a political subdivision, such as county, city, town, or village. The term also designates bonds issued by state agencies and authorities. In general, interest paid on municipal bonds is exempt from federal income taxes.

net asset value As applied to mutual funds, this is the market value of underlying securities divided by the number of mutual fund shares outstanding.

noncumulative A preferred stock on which unpaid dividends do not accrue. Omitted dividends are, as a rule, gone forever.

no-load funds Mutual funds that do not charge any commissions on their sales. To buy these, you may have to contact the company directly.

odd lot A block of stock consisting of fewer shares than the number customarily traded at one time (a round lot of 100 shares).

odd lot dealer A dealer who buys and sells odd lots exclusively.

open-end investment company (Also called mutual funds.) A company that has no limit as to the number of shares in itself that it may sell.

open order An order to buy or sell securities at a stipulated price that remains in effect until it is executed or canceled.

opportunity cost The rate of return on the best alternative investment that is available. It is the highest return that will not be earned if the funds are invested in a particular project. For example, the opportunity cost of not investing in common stocks yielding 8 percent might be 6 percent which could be earned on bonds.

over-the-counter The market for those securities not listed on any organized exchange.

paid-up insurance Insurance on which premiums are no longer due but remains in force.

par value The face or stated value of a bond or a stock. In the case of a stock, this is meaningless. However, in the case of a bond or a preferred stock, the par value generally indicates the dollar value on which the annual interest or dividends are to be paid.

participating preferred A preferred stock that is entitled to its state dividend and, also, to additional dividends on a specified basis upon payment of dividends on the common stock.

policy loan A loan made by an insurance company to a policyholder on the cash surrender value of a policy.

portfolio The securities owned by an individual or corporation.

preemptive rights The rights of existing stockholders to buy a prorated share of a new issue of common stock that a corporation may offer.

preferred stock Stock that receives preferential treatment over common stock both with respect to dividends and to claims on assets in the event that a corporation goes out of business.

price earnings ratio The market value of a common stock divided by its earnings.

pro forma Projected. A pro forma financial statement is one that shows how the actual statement will look if certain specified assumptions are realized. Pro forma statements may be either future or past projections. An example of a backward pro forma statement occurs when two firms are planning to merge and show what their consolidated financial statements would have looked like had they been merged in preceding years.

prospectus The official document that describes the shares of a new security being issued.

proxy statement The written permission to vote one's stock that one shareholder gives to another.

puts Contracts that give a holder the right to sell a particular security to the option dealer at a specific price for a specific period of time.

record date The date on which you must be registered on the books of a company as a shareholder in order to among other things receive a declared dividend or to vote on company affairs.

refinancing Same as refunding. New securities are sold by a company, and the money is used to retire existing securities. The object may be to save interest costs, extend the maturity of the loan, or both.

round lots The fixed number or block of shares, usually 100, which is the commonly traded unit on the organized exchanges.

short sales Selling securities one does not own by borrowing them from a broker. Later, hopefully when the price falls, they can be bought and repaid.

sinking fund Money regularly set aside by a company to redeem its bonds, debentures, or preferred stock from time to time as specified in the indenture or charter.

stock split An increase in the number of shares of a corporation brought about by a division of existing shares. A two-for-one split, for example, will result in two new shares for each old share that previously existed, making a total of three.

stock dividend A dividend paid in securities rather than cash. The dividend may be additional shares of the issuing company or shares of another company (usually a subsidiary) held by the company.

stop order An order to a broker to sell a stock if the price reaches a certain level. Sometimes also called a stop loss order. For example, if you buy a stock at $100 and it rises to $120 before falling again, you can guarantee a profit by putting in a stop order at, say, $115.

12b-1 funds These mutual funds charge a 12b-1 fee (up to 1.25 percent of average daily fund assets each year). These fees cover the costs of selling and marketing shares. The SEC passed Rule 12b-1 in 1980.

usury Interest that is in excess of what the law allows.

variable annuity An annuity contract with a life insurance company under which the dollar payments received are not fixed but vary (or fluctuate), usually with the price of common stock.

working capital A firm's investment in short-term assets—cash, short-term securities, accounts receivable, and inventories. Gross working capital is defined as a firm's total current assets. Net working capital is defined as current assets minus current liabilities. If the term "working capital" is used without further qualification, it generally refers to gross working capital.

yield Income received on investments. Usually expressed as a percentage of the market price of the security.

Recommended Reading

Personal Finance

Lewis, Allison. *The Million Dollar Car and $250,000 Pizza.* Chicago: Dearborn, 2000.

Liberman, Gail, and Alan Lavine. *Rags to Riches.* Chicago: Dearborn, 2000.

Pollen, Stephan and Mark Levine. *Live Rich.* New York: Harper Business, 1998.

Quinn, Jane Bryant. *Making the Most of Your Money.* New York: Simon & Schuster, 1998.

Ramsey, Dave. *Financial Peace.* New York: Viking Penguin, 1995.

Schwartz, James D. *Enough*[SM]. New York, NY 10128: MasterMedia Limited, 17 E. 89th St., 1995.

Tobias, Andrew. *The Only Investment Guide You'll Ever Need.* New York: Harvest Books, 1999.

Barron's

Bottom Line Personal (Boardroom Reports, Inc., 330 W. 42 St., NY, 10036)

Business 2.0

Business Week

Entrepreneur

Forbes

Fortune

Home Office

Kiplinger's Personal Finance Magazine

Smart Money

The Wall Street Journal

Insurance

Katt, Peter C. *The Life Insurance Fiasco: How to Avoid It.* West Bloomfield, MI: Dolphin Publishing, 1992.

Second Businesses

Business Use of Your Home. IRS Publication 587. Washington, D.C.: U.S. Government Printing Office, updated each year.

Dappen, Andy. *Shattering the Two-Income Myth.* Brier, WA: Brier Books, 1997.

Norman, Jan. *What No One Ever Tells You about Starting Your Own Business.* Chicago: Dearborn, 1999.

Tax Guide for Small Businesses. IRS Publication 334. Washington, D.C.: U.S. Government Printing Office, updated each year.

www.smbiz.com—small business taxes and management

Zbar, Jeffery D. *Home Office Know-How.* Chicago: Dearborn, 1998.

Taxes

Melvin, Sean P. *Settle Your Tax Debt.* Chicago: Dearborn, 1998.

Your Federal Income Tax. IRS Publication 17. Washington, D.C.: U.S. Government Printing Office, updated each year.

Estate Planning

Brosterman, Robert. *The Complete Estate Planning Guide: Updated to Include Tax Changes to 1998.* New York: Mentor Books, New American Library, 1998.

Leimberg, Stephan R., Jerry A. Kasner, Stephen N. Kandell, Ralph G. Miller, Morey S. Rosenbloom, and Herbert L. Levy. *The Tools and Techniques of Estate Planning, 11th ed.* Cincinnati, OH: The National Underwriter Company, 1998.

Index